SODOMETRIES

Renaissance

Texts,

Modern

Sexualities

Jonathan Goldberg

STANFORD UNIVERSITY PRESS

STANFORD, CALIFORNIA

Sodometries

RENAISSANCE TEXTS
MODERN SEXUALITIES

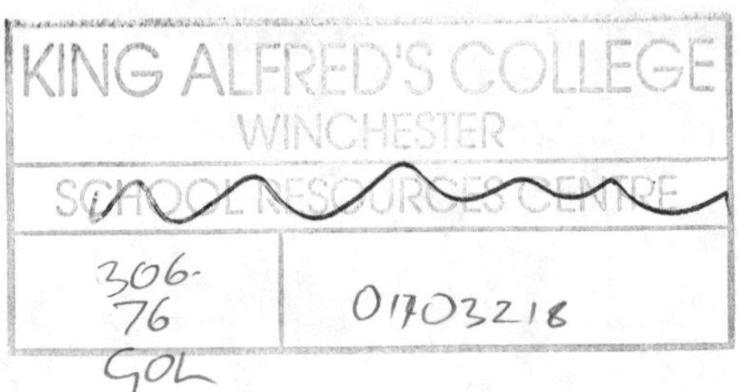

Stanford University Press
Stanford, California

Printed in the United States of America

CIP data are at the end of the book

The illustrations on the title page and the part title pages are excerpted from Plate XXII of Theodore de Bry, *Americae, Pars Quatra* (1594). Reproduced by permission of the Folger Shakespeare Library.

for

Eve

Kosofsky

Sedgwick

ACKNOWLEDGMENTS

A VERSION OF the first part of Chapter 3 of *Sodometries* appeared in the *South Atlantic Quarterly* 88 (1989): 107–26 as "Colin to Hobbinol: Spenser's Familiar Letters" and was reprinted in Ronald Butters, John Clum, and Michael Moon, eds., *Displacing Homophobia* (Duke University Press, 1989). An abbreviated version of Chapter 7 appeared under the same title in Andrew Parker, Mary Russo, Doris Sommer, and Patricia Yaeger, eds., *Nationalisms and Sexualities* (Routledge, 1991). A portion of Chapter 6 appeared as "Sodomy in the New World: Anthropologies Old and New" in *Social Text* 29 (1991): 46–56.

Parts of this book were delivered as lectures: I am particularly grateful to Andrew Parker for a stimulating visit to Amherst College (and to Marguerite Waller for her response to a version of the Marlowe chapter on that occasion); to Jonathan Crewe, who sponsored several trips to Tulsa University, not only to deliver versions of the Marlowe and Shakespeare chapters, but also to teach, along with Michael Moon, a graduate seminar on materials related to the third part of this book. In that context, it is a pleasure to recall the participants in that seminar (not least James Crewe), as well as the company of Barbara Correll (who subsequently has made it possible for me to deliver portions of this book at Cornell) and the hospitality and conversation of Katharine Crewe. To Michael Warner, I owe a visit to Rutgers, as well as the chance to appear in *Social Text*; once again, I thank him for support and, again, have the pleasure of anticipating work of his that will extend the scope and complexity of the arguments offered in the pages that follow. Stephen Orgel made it possible for me to deliver versions of the Marlowe chapter at MLA and at a Stanford Humanities Center conference; Marjorie Garber had a hand in the latter event as well as issuing an invitation to speak at Harvard; Thomas Roche had me to celebrate Spenser 500 at Princeton, where Anne Lake Prescott braved the word *sodomy* for the NEH tape recorders; David Lee Miller gave me the chance to deliver the same Spenser talk to his colleagues and students at Tuscaloosa, and introduced me to Jillana Enteen, to whose work I look forward; Geoffrey Harpham included me in a faculty seminar on gay and lesbian studies at Tulane, and Rebecca Mark invited me back to join her colleagues in their first gay studies conference. Thanks to Eve Kosofsky Sedgwick's Sex/Representation/Gender series at Duke, I delivered versions of the Marlowe and Bradford chapters; it is with pleasure that I recall the enthusiasm of Stanley Fish and Jane Tompkins on those occasions, as well as some friendly wrangling with Barbara Herrnstein Smith. The annual Gay and Lesbian Conference has been hospitable to me as well, and I am particularly grateful to Margaret Hunt for her encouragement. Members of the English Institute in 1991 offered enthusiasm and engagement when I presented materials drawn from the opening and close of this book, and I thank Susan Stewart for asking me to speak. I am grateful to Karen Newman and to David Riggs, the readers of this book for Stanford University Press, and moved by their generosity towards my work. They too have sponsored visits of mine to Brown and Stanford. This is the place to thank Helen Tartar for being a wonderfully supportive and immensely helpful editor.

I have tried out many of the arguments to be found in this book in classes at Johns Hopkins: my undergraduate Shakespeare students have listened to lectures and, at times, offered valuable resistance as well as evidence of gratifying persuasion; my graduate Teaching Assistants have also served as necessary barometers of my success. An undergraduate seminar that touched on much in the third section of this book also proved an important teaching and learning experience for me, not least because of the presence of Maria Farland in that course. Other graduate students who have been reading sixteenth-century literature with me for the past couple of years have been extraordinary allies in the thinking of this book. Several are named in the notes below; without making invidious comparisons among a group of superlative students, I would be remiss if I didn't acknowledge—with pleasure—how much I have learned from Elizabeth Hewitt, T. Sean Holland, Anthony Scott, and Jonathan Brody Kramnick.

It is with a group of friends with whom so much of my life has been shared as I was writing this book that I would end this page, thanking Michael Moon for the thousands of (extra)ordinary joys of his companionship and support, and acknowledging how much his work makes mine possible. Hal Sedgwick has smoothed any number of paths, helped make decisions, and provided calm; he can make restaurants appear in deserts. Eve Kosofsky Sedgwick has often been the first reader of these pages and has never—despite the pressures and pleasures of a complicated and demanding life—stinted in her generous and acute responses to them. I offer this book, however inadequate, as thanks. I wish I could write a sentence sufficiently gorgeous to acknowledge her work, her friendship, her courage, and her brilliance.

J.G.

CONTENTS

PHILOPONUS This poyson hath shed foorth his influence, and powred foorth his stinking dregges over all the face of the earth, but yet I am sure, there is not any people under the Zodiacke of heaven, how clownish, rurall or brutish soever, that is so poisoned with this *Arsenecke* of Pride, or hath drunke so deepe of the dregges of this Cup, as *Ailgna* hath, with griefe of conscience I speake it, with sorow I see it, and with teares I lament it.

SPUDEUS But I have heard them saye, that other Nations passe them, for exquisite bravery in Apparell: as, the *Italians*, the *Athenians*, the *Spaniards*, the *Caldeans*, *Helvetians*, *Zuitzers*, *Venetians*, *Muscovians*, and such lyke: now, whither this be true or not, I greatly desire to knowe.

PHILOPONUS This is but a visour, or cloke, to hide their Sodometrie withall: onelye spoken, not prooved: forged in the deceiptfull Mint of their owne braynes.

—Phillip Stubbes,
The Anatomie of Abuses

PREFACE

SODOMETRIE is a synonym for *sodomy* current in English from around 1540 to around 1650, the *Oxford English Dictionary* notes. The word has been chosen to title this book not only because of its historical pertinence to the Renaissance texts to be discussed, but also for its nonce-word suggestiveness, as if sodomy were a relational term, a measure whose geometry we do not know, whose (a)symmetries we are to explore. The *OED* pronounces the word obsolete, but its suggestiveness is not historically confined. The feel of the word points to the procedures in the pages that follow, where what sodomy *is*—in those texts *or now*—can be delivered only through what is said (or what is not), through slippages capable of being mobilized in more than one direction. In those respects, the passage cited above from *The Anatomie of Abuses* (1583) may serve as an initial example. A dialogue ostensibly addressed to questions about improprieties of dress (a "contagious infection of Pride in Apparell" [B8r]) lights upon the word *Sodometrie* to do double work, at the least. Philoponus responds to Spudeus's claim that other nations have been as extravagant as the English in their dress by labeling his claim a sign of the "Sodometrie" of those who make such a claim. At once, the word *Sodometrie* serves to impugn their customs and their arguments; it names the truth of their falseness, the "visour, or cloke" in which they apparel their false apparel. "Sodometrie" is the word to reveal the truth, but it is also the word for all that is wrong in their behavior, their thinking, their language, their dress. The instabilities of this moment are part and parcel of the "contagious infection" the text both sees and perpetrates, the "poison" that spreads uncontrollably, violating borders and differences—upside down, inside out, animal/human—as the very name of the poison ("*Arsenecke*") suggests when it is decomposed into its anatomical parts. Once false apparel is so falsely/truly named, the text riots in a proliferation of sites upon which sodomy fastens: the false claims of other nations, dark races, the frozen east, the sultry south, the lower classes and country lads. Always elsewhere, the home of sodomy here is called "*Ailgna.*" What land is this, however, and in what language has it been written? England, otherwise; "our" literature and history written in the language of sodometries.

SODOMETRIES

Renaissance

Texts,

Modern

Sexualities

CHAPTER 1

In November 1990, just a few months after the Iraqi invasion of Kuwait, and in the midst of U.S. preparations for war, an ad for a T-shirt appeared in *Rolling Stone* magazine. "Americans, Make a Statement," the ad read; below it was displayed the image that "Americans" might sport: a U.S. flag appears in the background, partially obscured by a camel; superimposed on the camel's rump—obligingly turned to meet the viewer's gaze—is the face of the Iraqi leader, smiling, slightly open-mouthed, his head swathed in Arab headdress. What statement were "Americans" to make? A sentence surrounds the picture; it reads: "America Will Not be Saddam-ized."[1] The statement equates Saddam Hussein's invasion of Kuwait with rape, and implies that all forced entries are acts of sodomy. Saddam Hussein is, thereby, represented as homosexual, as the highly stigmatizing depiction makes clear. Saddam's head is where the camel's tail would be; hence, the face, quintessentially human, is, in this image, animal; Hussein's mouth replaces the camel's asshole, and the reversal of front and back also implies an equation of anal and oral sex. Homosexuality, thus linked to bestiality and to indiscriminate, promiscuous sexual behavior, is further tainted by all

the ways in which the face reads as foreign—heavy black holes for eyes and mouth, black lines for eyebrows and moustache; racial difference is insistent, while the headdress—not usually worn by Hussein—is feminizing. Although Saddam Hussein is declared to be a sodomizer, the homophobia that fuels the picture aggressively sodomizes him.

Appearing in *Rolling Stone,* this ad could be regarded as aimed at a particular audience—presumably, a youthful rock cult one. Yet the appeal of such an image hardly can be confined to a rock 'n' roll crowd of whatever age, nor relegated to a particular segment of the population. Moreover, the work that the ad does is not only a manifestation of popular culture or dismissible as such. For the image trades in a militaristic *imaginaire,* one that frighteningly seemed all too available as military briefings saturated the media during the U.S. war with Iraq. The T-shirt is part of a war effort licensed by Congress and the White House. Nonetheless it would be a mistake, I think, to regard such saturation as complete or as entirely successful. For the T-shirt logo and image, however complicit they might be with the recruitment of *Rolling Stone* readers for the campaign of military mobilization, is also knowing, almost witty. Indeed, the shirt says something that otherwise remained buried, virtually unspeakable and unacknowledged on the airwaves and in most newspapers, which were happy, it appeared, to report the news as the military supplied it: the shirt declares the complicities of racism, sexism, and homophobia mobilized by the war. A certain amount of demystification is performed by the image; it might even be thought to empower its wearer with a degree of knowledge.

For the statement made by this T-shirt is not an entirely straightforward one. Perhaps only to my Renaissance-trained eyes, the shirt seems amenable to a reading that might recognize in it not only the complex overdeterminations of the present moment—confluences and conflicts within and between popular culture, the media, late-capitalist commodification, the military, the government—but also certain strange historic overlaps. Structured as the image is by confusions of before and behind, head and tail, flag and camel, the statement it makes seems to me if not "utterly confused," to borrow Foucault's characterization of sodomy before the advent of modernity and the modern regimes of sexuality, at the very least confused *with* those supposedly archaic registers.[2] As in the "ancient civil or canonical codes" to which Foucault alludes (43), sodomy is equated with bestiality, as it is in the first English sodomy law, passed during the reign of Henry VIII, which punishes with death those convicted of "the detestable and abhomynable vice of buggery commyttid with mankynde or beaste";[3] as in that formulation, the sexual act lacks specificity—it might be oral or anal sex, performed by "mankind" or with an animal. Insofar as Saddam is feminized—or, indeed, insofar as Kuwait is thought of as a woman taken from behind—crossings of gender, so-called unnatural sex, in the favored language of Blackstone for instance, even the trope of inversion that serves as one major definition of homosexuality from the nineteenth century on, also are implicated in the image. Fantasies that equate homosexuality with molestation are involved. Sodomy as the vice of Mediterranean/Islamic cultures, a recurring notion in English Renaissance texts, seems available too.

If the image traffics in these highly sedimented registers that go back over several historical periods, all more or less out of date, one might have supposed, the representation is organized by a classical trope, *histeron proteron*, anglicized by George Puttenham, the Elizabethan Kenneth Burke,[4] as the preposterous. Puttenham defines the trope as a form of disordered speech in which the cart is put before the horse; *histeron proteron* borders on the tropes that Puttenham finds "notoriously undecent";[5] yet the preposterous, he opines, is "tolerable inough, and many times scarce perceivable" (181). Part of the work this image does can be understood in these terms: it borders on obscenity, yet locates indecency in what Saddam Hussein has done, not what the image does. Interestingly, among Puttenham's examples of the preposterous is a line of poetry in which the speaker first claims a kiss and then departs. Puttenham worries about whether that order is backwards or not and decides finally that on this question, "yong Courtiers" (181) can decide. The preposterous is thus a trope involving questions of sexual decorum; although reversing before and behind could mean crossing over the boundary that separates licit from illicit behavior, it might as easily be a question managed by those who do it all the time, and have the capacity to make such transgressions seem utterly ordinary. These confusions—and normalizations—of before and after also may guide our reading of the historical sedimentation of the image. If this shirt says we will not be sodomized, it also demystifies what must be done in order not to be in that supposedly passive position. For the ad does not simply invite "Americans" to make a statement, it calls for action. If the American flag has been desecrated, covered and recovered by the images of camel and Saddam's face, a reversal of the image is called for by the image's own reversals. What are "Americans" to do? Aim at the bull's-eye, the target on the camel's rear; clear the space so that the flag will be uncovered. "We will not be Saddam-ized"; the flag that is unfurled behind will come before, as a missile of penetration. Within the tropologics of this reversible statement, if we say that we will not be sodomized, our actions will reverse that deplorable condition. In a word, "America" says, "we will sodomize."

Saddam—homosexual, bestial, foreign, inhuman, feminine—is

the target of a proper masculinity: America's degradation is nothing less than its being placed behind, its assuming a passive position (feminine, homosexual) in a sexual act that the image asks its viewers to reverse. In the layout of the shirt, the word *America* appears above the image, the rest of the sentence below it. Momentarily, it might appear as if the word *America* titled the image. To read the image that way would be to produce, in Puttenham's terms, an indecency, an image of America that includes the foreign, the homosexual, the woman, an America, in a word, that has subscribed to cultural pluralism; all this follows from the equation of Kuwait and America upon which the image depends and which it also disavows. Rather, to read the image and statement properly—which is to say, backwards—we must produce something that will not seem reversed at all. Imperceptibly, as Puttenham suggested, the image can be made tolerable enough so doing, and the complicities upon which it trades can be effaced. Even as "America" is invited to perform an act—Saddam's act—that act must be read and done otherwise. But the image only knows front and behind, and it trades in the equation of oppositions. Unavoidably, the image asks us to be sodomites, a message delivered quite explicitly by another T-shirt in support of the war; it depicts a missile and bears the logo: "Hey Saddam This Scuds [*sic*] For You!!"; the missile's target is Saddam's rear end.[6] If Saddam is blasted away, if the homosexual is destroyed, it would be impossible ever to suppose that proper male aggression could be misrecognized as sodomy. First, these images misrecognize Saddam's aggression as sodomy, then they claim the rights of aggression.

Looking at these images, we're not merely engaging in the vagaries of the signifier—Saddam's name is an accident that makes it available for a colonial *imaginaire* that could proceed without his name—nor are we simply dealing with the ever-crossable and heavily policed border between the homosexual and the homosocial, the terrain of homophobia and homosexual panic. These representations raise some further questions: What place is sodomy assumed to have in the mind of the "America" being addressed? What is the purpose in these contemporary images of a sexual order whose confusions Foucault assigned to historic regimes before the advent of sexuality, indeed to a past that would seem to have been replaced by the regimes of modernity?[7] How and where does "that utterly confused category" survive and what work does it continue to do? Perhaps these are questions likely to occur only to someone who works "in" the Renaissance, but it will be my argument that an inquiry into the ancient codes is not sealed off in some antiquarian preserve. Indeed, that the invocation of historic difference—even the differences between the sodomite as "nothing more than the juridical subject" of forbidden acts and the homosexual as "a personage" (43) that Foucault so persuasively and magisterially laid out—cannot be used as a way of cordoning off the past from the present. The productive value of sodomy, even today, should not be underestimated. We need only recall the 1986 U.S. Supreme Court decision in *Bowers v. Hardwick* (106 S.Ct. 2841), with its declaration that the Constitution of the United States recognizes no fundamental right of privacy for consensual acts of what the court termed homosexual sodomy, to see that the attitudes in these images are officially sanctioned ones. I turn to that decision here for the clearest evidence that the confusions of before and behind in which the image trades represent historic confusions capable of lethal mobilization.

A *University of Miami Law Review* piece, cited by Justice Byron White in his majority opinion in *Bowers v. Hardwick* (2844), contemplates, in its concluding pages, the effects the decision of the court might have.[8] First, opining that to uphold Georgia's sodomy statute would have no effect whatsoever—since states could continue to criminalize sodomy or not—the essay proceeds to the "major impact on both constitutional doctrine and on our society's view of homosexuals" that overturning the law would have (638). "A decision extending the right of privacy to homosexual activities could legitimize the gay rights movement," the essay concludes; "a contrary decision might reinforce negative attitudes toward homosexuals" (638). Within two pages, the affirmation that the "consequences of denying homosexual activities the protection of the right to privacy would be few" (636) leads to the recognition, faced, it would seem, with utter equanimity, that such a decision would license and endorse homophobia. Justice

White never acknowledges that effect as a consequence of his merciless decision—he, too, claims that the decision leaves each state free to pass the laws it chooses and thus declares that the opinion of the majority "raises no question about the right or propriety of state legislative decisions to repeal their laws that criminalize homosexual sodomy, or of state-court decisions invalidating those laws on state constitutional grounds" (2843). Rather than noting that he knows he is promoting and encouraging homophobia, White only acknowledges the *Miami Law Review* article as a source for its historical survey of sodomy laws. Under the cover of what passes for history, White evades—and ensures—the consequences that he pretends the court's decision was not meant to unleash.

Drawing on previous decisions that define the fundamental rights guaranteed by the Constitution as those "'implicit in the concept of ordered liberty' such that 'neither liberty nor justice would exist if [they] were sacrificed,'" and as "'deeply rooted in this Nation's history and tradition,'" White wrote: "it is obvious to us that neither of these formulations would extend a fundamental right to homosexuals to engage in acts of consensual sodomy. Prescriptions against that conduct have ancient roots" (2844). White refers at this point to a page of the *Miami Law Review* essay that declares that "current state laws prohibiting homosexual intercourse are ancient in origin" (525), and which offers as examples Plato's *Laws,* the Sodom and Gomorrah story, a sentence from Leviticus, the burning of "homosexuals as heretics" in the middle ages, and the English statute of 1533 cited earlier. Governing this presentation of history is a slippage from sodomy to homosexuality that occurs in the course of a single sentence. The historical review opens, "At common law, and at one time by statute in every state of the United States, sodomy was a criminal act" (523). Next sentence: "Traditionally, states have considered homosexuality to be 'sinful, sick, and criminal'" (524).

Several commentators have pointed out the superficiality of this history, its fundamental errors in equating sodomy with homosexuality, as well as factual errors in Justice White's next historical pronouncement, that "sodomy was a criminal offense at common law and was forbidden by the laws of the original thirteen states when they ratified the Bill of Rights. In 1868, when the Fourteenth Amendment was ratified, all but 5 of the 37 States in the Union had criminal sodomy laws" (2844–45).[9] Not only are White's numbers suspect, but the content of sodomy laws changed in the course of the years; what is effaced in this history is that ancient sodomy laws *and the Georgia statute under consideration* do not distinguish between hetero- and homosexual sodomy, that it is only in twentieth-century legal formulations that oral sex—the crime that Michael Hardwick was caught performing in his own bedroom—explicitly is included in the definition of sodomy—in the nineteenth century, it explicitly was not.[10] The Supreme Court decision tacitly upheld the right of heterosexuals to perform sodomitical sex and denied that right to homosexuals. Yet, it also defined homosexuals as those who perform that act, and several post-*Hardwick* decisions have affirmed that homosexuals now are by definition a criminal class.[11]

Those who have written about the historical errors in White's decision have taken it to task for its highly prejudicial account; much the same is the case for his source, and it is, it hardly needs saying, amazing to find Plato's *Laws* invoked as the touchstone for ancient Greek attitudes towards sex between men; by referring to the Sodom and Gomorrah story as a "legendary account," the *Miami Law Review* piece (525), it might be added, is more circumspect than White, or than Justice Warren Berger, whose concurring opinion invokes "millennia of moral teaching," and includes an approving citation of Sir William Blackstone's description of sodomy as " 'the infamous *crime against nature*' as an offense of 'deeper malignancy' than rape, a heinous act 'the very mention of which is a disgrace to human nature,' and 'a crime not fit to be named' " (2847). But more to the point here is a consideration of what has happened when sodomy, that utterly confused category, one of whose confusions lies precisely in failing to distinguish nonprocreative homo- and heterosexual intercourse, is invoked in *Hardwick,* but now to secure the very difference between homo- and heterosexuality. Here it's worth remarking, as the dissenting justices did, that the Georgia statute in question in

Bowers v. Hardwick was hardly an ancient one at all, having been enacted only in 1968, replacing at that time a sodomy law aimed solely at homosexual sex. That earlier law had proved to be too specific, had been found, for instance, not to obtain when two lesbians were brought to trial.[12] It is possible that the law was extended to include heterosexuals for fear that the earlier law might be challenged as unconstitutionally prejudicial; perhaps the only way to ensure that the law could cover all possible cases lay in not specifying sexual orientation. For, it has to be added, that however written, Georgia's laws, like those of other states, when enforced, have been used for the most part against men or women presumed to be gay or lesbian. But it was recognized that that practice could only be shielded—indeed would only be possible—if the law pretended to equality. The Supreme Court decision vacates the need for that pretense.

Between the codes of the colonies and the states of the union in 1861 and modern statutes, a change had occurred, the one that Foucault's argument details: from the sodomite, the juridical subject defined as anyone performing a sexual act not aimed at procreation within the bonds of marriage, to the homosexual as a particular form of identity. The 1968 change in Georgia's law tallies with the statutes on the books in the 24 states that continue to criminalize sodomy (only seven states restrict their sodomy laws to homosexuals). These laws, at least as written, do not discriminate overtly between identities. Acts are criminalized, not identities. Laws that would seem *textually* to evidence a continuity with the ancient statutes are *contextually* quite different, however. Earlier sodomy laws were directed solely at acts because it was presumed that anyone might do them; homo- or heterosexual identity was not in question. Nonetheless, those who have attempted to make the historic argument that the ancient statutes have nothing to do with the present have erred, not in insisting that sodomy and homosexuality are different, but in assuming that because sodomy comes from an older regime it no longer has a function. Paradoxical as it is, the decision of the Supreme Court, distinguishing homo- and heterosexual sodomy, follows from the modern regimes in which homo- and heterosexual identities are presumptively distinct. That presumption about identities allows the same act to read entirely differently when performed by persons who are assumed to embody these identities. The Foucauldian insistence that the sodomite is not the homosexual ignores not only the persistence of the sodomite as a means of defining homosexuality, but also how unstable the modern regime of supposedly discrete identities is. For when the Supreme Court attempts to define an identity through an act that it also permits to those whose identities are not defined by the performance of the same act, it leaves open the question of where heterosexual identity resides beyond the affirmation of a difference that has no content, an identity in other words that is defined by no specificity of acts but only by claims to be an identity.

These questions touch on the definitional impasse that Eve Kosofsky Sedgwick explores in *Epistemology of the Closet,* the difference between minoritizing definitions of homosexuality (which, she notes, have often been the basis for legal claims—about the rights due to a despised minority) and universalizing claims—those that declare that sexual identities take place across a continuum that artificially divides one sexual preference from another. The latter as she suggests might well be associated with the ancient regimes of the sodomite insofar as sodomy was assumed to be a temptation anyone might succumb to, rather than a marker of identity.[13] In this light the illegitimacy of the Supreme Court decision lay in its use of the equation of sodomy and homosexuality to attempt to separate the homo- and heterosexual on the basis of sodomy; the fault, that is, lay in the assumption about the relation of acts to persons, in the presumption of unbridgeable difference. It's that presumption that also underwrites the opinion of the dissenting justices, couched as it is in the language of liberalism, of individual rights and the right to privacy. As one law review essay has suggested, to protect homosexuality through arguments about the right to privacy offers no safeguards for homosexuality as a social identity—it assumes that homosexuals are defined solely by private sexual acts;[14] hence, as Robert Caserio has commented, both majority and minority views in the *Hardwick* decision agree that if homosexuals have any place at all it is the closet.[15] (The majority would have that closet barred and padlocked, of course.) Both views would keep homosexuality and homosexuals invisible. Public space is presumptively heterosexual; hence the Americans addressed by the T-shirt with which we began can engage in acts of sodomy—even acts of homosexual sodomy—on the presumption that such acts do not define heterosexuals. To base rights for homosexuals on minoritizing definitions or in the right of privacy allows for the belief, now made law in *Bowers v. Hardwick,* that homosexuals and heterosexuals are so immutably different that their acts could never be the same—even when they are. As in the ancient codes, sodomy continues to perform the work of categorical confusion that is necessary to maintain the state. The alternative to this, as Janet Halley has suggested, would be the recognition that the difference between homo- and heterosexuality is always being breached, that in furthering the regime of the closet, the *Hardwick* decision attempts to secure sexual difference even as it ensures mechanisms for homosexual invisibility—that is, guarantees that some gay-identified persons will pass as straight and that some straight-identified persons may be taken as gay. Her argument in support of the extension of equal rights to a public space of gay identity lies in the recognition that one can never know what homosexuality is or who is a homosexual.[16]

Or a sodomite. It is a remarkable fact that in many of the states in which sodomy remains a crime, the language used is identical to that found in Renaissance or colonial American statutes—25 Henry VIII c.6 cited verbatim, for example, in Massachusetts, Michigan, Mississippi, Oklahoma, Rhode Island, and South Carolina, and with small variations elsewhere;[17] a Maryland court just a few years ago ruled that its law against "unnatural or perverted practice" was perfectly correct, not in the least vague, because *we all know what it means* not to say more specifically what the crime not to be named among Christians is.[18] But do we? States worried that such language is too vague have tried to specify the acts; this means that in different states, sodomy is variously defined; most often it is any act involving the genitals of one person and the mouth or anus of another; in some states, the tongue is added; in two, the hand; Texas adds to these that the introduction of any foreign object into a sexual organ constitutes an act of sodomy. In Missouri, a man who placed his hands on the clothed crotch of a police officer was found guilty of sodomy. The laws and the ways they have been enforced revel in fantasies of sexual acts that are limited only by the imaginations of the legislators—all of whom, we are to presume (they depend on it), are straight. Certainly our Supreme Court justices are; hence, while they keep intoning the phrase "ancient roots" and can't let go of the word "fundamental," we couldn't possibly hear sodomy in their language.[19]

How is it then that these acts are protected when performed by heterosexuals? How are heterosexuals differentially defined if their performance of these acts does not make them sodomites? The answer, as repetitiously intoned in *Bowers v. Hardwick* as is anything in the decision, is the institution of the family. Justice White's denial of a constitutional right to perform homosexual sodomy was situated in his affirmation that there is "no connection between family, marriage, or procreation" and "homosexual activity" (2844) and his definition of what is "deeply rooted in this Nation's history and tradition" (2846) as virtually synonymous with the family. Like sodomy, however, the family also is an empty concept—without content—even as it is taken to be the content of prior decisions involving the right to privacy. This is stunningly revealed in the *Miami Law Review* piece that White cites; having laid the ground for the Supreme Court decision by showing that previous privacy decisions have always taken place in the context of cases involving the married or marriageable couple or the families that result from marriage, and by indicating how often those earlier decisions have gone out of their way to exclude gays from them, the *Miami Law Review* piece attempts, rather half-heartedly, to argue that such decisions need not be so straitened, that there could be room for consensual homosexual sex within a broadened definition of the family. For, as the writers note, the family could be redefined not in terms of legal ties but in terms of affective ones, in ways that would validate what presumably makes the family a valuable, virtually sacred, institution—monogamy, care, long-term commitment, and so on. But, following this logic, the *Review* is forced to conclude that to extend the family by defining it in this way might well mean that any number of married couples would no longer be protected by previous rulings. "The definition of family need not depend upon the sexual practices of its members but by the presence or absence of the attributes enumerated above," the *Review* concludes a section attempting to reconcile the traditional family to the equally long-standing liberal tradition that protects the individual. "The relationship must meet *all* the essential attributes to qualify for protection," the article continues. "Even a heterosexual relationship that is promiscuous would not qualify. Thus, the protection is for certain types of intimate relationships, and not for homosexuality or heterosexuality per se" (592).

There is, in this conclusion, a certain air of desperation, as the writers attempt to find what defines the value of the so-called family. Clearly, this was not a path down which the justices were willing to tread. By not giving any content to the concept of the family, *Bowers v. Hardwick* affirms that married or marriageable couples can perform any sexual acts in their bedrooms with complete impunity. But this also reveals that the private domain is defined solely in its relation to a public identity and to the laws that allow marriage only for male-female couples. (This ramifies to the defense of the individual offered by the dissenting justices, and not only to the regime of the closet noted earlier, for the individual affirmed, especially by Justice Stevens, is pronomially and presumptively male; even as equal rights for homo- and heterosexuals are affirmed by him, the rights are allotted, it appears, only to men.) Clearly enough, such privacy is shielded from public scrutiny because only some persons are allowed to have public identities. In that light, it seems worth arguing that so-called rights of privacy are shams; the bedroom has been policed beforehand. Freedom to do what one wishes is allowed only to those whose sexual acts the state will or could legitimize through the institution of marriage.

The consequences of this view are manifold. As Sylvia Law has argued, *Bowers v. Hardwick* depends throughout on a patriarchal view of sexual relations one might have thought to have been overturned in part by the very decisions about the rights accorded the family that the court cites as precedents;[20] of course, the most important of these is *Roe v. Wade,* and in a brief but telling essay, Norman Vieira has shown how *Bowers v. Hardwick* systematically undermines the principles at stake in that decision.[21] As he sees it, *Bowers v. Hardwick* was a rehearsal for overturning *Roe v. Wade.* "Given the striking conflict between the *Hardwick* opinion and the rationale of *Roe,* it must be asked whether the real target of the *Hardwick* case was homosexual sodomy . . . or the right of privacy in general and the *Roe* decision in particular," he concludes (1186). Both Law and Vieira contend that gender regulation is at the heart of the decision, and they are certainly right. Their arguments suggest that, once again, the line between homosexual and heterosexual is breached, and the very attempt to cordon homosexuals off as a criminal category fetches its arguments from ways in which the court wishes to enforce not merely heterosexuality but heterosexism. Law claims, convincingly, that the decision implicates the subordination of women within patterns of male domination; "the censure of homosexuality cannot be animated merely by a condemnation of sexual behavior," she argues (as I have been too), since the court allows the same sexual acts to be performed by heterosexuals. "Instead," she concludes, "homosexuality is censured because it violates the prescriptions of gender role expectations" (196).

Law's formulation that the decision was not, in her words, "merely" about homosexuality, like Vieira's claim that the "real target" in *Hardwick* was *Roe v. Wade,* runs the risk of the effacement, the rendering invisible of homosexuality that Law acutely sees is an aim in *Bowers v. Hardwick.* While there is no denying the importance of suggesting that the decision was not solely about gay rights, the way that point is made in both of these arguments conveys the unfortunate suggestion that the decision was important only insofar as it bears upon the relations between men and women, or upon a woman's rights to the control of her body. Rather, it is crucial in working out the implications of *Bowers v. Hardwick* not to seek to hierarchize oppressions but to trace the overdeterminations and discontinuities in the decision. Law is clearly on the mark, for example, when she notes that the patriarchal family affirmed by the decision is presumptively white and middle class (232–33); the decision has racist implications, and to begin to address them, one would want to note that historically sodomy laws have been used against blacks and immigrants far more often than against native-born whites.[22] One would want to pursue, as others beside Law have, following remarks made by Justices Blackmun and Stevens in their dissenting opinions, the startling relation between miscegenation laws and sodomy laws; African-Americans and whites were legally given the right to marry each other only in 1967, and the refusal to allow members of the same sex to marry is the Catch-22 that the Supreme Court depends upon when it separates the family from same-sex couples.[23]

When Law and Vieira depend upon the hierarchy in which the "real" significance of *Bowers v. Hardwick* involves male-female relations, they relegate homosexuals to a minority position, a consequence of the liberal values both writers uphold. By collapsing questions of sexuality into the "more important" realms of gender, homosexuality is allowed salience insofar as it seems assimilable to heterosexuality, insofar as same-sex relations are taken to be no different from cross-sex ones, a liberal tenet espoused as well by the dissenting justices in *Bowers v. Hardwick.* Yet the consequence of this assimilationist view is to deny differences that sexuality makes, and it is, once more, to model homosexuality in inversion, in the assumption that in any sexual relation, one person plays the male role and the other the female role, whatever their actual genders might be. Granting that the family that White appealed to is as atavistic an institution as the sodomy invoked to secure differences between hetero- and homosexuals, one must also suspect the implicit family structure, however liberalized it is, in Law or Vieira.

Once again, one may be struck by how these arguments resonate against Foucault, this time recalling his distinction between the apparatuses of alliance and sexuality, the former his shorthand term for the regulatory regimes that surround marriage, kinship ties, and inheritance and that define the boundary between licit and illicit sexual acts in the ancient codes. As Foucault frames his argument, alliance was what the ancient laws and codes were all about, and the confusion of sodomy with a host of illicit activities resulted from the ways in which the laws put married procreative sex on one side of the line, and everything else on the other. The proliferating deployment of sexuality from the eighteenth century on, as Foucault argues, focused its attention everywhere but on the couple that was at the center of the older regimes, on a whole series of potential disruptions to the norm of married life. As Foucault puts it, a silence surrounds the couple—"it tended to function as a norm, one that was stricter, perhaps, but quieter" (38)—while sex speaks noisily everywhere else. While, as he argues, alliance does not disappear, but gives the law to sexuality, sexuality eroticizes alliance. Remarkably, given the ties between alliance and the law—the link affirmed by invocations of the family—*Bowers v. Hardwick* allows the family to be the sole domain of sexuality. Ruling against the legitimacy of sexuality elsewhere, the perverse implantation is reimplanted within the couple. The silence that makes the family as undefinable as anything in the decision allows it all forms of sexual perversity. The justices and the legislators dream of a perversity that homosexual sodomites perform, and, believing such acts go on only there, license the same acts where they do not dream they occur. Where they really occur, and not only in the fantasies of these supposedly straight men.

Oddly enough, then, we return with this point to a strange continuity with the old supposedly outmoded regimes of alliance. For if the point about the ancient laws was that they imagined that anyone might perform illicit acts, the new regime, clinging to the family, believes it can be allowed anything because it cannot imagine it doing what is allowed. Homosexuality, as Sedgwick has argued, is the modern locus of the secret; but the secret is not simply sutured to those who identify as or are identified as homosexuals. Homosexuality is also the secret inside of heterosexuality, nowhere more blatantly so than in the nonrecognitions that structure the *Hardwick* decision. If many gay men and women would just as soon have nothing to do with the family, and might agree with Justice White—though without appreciating his brutality and nastiness when he declared that any relation between the rights of family members and the rights of homosexuals is, in his words, "facetious" (2846)—it is because the joke is on the institution that so anxiously defends itself against its own bankruptcy, and that has been doing so in this country at least from the time of its first sodomy laws. Such, at any rate, can be argued following Jonathan Ned Katz and other historians' explanations of why the colonists were so intent on formulating laws against sodomy. It was a way of ensuring the patriarchal family.[24] And it requires only a glance at Alan Bray's crucial book, *Homosexuality in Renaissance England,* or his recent essay on friendship and sodomy in the sixteenth century, to see why.[25] For, as Bray argues, the hierarchies of Elizabethan society were oiled with sexual exchanges between men. Sodomy is not, as he sees it, so much a set of forbidden acts as the performance of those undefined acts—or the accusation of their performance—by those who threatened social stability—heretics, spies, traitors, Catholics. Colonial American prosecutions were virtually confined to members of the lower classes, to those whose actions seemed to threaten the prerogatives of the patriarchs. To the alliances made through marriage, which are central to the legal apparatuses that Foucault details—and which remain central to them at the level of ideological production—there are, there were, these other privileged ties between men, not all of which were secured by the exchange of women or the normalizing function of marriage. Even the colonial family therefore is an ideological structure, inserting women to secure political relations between men, cloaking male-male sexual possibilities (those that accrue to men as they are granted access to each other within a public sphere) with the thin veneer of family life as the sole domain of sexual behavior. The regimes of modernity have only furthered these illusions, and homo- and heterosexuality have been the means of securing supposedly unbreachable differences. The ancient family is the ideological linchpin of these misrecognitions, the speakable nexus of human relations to which the law remains atavistically—and productively—sutured.

~

As the foregoing pages have suggested, *Sodometries* undertakes an investigation of sodomy in the Renaissance on the supposition that such an inquiry, however much it is attentive to the alterity of the past, is not simply a piece of antiquarianism. The crucial starting point for this work, as I have indicated, is the introductory volume of Foucault's *History of Sexuality*, and in particular his epochal pronouncement—epochal in more than one sense, since so much work in the emerging field of gay studies has been devoted to elaborations and modifications of Foucault's schematization—about a transformation late in the nineteenth century: "The sodomite had been a temporary aberration; the homosexual was now a species" (43). If, as I've suggested, pressure can be put on that statement, in order to recognize how the "utterly confused category" is mobilized now, it is also the case that sodomy is not a self-evident category in the Renaissance. Foucault says as much, labeling it as confused; in the work that follows, those confusions are traced, mapped, and the work that sodomy does is explored in several Renaissance contexts. Although the pertinence of such studies to the present guides these investigations, the present—at least the politics of the present moment—is engaged directly again only in the final pages of this book, and there only through one instance to glance at some—by no means all—of the locales in which homophobia currently is produced. Yet it is my guiding supposition in the pages that follow that by exploring some of the terrains of confusion in the Renaissance, I am also exploring sites of present confusion, and that readings that are as attentive and as unpresuming as I hope the ones that follow are, can indicate both the bankruptcy of the concept of sodomy, as well as the work that the term has been able to do—and continues to do—precisely because the term remains incapable of exact definition. Always mobilizable because of its confusions, it is also always capable of deconstruction.

In pursuing this topic, I have been guided above all by the

arguments of Alan Bray. Bray's work follows upon Foucault's and is intent upon one of the confusions of the antecedent sexual order summoned up by the specter of the sodomite. If, as Foucault argues, "sodomy was a category of forbidden acts," and "their perpetrator was nothing more than the juridical subject of them" (43), then, as Bray insists, it is impossible to call anyone in the Renaissance a homosexual, virtually impossible to believe that anyone might self-identify as a sodomite. But if, on the other hand, sodomy named sexual acts only in particularly stigmatizing contexts, there is no reason not to believe that such acts went on all the time, unrecognized as sodomy, called, among other things, friendship or patronage, and facilitated by the beds shared, for instance, by servants or students, by teachers and pupils, by kings and their minions or queens and their ladies. Thus, although sodomy is, as a sexual act, anything that threatens alliance—any sexual act, that is, that does not promote the aim of married procreative sex (anal intercourse, fellatio, masturbation, bestiality—any of these may fall under the label of sodomy in various early legal codifications and learned discourses), and while sodomy involves therefore acts that men might perform with men, women with women (a possibility rarely envisioned),[26] men and women with each other, and anyone with a goat, a pig, or a horse, these acts—or accusations of their performance—emerge into visibility only when those who are said to have done them also can be called traitors, heretics, or the like, at the very least, disturbers of the social order that alliance—marriage arrangements—maintained. As a book like Ian Maclean's *Renaissance Notion of Woman* suggests, the place of the institution of marriage in the period, its integuments with legal, medical, scientific, philosophical, psychological, and theological discourses, were manifold.[27] Marriage is the social institution whose regulatory functions ramify everywhere. Sodomy, as Bray suggests, fully negates the world, law, nature. Hence the unlikelihood that those sexual acts called sodomy, when performed, would be recognized as sodomy, especially if, in other social contexts, they could be called something else, or nothing at all.

Bray's historic work raises formidable questions—not least in the areas of ontology and epistemology, that is, questions about what sodomy is and how it may be recognized. It also suggests that any inquiry into such questions will never deliver the sodomite per se, but only, as my title suggests, sodometries, relational structures precariously available to prevailing discourses. It has therefore seemed to me that sodomy is, in the Renaissance—and after—a site for deconstructive reading, a site that produces a deontologizing effect. This is not to say—to dismiss as summarily as possible a prevailing misreading of deconstruction—that sodomy has no worldly effects. Many people died in this period (and well into the nineteenth century) under the label. Many people performed sodomitical sex without being so classified. Sodomy allows and disallows both. A deconstructive analysis seeks to see what the category enabled and disenabled, and to negotiate the complex terrains, the mutual implications of prohibition and production.

Bray's work—or Foucault's for that matter—has yet to have the kind of impact that one might have hoped it would have had on historians whose work concerns the history of sexuality, and much remains to be done in the archives, in the analysis of the various codes to be found in any number of sites, or in the workings of the law. The empirical investigations that have been performed in these areas suggest how complex the terrains are, and draw attention to national and regional differences, spaces that sometimes are but a few miles apart, formidable differences even across relatively short historical periods, disjunctions at any given moment from place to place.[28] The work that follows occasionally glances—as have the preceding pages—at such historical questions, especially in the final section on sodomy in the new world, but the focus is less on the legal codes or the law cases that will deliver records about sodomites, and more on the question of literary representation. It is here, of course, that this book also touches on present concerns, especially the ways in which readings of Renaissance literature may connect with current political realities. As no one needs to be told, the academy has been under continual assault, from a number of quarters (some of them, of course, well within the academy), for its promotion of what is sneeringly called political correctness (that is, the engagement of a growing number of critics with questions of race, gender, and sexuality), but it is also the case that within Renaissance studies these questions have been circulating too, most notably in the less-than-comfortable relations between the most important critical interventions in Renaissance studies—those represented by the New Historicism and by feminism. The pages that follow are everywhere enabled by that work, but also seek to pose some critical problems raised by it. I've had, too, insofar as it seemed impossible to write this book and not to take on Shakespeare, to deal with more traditional criticism (Shakespeareans are, when so self-identified, definitionally coincident with that designation), but I've been less concerned to point out its most egregious lapses (Joseph Pequigney's *Such Is My Love,* however banalizing and dehistoricized its readings are of what it calls homosexuality in the sonnets, nonetheless does a thorough job of demolition when it takes on prevailing desexualizing readings of those poems),[29] than to suggest how it, like the more "advanced" historicist and feminist work produced around Renaissance texts (including Joel Fineman's formidable *Perjured Eye*),[30] functions under the assumption that the only genuine form of sexuality one might find in them is heterosexuality.[31] True as it is that historians have, for the most part, proceeded as if Foucault had never written, literary critics, even those who invoke his name, have with only a few exceptions written about Renaissance sexuality as if the historic divide that Foucault outlined had no pertinence for Renaissance texts. Thus we have had, on the one hand, discussions of power that simply fold sexuality into them, and thereby efface sexuality (love is not love, any number of Renaissance historicists affirm, although Foucault argues for the inevitable entanglements of sexuality and power), or discussions of gender as if the only forms of power involved were those that determine the inequality between the sexes (arguments therefore that take the repressive hypothesis as a transhistorical truth rather than, as Foucault argued, a particular historical production within the regimes of modernity, and which collapse questions of sexuality into questions of gender). In seeking to address questions of sexuality, and in posing these questions to these critical practices, I hope that I am doing more than waving the banner of political correctness. I trust too that what I have to say to my colleagues in the Renaissance will not be received as a dismissal of their work, but as a call for engagement with the issues raised in the pages that follow.

In invoking the name of Foucault, I should immediately add that the pages that follow are hardly doctrinaire in their allegiance to his work. I've already suggested ways in which I believe his historical narrative is more complicated for present sexual arrangements than his schematizations allow, and I think that is true too for the Renaissance. I've allowed myself to refer to sexuality in the Renaissance recognizing that strictly speaking such a locution is preposterous. Yet, if one cannot (one cannot) proceed under the assumption that hetero- and homosexuality are to be found in Renaissance texts, but if, also, one cannot expect to find sodomy in these texts as sites of self-identification—if, that is, the only nameable sex in the period is that engaged in by the married or marriageable couple—a refusal of the term *sexuality* for these texts could all too easily suggest a desexualizing of them. Rather, I seek the sites of sexual possibilities, the syntax of desires not readily named. In wanting to claim these sites for sexuality, I do not mean to suggest that anyone in the period, or that characters represented in literature, have modern sexual identities, and I have tried to be careful not to suggest that. But I have wanted to see how relations between men (or between women or between men and women) in the period provide the sites upon which later sexual orders and later sexual identities could batten. I've had to move therefore between the recognition that the Renaissance does not distinguish two forms of sexuality as if they were totally distinct and my sense of the precariousness of the present aegises which declare that impermeable boundary now to be in effect. This is, once again, to suggest why a deconstructive method of reading has seemed to me the only way to approach these questions, and why, too, certain risks—including the risk of dehistoricizing (if we take Foucault's schema to *be* history)—also have had to be chanced.

In thinking about how forms of sexuality whose only official recognition of them in the period took place under a stigmatizing label that meant that such sexual practices could never be recognized *as* sodomy, I've drawn freely upon Sedgwick's *Between Men* (which has, among its other virtues, the distinction of offering the only satisfying reading of Shakespeare's sonnets that I know), and particularly upon her notion of homosocial relations.[32] It is through that concept that her work approaches Bray's, since homosociality suggests a continuum of male-male relations, one capable of being sexualized, though where and how such sexualization occurs cannot be assumed a priori. One way in which Sedgwick's term has been deployed, however, has been to slight possibilities of sexuality. Reading Renaissance texts for sodomy—and for sodomites—involves rather seeing the ways in which normative bonds that structured society also allowed for sexual relations. It means, to glance at the most exciting work in feminist studies that I know, to allow the gender trouble (to borrow Judith Butler's title)[33] that follows from the incoherence of sexuality, to ask of sexual identity the question that Denise Riley asks of gendered identity, am I that name?[34]

The book that follows takes up a number of Renaissance authors as well as several spheres of cultural production, in particular, the court as a locus for the formation of a new vernacular high literariness, and the theater, especially as it serves as a site of denunciation for its transgressions of norms of gender and sexuality. In reading some texts by Spenser, Shakespeare, and Marlowe, among others, I have not proceeded as if my aim were to cover the field. Much remains to be done, and there are pointers in the pages following to some—by no means all—of the places where it might occur. To read for sodomy—for sodometries—is to read relationally, and a focus on male-male sexual possibilities or on male authorship also has involved necessarily observations on sociopolitical formations, on the possibility of female authorship, indeed on a range of questions that cannot be disentangled from the central subject matter of this book. I trust that what I have said already, and that the pages that follow, suggest why sodomy is not a subject that can be approached on its own, and why, however long this book is, it only serves as a beginning for investigations that I hope will follow from it, and that will offer more subtle and exacting readings, ones, I believe, that might transform utterly our sense of what Renaissance texts are about, where produced, and in whose interests.

This book looks at literature for most of its pages, but it can't be said that literature per se is its focus, and in that respect too it seeks to ally itself with the promise of New Historicism and feminism—the promise, let us say, of the transformation of literary studies into a branch of cultural studies. We all know by now the formula of the New Historicist essay—an opening glance at some piece of exotica, preferably colonialist, and then a reading of a literary text that reveals its complicities with the colonial encounter. The structure of this book reverses that procedure, ending with colonial ventures, and particularly at the systematic persecution of sodomites in the New World (a topic not much in evidence in the vast explosion of postcolonial studies, although for many Renaissance accounts, the native populations are considered simply to be a society of sodomites).[35] This reversal of procedure, at the very least, means to suggest the worldly consequences of literature. In the final chapters of this book, Renaissance England is not the site of investigation, and the book moves from the earliest encounters in the new world to a proto-American text, Bradford's *Plymouth Plantation.* Tellingly, in Bradford's account, the sodomite is discovered as a fellow Englishman, and the exalted bonds that link the male community of fellow believers is separated by only a hair's breadth from the abjected image of the sodomite. Bradford's text brings sodomy to the New World in a way that crosses the divide between self and other, Englishman and native inhabitant, and that redivides the terrain along lines of class, as he attempts to erect a division between the patriarchs—the founding fathers of a new nation—and the dissolute "strangers"—the lower classes that joined the community but were not really a part of it. Accusations of sodomy in seventeenth-century New England are ways of policing emerging social and class relations. It is with Bradford's text that I end because in it I think we can see another "fundamental" national tradition than the one the Supreme Court cited in

Bowers v. Hardwick; it is there that the work I've done in the Renaissance comes home, as it were.[36]

The preceding pages, starting with their citation from Puttenham, enact in brief the shape of the arguments conducted in the pages that follow. Each pair of chapters attempts first a more generalized survey of the field—formations of high literariness in sixteenth-century England, New Historicist readings of those formations, and then the examples of Spenser and the writing of the Countess of Pembroke; antitheatrical tracts, feminist commentators on cross-dressing, and then the examples of the practices of Marlowe and Shakespeare; colonial accounts, and then Bradford. In all that I've written, I hope that the pressure of the Supreme Court decision—as one privileged instance—can be felt. The justices' fundamental confusion, iterated in the laws still on the books, about whether homosexuals are a category of persons or the juridical subject of acts, resonates against the Renaissance confusions. The Supreme Court decision enacts a sodometry, affirming an identity on the basis of acts, legitimizing an act in one situation that it stigmatizes in another. This is not all that far from the position of sodomy in the Renaissance.

It is not only under the pressure of the Supreme Court decision, with its invitations to an escalation of homophobia, not only the assaults on political correctness, with their similar energies, not merely the recent war and its unveiling of the oldest arsenals of hatred coupled to the newest technologies, that put pressure on the work that follows. I think too of much writing about AIDS in the media and in announcements issuing from the centers of power, in which divisions in the population have been affirmed, and the worry expressed has been that the disease might spread from its gay origins—as it is popularly imagined—to the general populace. The disease offers the most awful specter of the interpenetration of these two supposedly divided spheres—gays and straights, so-called risk groups and those supposedly free from worry. It suggests that in sexual acts separate identities cannot be secured. Everything that our society abjects—gays, blacks (for, of course, the other supposed origin of AIDS is Africa), the underclasses—threatens to declare itself part of the body politic.[37] The lethal energies directed against those who have AIDS or are HIV-positive are the latest episode in the persecution of sodomites; people with AIDS are our culture's version of the Elizabethan monster with his heretical beliefs, or the colonialist's promiscuous natives and degenerate underclasses. In our culture, at this moment, in many quarters, AIDS and homosexuality are considered to be synonymous, and AIDS serves as the present site for the lethal confusions that, in the Renaissance, were called *sodometries.*

'Wee/Men': Gender & Sexuality in the Formations of Elizabethan High Literariness

PART ONE

CHAPTER 2

UNDER THE AEGIS of the New Historicism, thanks especially to the work of Louis Montrose,[1] George Puttenham's *Arte of English Poesie* has become a master key for understanding the relations between literature and sociopolitical formations in the Elizabethan period, particularly as they take place within courtly culture. Puttenham's authorizing role for recent critical practices also has been duly noted—by Jonathan Crewe, whose work on Tudor and Elizabethan literature is implicated everywhere in the pages that follow.[2] As Crewe admits (171 n. 3), Book II of Puttenham's *Arte,* devoted to "Proportion" (to questions of metrics), has proved largely inassimilable to his and others' historicizing projects; perhaps for that reason, the final anecdote in Book II to which I will be turning has gone virtually unnoticed (Rosemary Kegl is the only commentator on it that I know).[3] Puttenham offers a story in the spirit of "solace" after the "scholasticall preceptes" that have preceded it, but the anecdote is not entirely irrelevant to questions of "proportion" since it hinges on an ambiguous quatrain in which problems of reading at their most material level are involved: whether the word "weemen" is to be construed as "we men" or as "women," whether "any" is or is not "a nie, or neere person to the king."[4] These are material questions in several senses of the word since they engage the relation between written and spoken forms of language, and depend upon the question of spacing and differentiation through which (to follow a grammatological argument) any possibility not merely of signification but of being can be said to arise. Such questions begin to suggest that Puttenham's inquiries into the "scholastic" matter of metrics could impinge upon his sociopolitical project, and that the disposal of words could be as telling as the uses of genre and trope that occupy Books I and III of the *Arte.* That possibility I would leave now as simply that, since it is not my aim in this chapter to engage in a philosophical investigation of such linguistic issues. Rather, my interest in the anecdote has to do with the various boundaries broached and opened by the terms "weemen" and "any," which is to say, with questions of gender and social distance.

Such an interest, of course, returns us to more familiar ground in the criticism of Puttenham, since gender and social distance (especially questions of class mobility) are by no means unfamiliar topics. Indeed, the verbal prevarications in the anecdote would seem perfectly suited to the subject of a recent essay by Jacques Lezra[5] that (rather obliquely) engages the work of historicist and feminist criticism of the Renaissance, and reads those projects towards an aporetic impasse in Puttenham's text, making it forever impossible to pass easily from it to the determinations that such criticism offers. Lezra suggests instead a different route, through indeterminacies of the sort that the episode at the end of Book II of the *Arte* also displays. His essay forcefully calls into question the belief that history would somehow be a real that had not passed through language or one that could leave language behind. Implicitly, then, historicists who have read Renaissance texts for the singular "truth" of social reformations are asked to pause in their readings of texts and to register a textual remainder not assimilated in their transportations of the text to an elsewhere, an *hors texte.* In Lezra's attentiveness to the abyssal structures of writing, especially, as in Puttenham's case, to a text that is written almost entirely through examples and anecdotes, the notion of a unified text is interrupted. The passage from logic to rhetoric remains suspended; with it, the distinction of male and female that often goes hand in hand with the supposedly entirely differentiated linguistic gestures of (male) logic and (female) rhetoric also comes into question.[6]

The anecdote at the end of Book II of Puttenham's *Arte* could be read along these lines; were we to do so, we would return to the philosophical/linguistic issues raised earlier, and to questions of historicity at the highest level of generality. These are questions to which I am sympathetic,[7] yet I would like (without losing sight of the problematic that Lezra raises) to mobilize the reading of this anecdote to more limited historical concerns, to questions about sexuality that criticism of the Renaissance has not yet raised in its considerations of the relations of literature to gender and class mobility. Granting that the indeterminacies in Puttenham's story cannot lead transparently to some determinate historic, gendered ground does not mean that the only place his story can be read is in its reading, or that its aporias are only textual impasses. The logic of textuality that is the logic of historicity means also that the virtually unbounded possibilities of difference are relatively bound within any textual/historic instance. In this case, disposals of sexuality that do not subscribe to the supposed differentiations of modern object choice as determinants of sexualities provide a locus for my reading. Puttenham's story is of critical interest to me because it suggests that the relations of literature to social formations that have been read could be read differently once such questions about the historicity of sexuality are taken into account.

We need the anecdote, however, before I anticipate my argument any further.

Polemon, "an honest plaine man of the country, but rich" seeks the king's favor; Philino, a courtier, offers his help for twenty crowns, and delivers it "in manner of an Oracle," uttering these lines while hidden behind an arras:

> *Your best way to worke—and marke my words well,*
> *Not money: nor many,*
> *Nor any: but any,*
> *Not weemen, but weemen beare the bell.* (147)

Polemon responds to "this doubtful speach" by taking "the pleasanter construction," and brings his eighteen-year-old daughter to court. She pleads for her father and pleases the king. Thus, Puttenham moralizes, the suitor obtained his suit, and Philino saved his skin, since whatever way Polemon had understood his verses would have been right. "*Philino* served all turns," Puttenham concludes, like the rattlemouse (the bat) who refused to align himself either with the birds or with the beasts when they were at war and who, besides, managed to prey upon a poor husbandman who had no wife to guard his goods.

Puttenham's anecdote seems made to order for the various ways in which his text has been construed. It houses, for instance, the paradigmatic story that Louis Montrose reads, insofar as Polemon's career parallels that movement "from the carte to the schoole, and from thence to the Court," finally to be "preferred . . . to your Maiesties service" (304), the story of preferment and social mobility that Montrose takes to be central to Puttenham's *Arte.* Polemon's schooling passes through the "scholasticall" knowledge of the intricacies of verses capable of being doubly construed; he makes his way to the king through a poem that would seem to epitomize the strategies of dissimulation necessary for courtiership. Indeed, Puttenham compares Philino's poem to the oracle of "the Sybils and sothsaiers in old times" (147), making his story, however contemporary its feel, nonetheless an archetypal one. So much so, in fact, that the story also supports Jonathan Crewe's reading of Puttenham, in which the strong poet rivals and threatens the monarch; Philino's dissimulations, after all, seem mainly to serve *his* turn and to keep him safe; moreover, the final analogy compares him to a crafty bat that "shunned the service of both Princes" (148), the lords of land and sea. In the opening pages of his *Arte,* Puttenham had made clear that the voices of gods really are those of poets, and that their initial function was to reprehend rulers under the guise of their own divinity. Behind the arras, Philino speaks in an unrecognizable voice, one which, if marked well, is doubly marked. Yet those duplicities, in Rosemary Kegl's reading of the episode, are not really difficult to see through; Polemon's "pleasanter construction" of the verses and their imperatives is, she claims, the only happy solution to the puzzle. Male preferment and male pleasures all depend upon the exchange of women. The solution is overdetermined, for the king whose pleasure is being served is, as we are told in the first words of the story, the protagonist of a play by Puttenham called *Ginecocratia,* "a person very amorous and effeminate," who "therefore most ruled his ordinary affaires by the advise of women either for the love he bare to their persons or liking he had to their pleasant ready witts and utterance" (146).

These three readings of the story are not the same, of course: Montrose's depends upon the possibility of an accommodation of interests through shared strategies of dissimulation; Crewe's upon a sense of warring interests for the control of cultural production; Kegl's upon a bottom line of gender difference that Crewe also reads in the opposition of strong male poets to the queen. The story allows these interpretations easily enough once each of the critics is imagined as reading from the position of one of the characters in it, Montrose as Polemon, Crewe as Philino, Kegl as Polemon's daughter; each critic reads Puttenham as he addresses (or, in the case of Polemon's daughter, suppresses) the interests of those involved. Which position Puttenham might be thought to occupy is more difficult to say; he is, after all, summarizing a play of his own. Lezra's prospect of an abyssal intertextuality is opened further since the happy solution that the plot offers would have been as happy had it ended entirely otherwise, as Puttenham makes clear commending the "subtletie" of the "accent and Ortographie" in the disposition of "any" and "weemen." Although Puttenham clearly is closest to Philino, the verse he composes also throws closeness ("a nie") into question; proximity even here might only approximate. Identification could remain indeterminate.

Kegl has claimed something like this when she describes Puttenham as speaking from "a destabilized, decentered subject position" (185), a place, she argues, that he claims from women. Just as Polemon's daughter in the story vehiculates male desire, so Puttenham moves, dissimulating his desire as an ability to be everywhere, to satisfy simultaneously all desires. While women, Kegl argues, are undone by the contradictory demands of their oppression, Puttenham's "undoing" masks his predations—the success he would have no matter how the story turned out. Were that true, however, Philino's position would not be Puttenham's. Kegl sees Puttenham as the batlike courtier; but, recall, Puttenham's bat has returned to country predations and serves no king. "And ever since sate at home by the fires side, eating up the poore husbandmans baken, halfe lost for lacke of a good huswifes looking too" (148). This ending would seem to deny the indeterminacies of Philino's verse, since the bat who served no master winds up in a limited sphere in which to work his predations, an impoverished country scene where he is not even a retainer in the country house of someone like "rich" Polemon, and certainly not at court. The bat is situated in a strange domestic arrangement, consuming the provisions a wife might have kept him from having, sitting by the fire very like the poor husband himself. If this domestic idyll masks courtly ambition, it looks too like the outcome if a less pleasant construction had been made, the one that Polemon avoided, in which his body—a male body, rather than his daughter's—would have been offered to the sovereign, and in which, had that failed to please the king, he would have served only as Philino's prey. But had that happened, Philino, too, like the bat, might have found himself no longer at court. The bat's neither (beast) / nor (bird) seems fundamentally to contradict the logic of Philino's either/or verses; Puttenham's moral, praising indeterminacy, seems to turn upon itself.

The point of the ending of the story thus might be that the knowledge displayed in the poem cannot maintain its indeterminacy forever, that the decentered subject position that Puttenham occupies is also an imperiled one even as it is an empowering one, and that *knowing* that is not the same thing as being able to do anything with one's knowledge; or, to extend the point, that Puttenham's "decentered" position is not *tout court* a site of totalized empowerment. Furthermore, the story's ability to accommodate what might be mutually exclusive possibilities (of the antagonism that Crewe and Kegl read or of the reconciliation that Montrose argues—the prevarications, in a word, between "any" and "a nie") points to the insecure grounds upon which each of these readings depends. As Puttenham's *Arte* forever reminds its readers, especially in its chapters on decorum, there are finally no rules for courtiership. The desire of the sovereign remains incalculable (in this anecdote it is scarcely represented); a king notorious for his preference for women might sometimes prefer a man even if in this instance he did not. The prevarication "we men" / "women" at any time might be decided one way or the other. Moreover, while either a man or a woman could become the preferred one (hence man and woman could be exchangeable identities), the simultaneous occupation of the singular, doubly marked spot ("weemen"), seems impossible. Hence, whatever difference gender makes, that difference is not accounted for by the double desire that Philino's verses imply.

From this perspective, we can see that Polemon's "pleasanter construction" of the oracle that might be taken to mark him as an "honest plaine man" hardly is sustained by the less than plain way in which his daughter is introduced, "apparelled as gay" as Polemon can imagine, a daughter who, besides, knows how to "behave her selfe in countenance and also in her language." We don't know what she says to win the king's favor, but we have been told it is either women's bodies or their wits that please him. This woman's body is covered gaily, and her wit also has been trained. She knows how to present a countenance, a face that may or may not be her own. Polemon thinks of his daughter after he hears the oracle, a voice that might be that of a sybil or a soothsayer, a voice, that is, that might be male or female, and which cannot be heard to have said distinctly "we men" or "women." It's spoken behind an arras, and it produces in Polemon the thought of a dressed-up daughter. In a word: Polemon's daughter matches Philino behind the arras and his cloaked language; which is to say that it is not clear that her successful suit is simply the product of her gender. The "pleasanter construction" involves the pleasantly constructed daughter who seems already to have read or to embody Puttenham's ambiguous *Arte.* Thus Polemon's "plainness" is complicated by the very trajectory that produces the "pleasanter construction." Moreover, however much the daughter is represented as a duplicate of Philino, the outcome of the story does not sustain the analogy, for it is not clear that the story is simply that of Philino's triumph or that his success merely matches the daughter's. Philino thinks he is playing a con game with simple, honest Polemon; however empowered he is, there also are indications of his limits. "A merry companion at Court" (146), Philino nonetheless appears unable to do anything for Polemon except recite his oracle to him; he does not bring him any closer to the king. Rather, it is only after the daughter appears that Philino can guide her to other lords, only after *they* (not Philino) approve of her that she finds herself in the presence of the king. Philino gets his twenty crowns; it's not apparent that he gets anything else. Hence, while his oracle seems designed to serve the ideological function of suggesting that money never moves the king, it also exposes what might otherwise remain unremarked, monetary exchanges which seem to give Philino only a limited entree in a circulation that exceeds his calculations. For the final bat/man idyll might also suggest that Polemon and his daughter succeed in ways that Philino cannot once the pleasanter construction happens to please the king.

These complications, fostered by the prevaricating identity of men and women, suggest how difficult it would be to say that the story exactly supports any of the critical positions that first seemed to find their exemplification in the tale. However much the story might look like Montrose's machine for the mutual satisfaction of king and courtier, it would also appear to depend upon incalculable and multiple interests that are only marginally represented and yet are crucial to the story: what are the lords up to? what interests do they represent? how did this daughter get educated? is there nothing in these exchanges for her? And to Crewe's reading, one would want to ask whether Philino is a strong poet or a court jester, whether twenty crowns represents much of a triumph (how near to the crown do those crowns get Philino?)—one would want to ask, too, how far Puttenham identifies with his mouthpiece in a story that seems to be about mouthpieces and ventriloquism, a series of displacements that also might displace Puttenham. Finally, one would have to ask whether gender poses some bottom line in this story, whether reading the daughter as a counter in exchanges between men has not devalued her even further than the story does; whether, also, Puttenham's investment in her is, as Kegl argues, her divestment.

The undecidability that my reading points to has a bottom line as well: not that of language per se, but of the relationship between acts of signification (relations of proximity between signified and signifier which can never be relations of identity) and the sexuality that the oracle bespeaks and that Philino "knows" (is it what has assured him his slippery place as "merry companion"?). How are we to read the overlap of "we men" and "women"? The multiple interpretive possibilities that the story seems to sustain and yet to contradict return us to that question, and thus to the indeterminate desire that the verse represents. How is gender difference produced if the trajectory of desire is not determined by the gender of its object? However much it might seem (as Kegl contends) that there is only one possible way to construe the king's desire, Philino's verses suggest otherwise, his position as "merry companion" implying the intimate source of a knowledge that is otherwise unrepresented in the tale (we never see Philino in the company of the king). If we take that trajectory of desire into account, issues that might be thought of as separate in the story—issues of class (male mobility) and gender (female subordination)—cannot be stabilized or sealed off one from the other. In a word, this story does not presume that there is only one form of desire.

That assumption is one all the critics share: that male self-promotion and ambition are propped on (hetero)sexual desire but are not themselves to be thought of as sexual. Yet when the daughter and the verses are in the same position it becomes difficult to maintain that distinction, hard to know whether merry companions and witty daughters do not potentially share the same space in relation to sovereign desire. One thing that is clear, however, is that the critics assume that there is only one form of desire—heterosexual. The pleasanter construction is, no doubt, more pleasant precisely because it appears to stabilize gender and male prerogatives. But much in the story suggests that not all of the desires represented in the story are calculable within a heterosexual matrix. Most of all, of course, it is the king's desire that seems at once blatant and at the same time utterly obscure: there would be no need for the oracle, after all, if it were always the case that a woman was the way to the king's favor. But if the bottom line is a desire that could go either way, if the route to promotion could be either through women or man-to-man, then women are not simply in a position of displacement. Indeed, it is possible, as I've suggested, to read the tale as one in which simple Polemon betters wily Philino, though it would be naive to suppose that winning his suit simply brings to an end the rich countryman's engagement with the court. One might wonder too whether the daughter who paved the way to Polemon's success is represented in the final analogy, failing to safeguard the domestic sphere.

Puttenham's story, in short, is written, as Kegl suggests, from multiple sites of identity and poses possibilities of reading that seem endless and incalculable; however much the tale seems bent on mystification, it would be a critical mystification to believe that Puttenham writes from a position of control conferred upon him thanks to his gender or to his proximity to the court. For it is both those attributes that the verses prevaricate; their unsure ground sends us back to the unsure ground of a desire that in its very indeterminacy always is determining, but never the same way, the possibilities of positioning that circulate in the story and that are marked as locales (court/country), gender (male/female), by the double suits (of father and daughter) and the double-voiced double desires of Philino, in the position of knowing either/or and perhaps, at the end, transformed into the bat who is neither/nor and, at least from the perspective of the court, virtually nowhere.

Although the anecdote has already been made to bear a large interpretive burden, if we are to read it in terms of the histories it implicates there is one clue in it that needs to be pursued further. It is suggested by the title of Puttenham's play, *Ginecocratia*. Ostensibly the rulership here is that of a man ruled by women, an "effeminate" man. But what if "his" sex was a masquerade, if the ambiguous genitive of the title, the rule of women, allowed for a monarch of either sex? If this were, in short, a play about female rule? Who is this story about, who is the monarch in it, Henry VIII or Elizabeth I? To raise this question will allow us to take note of an analogy that runs throughout Puttenham's *Arte,* between *that* father and his daughter; it will also allow us to consider a topic that has engaged much recent criticism, the gender of Elizabeth I. Ultimately, it is my aim in the pages that follow to think about the role that sexuality (as glimpsed in this anecdote in Puttenham) plays in the making of courtly makers at the court of both Henry VIII and Elizabeth I and in the formations of courtly literariness.

That the monarch in this anecdote could be either Henry or Elizabeth is not, after all, a very unlikely supposition. Critics (especially Louis Montrose[8] and Leah Marcus[9]) have shown how Elizabeth's representations occupy every possible gender position: that, as Montrose emphasizes, the queen represented herself in all the sites of femininity (as determined by marriage and as undermined by her): virginal maid, wife, and mother (to the nation). But equally so, as Marcus insists, she preferred, more and more, to call herself prince, to figure her "other" body (the immortal body of the state) as male. Since that body never dies, Marcus argues, Elizabeth virtually "solved" the succession problem by prevaricating her masculinity as a self-perpetuation: the prince could succeed himself. These masculine self-representations were developed, the critics argue, precisely because the rule of woman (the very title of Puttenham's story) was problematic, virtually contradictory if not (as John Knox affirmed) monstrous.[10] Yet, the bisexed body raised in response was, the critics also suggest, monstrous too. Among other things, the division of the body as natural (female) and politic (male) is not easily maintained. Perhaps that accounts for the fact that a strong strain of discomfort runs through the critical discussions of the queen's strategies. It suggests too that the image did not simply serve an ideological function, that representation impinged upon the "reality" of the queen's body.

Thus, although Montrose devotes page after page in "Shaping Fantasies" to the threatening image of the Amazon, he distances the queen from the image of a masculinized woman who has no need of men, preferring instead to see her solicitations and refusals of desire as the real calling card of a hyperfemininity: "the Queen herself was too politic, and too ladylike," he assures his readers, "to wish to pursue the Amazonian image very far" (77).[11] The "beyond" of the woman praised as "beyond her sex" stops short in this account. Marcus, too, writes happily about the queen's bigendering in *Puzzling Shakespeare* so long as it seems to be as playful as she takes Shakespearean comedies to be; but when the queen dons armor at Tilbury, Marcus represents her as threatening—as an Amazon, a witch, a monster; her way of taming these images is to worry about whether or not they are, as she terms it several times, "deviant."[12] Indeed, Marcus exhibits some discomfort even when the queen's "flirtatious feminine side" (as she puts it) served to frustrate the desires of her courtiers. As Marcus sees it, at such moments the queen apparently denied her "femininity" by using "her chosen epithet 'prince' to cool potential suitors" (59). Both Montrose and Marcus are fond of describing the queen's gendering as "anomalous" (freakish?) and both have recourse to "androgyny" as a way of describing and softening the "anxiety" (another favorite term) that state is said to have provoked. It certainly provokes the critics.

That "anomalous" condition of the queen Puttenham represents too, as when he writes a "roundell" praising her, in which the encompassing circles of her power find their center in her "pricke" (113).[13] Puttenham's representation bears comparison with an image devised to adorn John Case's *Sphaera Civitatis,* in which the queen surmounts and embraces a series of circles that represent her virtues, a map of her *interiority* that also figures her control of every social sphere: she is everywhere, inside and out, yet also embodied in the empyrean, in the place of God—the locus of her immortal body politic. Her head rises above the circles; the image is, at once, phallic and vaginal, as endlessly prevaricating the relationship between inside and outside ("any") and male and female ("weemen") as the queen did at Tilbury, when the armor she donned pointed her viewers to "the heart and stomach of a king, and a king of England too." What king if not her father? What does this display of the virgin as virago reveal if not her virtuous, powerful, virile soul?[14]

Elizabeth donned armor only once; yet in her speeches she often invoked her father,[15] and she is reported to have posed before the Holbein image of the king, inviting viewers to draw the (obvious) conclusion that Sir John Harrington had no trouble making when he pondered her frequently ferocious behavior.[16] To treat her as "anomalous" is to assume that biological sex and gender are unproblematically sutured in "ordinary" cases and that heterosexuality assigns men and women to stabilized and opposing positions. That is the work that marriage as an institution is supposed to do, and Elizabeth, from her accession speech on, made clear that however her femininity was to be defined it would not be through that straitening and deforming institution. It is often noted that she violently opposed the marriages of her maids, and it is no doubt correct to assume that the queen sought to play a paternal role in disposing of them in marriage, as Montrose has argued. But it is also possible to understand that she wanted these unmarried women for herself, and not merely as her reflections. Once, at least, that desire was voiced, in conversation with the Spanish ambassador, when the queen's "pleasanter construction" of the way to solve the demand that she marry was her proposal that she be joined with Princess Juana, the queen playing the husband's part.[17] Philippa Berry, pondering (to cite the subtitle of her recent book) *Elizabethan Literature and the Unmarried Queen,* has insisted that images of the queen's marriage to her state be taken seriously insofar as they suggest a lesbian relationship, female queen married to female state. Berry reads such configurations as a kind of essential femininity (a problematic analysis since it ignores the masculinization in the Juana story, not to mention the further evidence that Marcus exhaustively presents), but she does offer a compelling argument—drawn from literature as well as accounts of the queen's appearance—that the queen was often represented surrounded by an exclusively female company, one that warded off men.[18] Berry's basic assumption is undeniable, that desire in the period cannot be read through marriage and its syntax of compulsory heterosexuality. Certainly that was not the queen's desire.

Elizabeth's refusal of marriage was not the ordinary thing for a woman in the period. Yet, I would want to argue, the possibility of the gender positions she occupied was not all that anomalous either. The desires she could play upon can be understood far more "normatively" once one dispenses with the notion that the institution of marriage corresponded to or was (or is) the only locus for sexual desire, once one allows too that desire does not take only one form. Heterosexuality and homosexuality are both misnomers in the Elizabethan period—as they are now. The supposed modern regimes of the supposed absolute differentiation of these desires, often assumed in discussions of Elizabethan literature, and certainly responsible for some of the critical discomfort with representations of the queen already noted, need critical analysis.[19] Marriage, we know, was an extension of patriarchal prerogative, and involved the disposal of women's bodies, securing them as instruments for reproduction. Elizabeth's "feminine" flirtatiousness, with which Marcus seems so uncomfortable, also points to the widespread evidence (in literature, for instance) that the desirable woman was the woman taken outside of marriage or (as the genre of comedy insists) the woman who is refused. Whatever marriage consolidated in the period, it also seems to have represented an end to desire. If desire occupied some terrain of the illicit and the extrajuridical, then Elizabeth's "anomalousness" positioned her in that captivating locus. If so, one can make sense of the slide in Marcus's analysis from the woman who whets desire by saying no to the position of the "prince": one need not, that is, assume that Elizabeth's "masculinity" was a turn-off, or suppose that male/male desire represents a condition of impossibility.

There are various ways of understanding the appeal of Elizabeth's sexuality: one could follow Christopher Pye in *The Regal Phantasm* and invoke the psychoanalytic configuration of the phallic mother. Perhaps even more to the point (it would still be Pye's) one could take stock of the ways in which *representations* of the queen would operate even when in the presence of her "natural" body (is there a body outside of representation?). Her dazzling displays refuse the stabilization of gender and cannot be flattened out as "androgyny"; they provoke imaginary identifications, siting the queen as a locus of contradictory drives that, from the vantage point of psychoanalysis, seem situated before the oedipal divide. I don't think that one needs to locate the play of Elizabethan desire within the discourse of psychoanalysis, however, although perhaps it is only by recourse to the unconscious and its contemporary theorization that one can move beyond the impasse represented by the normalizing critical procedures of Montrose or Marcus. To understand the queen's sexuality, and its relationships to Elizabethan sexualities, it seems crucial to invoke the historicity of sexuality, for it gives us ways of recognizing that what was regarded as *illicit* in the period can be connected to the queen's refusal of the licit mode of disposing of the female body. In that light the queen's masculinity would not necessarily serve to bar male desire (Philino's verse suggests as much too, of course). Moreover, one could see that what is being done at the level of sexual desire also bespeaks a political desire—one that aligns the queen with her male progenitor. It is along these trajectories that political culture develops in the sixteenth century and, as I will be arguing shortly, in poetic projects like Puttenham's *Arte*.

Perhaps the easiest way to see the fundamental role that a different organization of sexuality might play in representations of the queen (or of the king in the position of "weemen") is suggested by a recent essay by Constance Jordan examining the Siena *Sieve Portrait.*[20] By now, it is no surprise to read the image of the queen in that picture as one that is heavily masculinized, a portrait of an imperial Elizabeth, solitary, posed between a storied column and the globe. She holds the sieve, an enormously complex and condensed image of, at once, the virgin and her abilities to penetrate, as Pye has remarked in his analysis of the image.[21] What Jordan adds to this analysis (besides some rather tortured attempts to read the enigmatic inscriptions on the painting) is an attention to the background of the Siena painting that is indeed worth pausing over. A man approaches in the far distance—mythologically he may be a latter-day Aeneas arriving at the court of a Dido who this time says no because she already *is* Aeneas the empire builder; Jordan suggests that the figure may represent Christopher Hatton, one of those suitors whetted and denied by the queen. His route to her is blocked and facilitated by a male couple that Jordan reads as

RIGHT: *The Siena Sieve portrait (detail)*

OPPOSITE: *The Siena Sieve portrait of Elizabeth I, attributed to Zuccari, Pinacoteca Nazionale di Siena (reprinted by permission of Soprintendenza per i Beni Artistici e Storici, Siena)*

if locked in a sexual embrace. She takes this couple to be a version of the "androgynous" queen:

> The figures of the procession are shown in attitudes sufficiently ambiguous to suggest that the queen's rule is again represented as governed by the notion of androgyny. . . . Were viewers to search for a clue to the meaning of the procession scene as a whole, they might well select the figure of the strangely posed guards. They stand together almost as lovers, the elder one open to the advances of the younger who, particularly, seems to represent man and also woman, to be at once phallic and uterine. In his doubleness, he serves as the imagistic equivalent of Elizabeth the prince. He is the *haec vir* to her *hic mulier.* (171)

Jordan's analysis is suggestive, though some of its assumptions require further probing. The young man, for instance, is said to be male and female on the basis of his "protruding doublet," which

Jordan takes to be both a "codpiece manqué" as well as a way of making his body appear pregnant (it is more likely, as Karen Newman has suggested to me, that the size of his doublet serves as a class marker). Such an analysis is further unfortunate in its assumption that "genuine" femininity would be represented by the pregnant body; Jordan makes that interpretive move, it appears, because she can imagine only that male/male relations involve one man playing the woman's part. Jordan loses the force of her insight—that the male/male relationship, differentiated by age in the picture, figures the queen, that a form of sexuality that does not depend upon gender difference is congruent with the bigendered queen. In this context it is worth recalling that when Elizabeth thought of marrying Princess Juana, it was their age and power differentials that allowed her to transpose the terms *husband* and *wife* onto the two women, that the scandalous marriage she imagined was not based on gender difference. It is such differences, rather than gendered ones, that the two male bodies display. In that light, it must be noted that these two men are not the only couple in the picture. Behind the Aeneas/Hatton figure a long-haired page boy follows; these two make another normative male couple, distinguished by age and social position.

In an analytic move fully congruent with those that Philippa Berry deplores, Jordan glances at another figure in the background of the *Sieve Portrait,* the "duenna figure" (smiling complicitously, Jordan opines), only to leave her out when the meaning of the procession is adduced. She can be read as occupying the place of transformation in the scene from an entirely male world (in which desire of men for each other is also in the service of the queen and her desire) to the male/female sexual encounter the scene seems to be suggesting and denying at once. Much as the duenna could suggest a continuum from one desire to another, it is also possible to read her as the figure most proximate to the queen and to the queen's desire—a desire for another woman. Montrose has remarked that Elizabeth was surrounded by thousands of importuning male courtiers, and a small number of (protecting?) women, as if that meant that the company of women was insignificant. One of those women is in this picture; is her smile one that registers that male/male and male/female desires need not be read as oppositional? Or one that registers that her proximity to the queen is the route that these men must take? It was literally true that access to the queen's body was in the hands of a small number of women; no approach to her privy chamber without passing by the female guard.[22] These women are the only people we can be sure were intimate with the queen's body. Elizabeth's remoteness in the Siena portrait (she stares off into the distance) is the counterpoint to her provocation of the desires of men for men, of women for women; she is the place where those desires could meet and cross without necessarily becoming identified one with another, without either of them ever assuming the position of male/female desire as it is supposedly controlled by the institution of marriage. Her remoteness is at once the position where *any* desire could be hers and where *anyone* could be *nie.* The represented body of the queen, the queen as seen only through the powers of representation, is a locus of the transformation of every sort of desire outside of marriage. It depends upon the spheres of sexuality that are not subsumed by marriage. It depends, in short, upon the overlaps of "weemen" that Puttenham's story illustrates.

How, then, might Puttenham's monarch also be Henry VIII? The obvious answer, that Henry was a great womanizer, only begins to answer the question, since it begs the knowledge that Philino displays. The "merry companion" has his historical counterparts, however. The king devoted to pastime and good company gathered around him a group of dashing young men, his so-called minions; by 1518, they occupied the privileged position of Gentlemen of the Bed Chamber. As David Starkey has argued, these men point to an important development in sixteenth-century kingship, the rise of the Privy Chamber as a locus of political power based in its physical proximity to the king. The chamber itself, Starkey argues, has its origins in the Groomship of the Stool: the man who attended the king on the toilet soon had control of his signature and his money. Puttenham's *Ginecocratia* can, without difficulty, be seen in this context: its insistence on a duplicitous textuality (in Philino's verses and in the daughter's educated appeal) matches the control of the king's signature, the dry stamp finally affixed by the last Groom of the Stool to Henry's last will and testament. Money, however mystified, circulates through the story. Were Henry's minions, those men closest to his body, sexually close? Cardinal Wolsey appears to have thought so when he attempted (unsuccessfully in the long run) to suppress the Gentlemen of the Bed Chamber. The minions were accused of "not regarding [Henry's] estate or degree," of being "so familiar and homely with him" that they "played light touches with him that they forgot themselves." And the king permitted it without rebuke or reproval, for they were "his very soul."[23]

Starkey reads Wolsey's opposition to the minions as the beginning of faction, the court divided by conflicting interests. Were these too love interests? Wolsey made himself and his court a rival mirror image of the king's (no Gentleman of the Bed Chamber he), but he was also capable of writing to Henry, as he began to lose his control over him, declaring "that there was never lover more desirous of the sight of his lady than I am of your most noble and royal person."[24] As the court divided—between the Boleyn faction and Wolsey—the cardinal continued to depend upon what Eric Ives refers to as his "magic" to sway the king even as he seemed to be opposing the royal will and the king's desire for Anne Boleyn. Ives appears baffled by the initial success of Wolsey's "magic." It is less puzzling, however, when we attend to the close of one of the love letters that Henry wrote to Anne at about the same time; complaining of her absence, he ends a letter saying it is "escrypte de la main de votre serviteur qui bien sovent vous souhait au lieu de votre frere," written in the hand of her servant who often wishes that she were where her brother was.[25] George Boleyn had been the king's page from the time the minions had first been drawn to the Privy Chamber; in 1528 he was promoted to Esquire of the Body. When Anne fell, charged with incest and adultery with her brother, charges of sodomy also were implied,[26] and not surprisingly, for as Alan Bray has reminded us, it was precisely the charge that would accompany treason and not at all unlikely to light upon the male/male sexual relations normally obscured under the guise of pageships and Privy Chamberers.[27] Henry's letter names a "place" his future queen and her brother could have shared.

This makes sense too of a rumor that circulated around another of Henry's queens, Katherine Howard, whose attentions to one of Henry's Gentlemen of the Privy Chamber, Thomas Culpepper, particularly piqued the king. The young man, the French ambassador wrote, "brought up in the king's chamber" ("nourry dès son enffance en la chambre du roy") had "usually slept in the king's bed" ("couché ordinairement dans le lict dudit seigneur") and had been advanced almost to the position of a blood relative ("traicté caressé et honoré aultant que s'il eust esté du propre sang dudict seigneur"); then in a show of "merveilleuse ingratitude," he repaid his master for all his favors and "caresses" by wishing to "share the queen's bed as much as he had the king's" ("voulloir estre particippant du lict de la royne aussi bien qu'il estoit de celluy du roy").[28]

How close the king in Puttenham's *Ginecocratia* might be to *this* Henry is suggested by two historical anecdotes offered later in his *Arte,* stories about Sir Andrew Flamock, Henry VIII's "standerdbearer, a merry conceyted man," whose wit (like Philino's perhaps?) broached even the limits allowed to someone "knowne to be a common iester or buffon" (274). In the first anecdote, the king, with Flamock at his heels, arrives in the park at Greenwich. Henry blows his horn, and Flamock, having "his tayle at commaundement," lets out a "rappe." Flamock's fart offends, but he manages to turn it into an artful statement that draws the king's laughter: "your Maiesty blew one blast for the keeper and I another for his man" (275). As Rosemary Kegl has remarked about this anecdote, Flamock manages to regain the king's graces by reassuming a properly subordinate position, thereby restoring a hierarchy violated when his desire seemed to rival the king's.[29] What desire, however, is in question here? What is the nature of the offense? Flamock has not merely made his fart equivalent to the sound of the royal horn; by equating what comes out of the king's mouth with what comes from his anus, Flamock has, as it were, put his "tayle" in the king's face, insisted, at the very least, that his anus is not at the service of the king. In the order that is restored, his "cleanliest excuse" places the "tayle" in a position no longer "unmanerly" or "uncomely." The story suggests—even as it effaces this fact in its witty solution—that there is a proper place for Flamock's "tayle" once it is not at his command; his "tayle," rather, serves the king. Having at first attempted to be in the king's place (to initiate desire), he takes up a position which, however subordinate, nonetheless imitates the king's desire or reveals a sexual impulse in his sounding horn. What is made proper and comely and, at the same time is covered by Flamock's witty solution, is the desire of a man for a man. At the end of the episode Henry has the gamekeeper, Flamock his man.

The second story also concerns a fart, but one that is less easily managed. Once again, the two men are at Greenwich, but this time the king desires "a fayre Lady . . . lodged in the tower of the Parke." The king begins a poem addressed to her, and invites Flamock to end it:

> The king began thus:
>
> *Within this towre,*
> *There lieth a flowre,*
> *That hath my hart.*
>
> *Flamock* for aunswer: *Within this hower, she will, etc.* with the rest in so uncleanly termes, as might not now become me by the rule of *Decorum* to utter writing to so great a Maiestie. (275)

Flamock ends the rhyme by, once again, insisting upon his "tayle"; this fart, turned into art, enrages the king: "he bid *Flamock* avant varlet, and that he should be no more so neere unto him." Flamock presumes upon his *nearness* to the king; the prevarication upon "any" in Philino's verse is in question here. Read in the context of that anecdote, Flamock's nearness and his insistence upon the anus sexualize their proximity. The two men have come courting a maid in the tower, however, a familiar homosocial scenario, and not only because the way in which Henry desires this woman, whether "for her much beauty by like or some other good partes" (276), matches the desire of the king in *Ginecocratia.* Like Philino, Flamock knows that the amorous king has desires of more than one kind; his versified fart voices the indifferent desire for "weemen" and suggests the (anatomical) place where that desire can be satisfied on both male and female bodies. Flamock fails to please the king here, just as, earlier, it is intimated, Philino's indifferent solution might not have worked either. But the reason is not because the king has only one desire, just one at a time. Decorum is the impossible, uncodifiable knowledge of proper timing and Puttenham's explanation of Flamock's error does not endorse Henry's desire (nor is the king in *Ginecocratia* approved when he is described as effeminate). Flamock has erred, Puttenham concludes, because "whome we honour we should also reverence their appetites, or at the least beare with them (not being wicked and utterly evill)" (276). Flamock may have turned "a pleasant and amorous proposition" into "lothsomenesse by termes very rude and uncivill" (276), as Puttenham explains his indecorum, but what is rude is not farting per se (not the anus) but the articulation of a relationship between male/male desire and the inordinate desire for women. Both are illicit, and sodomy is the name for an unspoken connection; Flamock's "fart," however much it euphemizes, comes close to saying the unsayable. When Puttenham describes the king's desire as not being "utterly evill," he condemns it and at the same time attempts to protect it from the revelation covered in Flamock's rhyme. (Similarly, Puttenham writes "etc." rather than the word "fart.")[30] Flamock's rhyme punctures the masquerade of courtly wooing by declaring the proximity of the king's "pleasant" desire to male/male sexual relations. Flamock's jests are not just rather tasteless bits of bathroom humor: they take us back to the Groom of the Stool and to the always breachable boundary between inadmissible and admissible desires. In the second anecdote, Flamock has breached a decorum of speech.

This is a decorum that Puttenham attempts to preserve in his telling of the story through the use of "etc." and in his qualified condemnation of the king's desire. Where he stands in relation to the desire that Flamock articulates is suggested much earlier in the *Arte,* when Puttenham considers how kings have rewarded poets in the past. "*Henry* the 8. her *Maiesties* father," he writes, "for a few Psalmes of *David* turned into English meetre by Sternhold, made him groome of his privy chamber, and gave him many other good gifts" (32). Henry's act parallels that of Francis I and Marot mentioned just before; a classical precedent appears several chapters later when Virgil's treatment by Augustus Caesar is recalled:

> he vouchsafed to give him the name of a friend (*amicus*) which among the Romanes was so great an honour and speciall favour, as all such persons were allowed to the Emperours table, or to the Senatours who had received them (as frendes) and they were the only men that came ordinarily to their boords, and solaced with them in their chambers, and gardins when none other could be admitted. (70)

One might be reading Alan Bray on the proximity of friendship to sodomy. Notice, too, that Henry's behavior here is slightly undercut: not in his granting of the rewards of friendship (shared beds and boards), I hasten to add, but by the implied unworthiness of Sternhold's accomplishments. Psalm writing is not the courtly making that Puttenham promotes. Nor is the explicitness of Flamock's rhyme.

If it is clear by now that Puttenham's *Ginecocratia* could as easily be about Henry VIII as Elizabeth, what remains unclear is how to read that analogy. Just as the moral of the Flamock stories is that there is no moral—no singular rule determining decorum—so the fact that either Henry or Elizabeth can be placed under the signifier "the rule of women" will not determine how they are so placed. Puttenham tells these two anecdotes about Flamock with a clear sense that Elizabeth may be reading them. "Etc." marks the spot of her reading and announces a decorum of what is *here* considered the properly speakable; it renders inexplicit what Flamock said, but hardly makes illegible the doubled desires that I have been describing. No more so than the "etc." that appears in the anecdote told just before the two Flamock stories, about a French princess barred succession by the Salic law, who, offended by a remark directed at her, said, "thou durst not have said thus much to me if God had given me a paire of, etc. and told all out, meaning if God had made her a man. . . . The word became not the greatness of her person," Puttenham concludes (274); while the princess had said "balls," Puttenham does not here. No Salic law barred Elizabeth's way to the throne, however, and elsewhere, in two rondels composed for her, she, like the "weemen" of *Ginecocratia* "beares the bell" (102) and the balls (as the center and circumference of every circle, vaginal or anal); she is even, we might recall, the "pricke" (103) at its center. Puttenham writes these lines for the queen as much as he writes his "etcs." for her. How is one to parse the proportions that govern the unspeakable and the admissible? Puttenham himself suggests that there is no determinate answer to such a question.

What he also suggests in the analogy between Henry and Elizabeth, between "we men" and "women," are possibilities of identification across genders facilitated by desires that are not limited by heterosexual choice or by the regulation of gender effected by the exchange of women under patriarchy, or by the system of marriage that institutionalizes those exchanges. Such an analogy also governs Puttenham's writing of English literary history, arguably the most consequential chapter in his book (I.xxxi), since his schema, in which Chaucer is the "father" of English poetry, and in which sixteenth-century literature may be divided between the accomplishments of Henrician and Elizabethan writers, continues to be standard literary history. As Puttenham writes it, by the end of Henry's reign there "sprong up a new company of courtly makers, of whom Sir *Thomas Wyat* th'elder and *Henry* Earle of Surrey were the two chieftaines" (74). "Now," Puttenham writes, history repeats itself, and "in her Maiesties time . . . are sprong up an other crew of Courtly makers Noble men and Gentlemen" (75). If, at first telling, Wyatt and Surrey are the two chiefs (paralleling Chaucer and Gower, "both of them as I suppose Knightes," Puttenham opines [74], quietly demoting father Chaucer to this paired position), at second telling Puttenham can "finde very litle difference" (76) between them. The pair of archetypal Henrician poets seems ready to join the undifferentiated crew of modern poets at the queen's court. She, it appears, steps into father Chaucer's place, or perhaps into her father's place, or is almost about to. She is proclaimed the greatest of poets, and her career lies before her, whenever "it shall please her Maiestie to employ her penne" (77). The kind of poem she might write,

Puttenham had already revealed in the opening chapter of his *Arte*: it is no different than the way she reigns, "making . . . the poore man rich, the lewd well learned, the coward couragious, and vile both noble and valiant" (21). Puttenham's description of these "poems" bespeaks the unspeakable, a courtliness constructed of euphemization and "proper" naming. But his literary history takes the same form when father Chaucer is made a partner in a male couple, or when the male couple of Wyatt and Surrey provides the prototype for the Elizabethan courtier. Elizabeth's "writing" in this new configuration makes her, at one and the same time, a "father" but also the master poet who can rename all sorts of illegitimacies.

How are courtly makers made? How is the analogy between these two moments in sixteenth-century literature to be understood? These are questions that criticism has engaged. Louis Montrose finds in Puttenham a testament to "the failures of Renaissance Humanism. . . . The *Arte* itself evolves from being a text in the tradition of mid-Tudor Humanism to one that propounds the decorative courtly style of the high Elizabethan period," he writes, and his text "represents, in little, the epochal transformation of the Orphic Poet into the cunning princepleaser."[31] As Montrose reads literary history, Puttenham can glance at the faults of Henry VIII only because he cannot criticize the monarch he must please. Clearly, as Montrose tells the story, Puttenham has it exactly backwards: the time of Henry VIII was the golden age. Making literary history the same as history *tout court,* Montrose conveniently ignores Puttenham's literary history and its insistent analogies between one set of courtly makers and another. It would be difficult, reading Montrose, to recall that there had been courtly poetry before the Elizabethan period, or that earlier humanists, like later ones, also had to be "cunning princepleasers" or pay the price.

Jonathan Crewe implicitly takes up Montrose's reading when he suggests in *Trials of Authorship* that the Elizabethan rewriting of Henrician culture performs a phallic investment in the earlier monarch, "a restoration of the potent 'member' to a symbolic figure whose lack of it in the first place is to be suspected."[32]

(Henry's inability to produce male heirs is what Crewe has in mind; George Boleyn's public announcement of the king's impotence, it is worth recalling, seems to have been his most explicit act of treason.) What this amounts to for Elizabethan writers, Crewe argues, for Puttenham (especially insofar as he may be thought of as the mouthpiece for Spenserian ambitions), is an attempt similarly to invest themselves, to assume a potency threatened by the queen. The stories of the Orphic poet, Crewe claims in *Hidden Designs,* are Puttenham's way of insisting on the role of poets in the making of culture; they represent a challenge to the queen and to political culture.[33] Crewe's analysis demystifies Montrose's idealistic investments in the Henrician age and reveals them as the echo of Puttenham—once, that is, Crewe has read Puttenham's idealizations of the queen as threats to expose her as the worst of poets; this is the very exposure, as I've noted, performed in the opening chapter of Puttenham's *Arte.* As Crewe reads Puttenham's description of the newly sprung courtly makers, they are a crew of "women's men" (*Hidden Designs,* 123), and the strongest of them, as in Puttenham's blazon, gives the queen "balls" ("*Her bosome sleake as Paris plaster / Helde up two balles of alabaster*" [251]) only to dismember her image.

Crewe's story is related to one we have seen before. The "effeminate" monarch is, indifferently, the woman ruler or the ruler ruled by women; male writers (or a critic like Montrose), from this perspective, defend against effeminization, thereby revealing their misogyny. Montrose idealizes Henry's court as an all-male domain in which high culture can be produced and deplores the sycophancy that accompanies the reign of women. In this light, Polemon's "pleasanter construction" was more pleasant precisely because he did not have to take up a position of subordination in relation to the ruler; giving his daughter to the king, he kept himself from the position that Flamock assumed the first time, when he put his "tayle" at Henry's service. But, as we have also seen, Puttenham does not simply endorse this equation; this suggests that Montrose is not exactly reproducing his position, that Crewe has not quite exposed it either. The king in *Gynecocratia* is effeminate in his relation to women, and elsewhere the very form of Puttenham's desire for advancement is found in Flamock's desire for the nearness of the friend or the Privy Chamberer. What is the place of this desire in Montrose's or Crewe's account? What role does it play in the making of courtly makers?

Montrose is silent about these questions: the only form of desire he recognizes is that of poets for the queen, and even that he sees as a pretense of sexuality in the service of ambition. Crewe, far more alert to the possibility of male/male sexuality when he writes of Wyatt and Surrey in *Trials of Authorship,* sees it, especially in the case of the later poet, as fatal (because it is explicit, not masked by Wyatt's craft). "To love in this way," Crewe sums up his account of how Surrey "touched" his servant Clere, and killed him in their erotic exchange, "is at once to court sweet death and to inflict it, indeterminately on oneself and another" (*Trials,* 67).[34] Surrey, Crewe is arguing, woos women the way he woos men (Henry, most notably, whose place he would have taken). Heterosexual relations mask homosexual ones, and for men to seek to touch each other in this way is fatal. The pathologizing goes further when Crewe discusses Surrey's relation to Richmond, Henry's illegitimate son, Surrey's alter ego and longtime companion. Their attachment is labeled adolescent, their sexual relations entailing "homosexual role-reversals"; Surrey is, by Crewe, "doubly doomed" (73): written as effeminate and as homosexual. But such too was implicit in Crewe's characterization of the "women's men" surrounding the queen. Is there another way to tell this story, to think of male/male relations outside of the stigma of effeminization or a misogynistically conceived but nonetheless privileged heterosexuality?

We might turn to R. A. Rebholz's notes in his edition of Wyatt's poetry.[35] Commenting on "It may be good, like it who list," Rebholz notes that although Tottel titled the poem "The lover, taught, mistrusteth allurements," "love is not mentioned" in the poem. "The assurances, therefore, could be other than amatory," he goes on to say; "they might, for example, be political or financial" (400). What Rebholz points to, of course, is one way in which Wyatt and Surrey came to seem the same to Puttenham: both poets had been narrativized by Tottel, their poems made to tell the amatory story that Montrose reads and demystifies, turning love into, for example, political or financial ambition. What such transformations conveniently do is supply a woman in poems that often do not explicitly name their point of interest. Rebholz believes, like Montrose, that these are alternative possibilities, as when he comments on the meaning of life and liberty in "If chance assigned": in an amorous context, power lies in the hands of a lady; but "if the context is other than amorous—for example, political" (428), Rebholz comments, then the poem deals with Wyatt's imprisonment, and life and liberty, by implication, are in the king's hands. Rebholz's alternatives, however, point to another alternative, one in which the languages of love for a woman and love for a man, the amorous and the political, have not been marked off and separated. One, that is, in which an address to a man might sometimes take exactly the same form as an address to a woman. The case is clearest perhaps in Wyatt's "The pillar perished is whereto I leant," a version of Petrarch's poem on the death of Laura and of his patron, Giovanni Colonna. Petrarch's poem suggests that both of these losses might be covered in the same language. Tottel entitles the poem "The lover laments the death of his love," and Rebholz notes that "this is not a love poem but Wyatt's lament for the execution of his patron" (357). An extraordinary statement: if "The pillar perished" is not a love poem, what is? Is love only possible between a man and a woman?[36]

To understand these alternatives, how complexly they work in Wyatt, we might turn to Joan Kelly's "Did Women Have a Renaissance?," an essay that subsequent work addressed to this question rarely has approached.[37] Kelly notices how the representation of women in a text like Castiglione's *Courtier* serves several functions at once: in the neoplatonic strains of the book that are most intimately related to courtly Petrarchanism, the lady is likened to the prince, a move, Kelly writes, that "both masks and expresses the new dependency of the Renaissance noblewoman" (44) under the domesticating pressures of bourgeoisification. The courtier represents as dominant the woman he dominates, and thereby displaces his attempts to exert power on the prince. But what he masks too is his "effeminacy," the fact, as Kelly puts it, that he can influence the prince only by submitting to him, by behaving "like a woman—or a dependent, for that is the root of the simile" (45). By that route, of course, gender is no longer sutured onto a biological body but is, rather, a term produced by structures of social relationship. The empowered woman of these representations stands in for, and displaces, a series of disempowerments, of court ladies and of courtiers. But the woman is also the site of a prince who might also suffer diminution. The courtier woos an image—of the prince-as-woman—that is also an image of himself.

It is easy enough to move from such an analysis to the point that Philippa Berry makes, that Petrarchan love poems in the Elizabethan period are narcissistic performances in which women only serve as vehicles for male desire and ambition. Such a reading seems to me to have overdetermined and limited the possibilities of reading that Kelly's schema could allow. Not, it must be granted, by Kelly, who resolutely answers her question about whether women had a Renaissance in the negative. A bit like Montrose, she too looks back to a golden age. For her it is the feudal period, not, as it is for him, the beginning of absolutism. Certainly, at any number of levels of social analysis, Kelly's point cannot be denied: the ideological production of domesticated, privatized woman in the Renaissance is one of the prime (and, it hardly needs to be said, dubious) accomplishments of the humanism that Montrose celebrates. Legal disenfranchisements of women in the period are real. Nonetheless, not even these massive closures are effective everywhere, and within the repressions and exclusions of women are also mechanisms that are productive—sites of resistance or of failure within the system, excesses or lacks. Kelly's complex analysis of how courtier and court lady could be substituted for each other suggests the possibility of instabilities in these regulatory measures.

This is a point developed in Barbara Correll's "Malleable Material, Models of Power,"[38] which similarly notes that male humanist anxiety about preferment at court often took the form of a fear of effeminization that was policed by the production of women in their texts. In those texts, women are placed in a subservient position, presented to show a proper use of subordination—to teach their husbands how to dominate them. Their "proper" position mirrors that of courtiers and humanists anxious to assure the king that they did not threaten royal prerogatives. What Correll argues, however, is that such representations of women could never be entirely guaranteed, either against the possibility of suggesting the effeminization of the men whose power they assured, or against the possibility that a woman might be given a means for her empowerment; in short, Correll points to "the uneasy presence of the socially constructed feminine, threatening to erupt from its place within the new cultural manhood" (257), threatening to erupt either in male/male relations or in the relations of women to men. This returns us to Wyatt and how to read poems that woo the king or a mistress in the same language. As Crewe implies (*Trials,* 43), Wyatt is, after all, the poet who knows where there is a hind and counts himself among those who come behind. What this means is that Wyatt's poems are traversed by desires that are not to be summarized as either hetero- or homosexual.

One effect of the Tottelization of Henrician verse was to make it appear to tell a single story, the story, as Crewe suggests, that Surrey's poems appear to tell as well. Crewe's demystification of that story need not lead to invariably lethal consequences. It would help, for instance, to see that while Surrey is the first writer of the hypermasculine Wyatt that criticism has gone on writing ever since (Greenblatt's chapter in *Renaissance Self-Fashioning* being, as Marguerite Waller has charged, its most recent exemplar),[39] Surrey also casts Wyatt in the position of Thisby to his Pyramus at the end of one of his elegiac sonnets.[40] This suggests that the role play that Crewe reads in only one direction could work both ways. It suggests that male/male and male/female desires could be regarded as supplementary rather than in the invidious relationship shaped by misogyny. Surrey, after all, writes several poems in which he speaks "as a woman" (Wyatt does too).[41] Yet the woman's voice is often the vehicle to express male/male desire. That such poems are spoken "by" women is as often imputed to them by their Tottel titles, just as "love" (for women) appears in his titles when something else might well be going on at the same time. Weemen. Among other things what might be going on in these "women's" poems is the possibility that that is just what they are. Surrey's "O happy dames," for instance, exists in a single Henrician manuscript, the Devonshire manuscript (BL Add. MS. 17492), and there it is written in Mary Shelton's hand. This fact has been viewed merely as evidence that she copied it out, but the Devonshire manuscript does have poems in it that were written by women. Mary Shelton has been denied authorship thanks to the evidence of what has been repeatedly called her scrawl.[42] The flyleaf of the manuscript reveals, however, that she could produce a signature in italic, a hand that shows that she was an accomplished writer (as learned in the ways of the court as Polemon's daughter). Is the "scrawl" of "O happy dames" the hand of a copyist or a composer? There is no way to know, and the fact that Tottel assigns the poem to Surrey does not decide the question.

Puttenham's *Arte* can be seen anew in this light too. Its address is not just to men on the make, but to women too. Several times, though no one has ever remarked the fact, Puttenham includes women and not just the queen among his readers. "Our chiefe purpose herein is for the learning of Ladies and young Gentlewomen, or idle Courtiers, desirous to become skilful in their owne mother tongue, and for their private recreation to make now and then ditties of pleasure, thinking for our parte none other science so fit for them and the place as that which teacheth *beau* semblant, the chiefe profession aswell of Courting as of poesie" (170).[43] The production of woman in Puttenham's text has been taken to tell a determinately misogynistic story of male violence directed against women. It's not that that story isn't there. But it is not the only one. We recall that Puttenham wrote his "etc." for the queen's eyes, but we may presume she could read beyond the mark that marked as well the space of her (not always unutterable) desire. We can recall too that Puttenham writes a paragraph that seems to recall the opening of Wyatt's second satire; "my mother had an old woman in her nurserie," he writes, going on to cite one of her riddling poems; it delivers a female enigma, the enigma of women's genitals, and having cited it, Puttenham worries about its "reprobate sence" (199). Might this rhyme nonetheless have pleased the queen? Or we might recall the story about the courtier who approached one of the queen's ladies, rocking a cradle and declared,

> *I speak it Madame without any mocke,*
> *Many a such cradell may I see you rocke.*
>
> Gods passion hourson said she, would thou have me beare mo children yet. (194)

"Hourson": the court lady's response voices the refusal of female domesticity and the bourgeoisification of woman. This is the voice of aristocratic protest, one that Kelly no doubt would be glad to hear. One can imagine too that the queen would have approved.

If one can read Puttenham's *Arte* as articulating multiple sites of reading and writing, one must conclude that the making of courtly makers depends, as I've argued throughout, on the possibilities of gender that follow from the indeterminacies of sexuality we first saw in *Ginecocratia.* Multiplicities of gender position—the possibilities that involve not treating all women as "woman" in Renaissance texts, that would involve recognizing that class also makes differences among women, that women are not all the same, and that Elizabeth's "anomaly" might well have been a potentially shareable position—to recognize these alternative possibilities in the writing of gender (alternatives most palpably available through a reunderstanding of sexuality) would mean that we might begin to be able to read Henrician and Elizabethan literature in ways that will deliver it from the single-minded story that some New Historicists have been telling, but also from the ways in which its feminist critics have replied (most damagingly when attacks on male critics place us in the Tootsie role, and homophobia—and misogyny—fuels the charge). Crewe's attempts to sidestep this argument, to open up sexual possibilities not written within a heterosexualized oedipal plot, have begun this project, but not, as I've indicated, unproblematically. There is more to be done.

CHAPTER 3

COLIN TO HOBBINOL The *Januarye* eclogue of Spenser's *Shepheardes Calender* is filled with Colin Clout's insistent complaint about the unresponsiveness of Rosalind. Not far from the close of this lament, the text exhibits an exorbitancy beyond its compulsive repetitiveness:

> It is not *Hobbinol,* wherefore I plaine,
> Albee my love he seeke with dayly suit:
> His clownish gifts and curtsies I disdaine,
> His kiddes, his cracknelles, and his early
> fruit.
> Ah foolish *Hobbinol,* thy gyfts bene vayne:
> *Colin* them gives to *Rosalind* againe. (55–60)[1]

A gloss for line 57, provided by the marginal figure of E.K., seeks to establish the propriety of the entrance of Hobbinol onto the scene of Colin's complaint: "His clownish gyfts: imitateth Virgils verse, Rusticus es Corydon, nec munera curat Alexis" (422). The reader is invited to open Virgil's second eclogue to line 56, in which the shepherd Corydon addresses himself and scores the folly of his suit: his gifts have not won Alexis. "Ah foolish *Hobbinol*": the line translates and transfers "rusticus es, Corydon" to Hobbinol, doubling the allusion, provoking exorbitant questions: not only the question of what Hobbinol's love for Colin Clout is doing in this text, with its monomaniacal lament for Rosalind, but also this one: if Colin is Alexis to Hobbinol's Corydon, is Colin thereby cast as Corydon in relation to Rosalind's Alexis? How far does the allusion to Virgil's eclogue go? Where does the literary allusion place the erotics of Spenser's text?

The questions begin to answer themselves, but only insofar as they point to an excessive economy, literary and erotic at once, of translation and transference. "It is not *Hobbinol,* wherefore I plaine"; Colin is not Corydon complaining about Alexis—*his* Alexis is Rosalind. The allusion establishes the genre of the *Januarye* eclogue through its Virgilian antecedent, and Colin's complaint transfers Corydon's, rewriting Virgil in a series of reversals. The iciness of January replaces the scorching heat of Virgil's second eclogue; Corydon burns in the first line of the poem: "Formosum pastor Corydon ardebat Alexim";[2] Colin freezes: "Such rage as winters, reigneth in my heart, / My life bloud friesing with unkindly cold" (25–26). Genre revision is also gender revision; Rosalind, the woman from "the neighbour towne" (50) who scorns Colin's rustic music, takes the part of Alexis, the urbane favorite of his master who cannot be persuaded of the pleasures of the countryside. E.K. gratuitously suggests the translation in a further gloss: "Neighbour towne: the next towne: expressing the Latine Vicina" (422), an exorbitant note that refers to no original Latin *vicina*; it suggests the "vicinity" of the *Januarye* eclogue nonetheless, for Spenser's poem translates Virgil's eclogue back to its model, the eleventh idyll of Theocritus, Polyphemos's lament for Galatea. The reversals of genre and gender are true to a doubled source.

"Ah foolish *Hobbinol,* thy gyfts bene vayne: / *Colin* them gives to *Rosalind* againe" (59–60). The analogical structure of this exchange of gifts (Hobbinol is to Colin as Colin is to Rosalind) repeats the generic transformation of the second eclogue, a doubling (giving again) that splits the same, rerouting Corydon's catalogue of gifts for Alexis. The same gifts pass from Hobbinol to Colin and from Colin to Rosalind; the same "vayne" effect is achieved in each case—it passes through several hands and is yet refused. Although it is the same, it is no one's and never proper, a text circulating from hand to hand, always out of hand, never arriving. Yet, this circulation within the same also opens difference, sexual difference most notably. For the circular structure further suggests that if Colin is Alexis to Hobbinol's Corydon, and Corydon to Rosalind's Alexis, he plays Rosalind to Hobbinol's frustrated suit. The homologies of this circulation place Colin at a split center, doubling himself; Janus-faced, he looks two ways—as in a mirror.

Mirror tricks of genre and gender: true, again, to the source. Colin looks at the "barrein ground" (19) and sees "a myrrhour" (20); Corydon looks at the sea and sees himself, in an ideal projection, as Daphnis, if the image does not deceive ("si numquam fallit imago" [27]). Corydon offers Alexis the chestnuts that pleased Amaryllis when she was his beloved (52); Colin passes Hobbinol's gifts on to Rosalind. Duplicating images, the same becomes different. In Virgil's poem, Corydon has loved Amaryllis and now loves Alexis to his sorrow; he might better, he says, have borne the disdain of Amaryllis, or have accepted Menalcas, unattractive as he is (14–16). In Virgil's Rome, such alternatives were possible—the love of boys and the love of women were not opposing categories.[3] And in Elizabethan England? "A Shepeheards boye (no better doe him call)": so is Colin Clout introduced in the first line of *Januarye.* Can this boy thus play the woman's part? Another Rosalind, Shakespeare's, playing the part of Ganymede in *As You Like It,* might reply, affirming the identification: "for every passion something and for no passion truly anything, as boys and women are for the most part cattle of this color" (3.2.387–89).[4]

Such a reading is policed from the margin in E.K.'s gloss on Hobbinol: "In thys place seemeth to be some savour of disorderly love, which the learned call pæderastice: but it is gathered beside his meaning" (422–23). E.K., whose earlier translation of *neighborhood* had granted proximity to vicinity, rules "disorderly love" out of "thys place" and "beside his meaning." Beside: exorbitant or parallel? The question, once again, involves the economies of exchange, of genre and gender. For, even as E.K.'s citation of Virgil suggests, the *Januarye* eclogue operates through displacement and replacement. Its "place" is translation, the mirrored spacing of a proximity; "thys place" is always "beside his meaning." The exorbitancy of allusion guarantees such proximity. And thus E.K.'s gloss registers its refusal of "disorderly love" by ordering it through an act of learned translation; this love properly speaks Greek (pæderastice) even as the poem's "neighborhood" is translated Latin. What is "gathered beside" is an exorbitancy written within the economies of exchange, the circulation of the gift and text: "for every passion something and for no passion truly anything," as Shakespeare's Rosalind puts it, the exorbitancy—something and nothing at once—of literature.

Even as E.K. rules out a reading, he rules it into the textual economies of the *Shepheardes Calender*; E.K.'s gloss continues with classical citations of a *proper* pederasty, the example of Socrates, to arrive at this conclusion: "And so is pæderastice much to be præferred before gynerastice, that is the love whiche enflameth men with lust toward woman kind" (423). Does this classicism—from Virgil's second eclogue to a platonized and delibidinized Socrates—secure the literary propriety of the text? Consider Erasmus's account of the second eclogue in *De Ratione Studii,* where Virgil's poem is chosen to illustrate pedagogic method. The poem, Erasmus says, will allow the teacher to discourse on friendship: "'The essence of friendship,' the Master would begin, 'lies in similarity.'"[5] Pairs of friends like Castor and Pollux are to be adduced, and then the poem may be read: "Now it is as a parable of unstable friendship that the Master should treat this Eclogue. Alexis is of the town, Corydon a countryman; Corydon a shepherd; Alexis a man of society. Alexis cultivated, young, graceful; Corydon rude, crippled, his youth far behind him. Hence the impossibility of a true friendship" (175). For Erasmus, Virgil's poem savors of disorderly love, "unstable friendship," differences that refuse the homeostasis of "similarity," identifications within the self-same and proper. From an Erasmian perspective, E.K.'s glosses—the poet "imitateth Virgils verse" (422), the learned disquisition on a proper pederasty—would be excessive; rather than placing Spenser's poem within the confines of classical purity, they overstep those limits.

Yet the "place" of that textual exorbitance, as we have remarked already, is within similitude; and even the Erasmian text offers a mirror. Among the exemplars of friendship adduced by Erasmus is "the beautiful myth of Narcissus" (175). "What has more likeness to ourselves than our own reflection?" Erasmus goes on to ask. His text, too, succumbs to the mirror effects of the *Januarye* eclogue, displays the same logic as the marginal (and exorbitant) glosses of E.K. and their double-edged reflections that attempt to "place" the poem within its sexual and textual economies, a place that escapes those confines by passing through the mirror. The excessive logic of the mirror of Narcissus may overcome the moral economies in which Erasmus would place Virgil's second eclogue—or those that regulate a reading of the *Januarye* eclogue: "The Mirror Stage of Colin Clout."

Thus Harry Berger, Jr., titles his complaint against the *Januarye* eclogue for its "self-indulgent" displays of "narcissistic metamorphosis. . . . Perhaps, to speculate idly, this confusion of literary and erotic motives informed the poetry addressed to Rosalind and affected her adverse reactions: perhaps she questioned the poet-lover's sincerity as well as his taste."[6] Whether she did or not, Berger does. His "speculations" pass through the mirror as he assumes the place of Rosalind, disdaining Colin Clout's narcissistic literary love; or when he occupies the place in which he muses, "why love a lass rather than someone or something more tractable—e.g., Hobbinoll or the 'refyned forme' of the woman as Idea—and more susceptible to the allure of Epanorthosis and Paronomasia?" (156). Berger reacts, exorbitantly, to Colin's line "I love thilke lasse, (alas why doe I love?)" (61) and to E.K.'s gloss, "a prety Epanorthosis in these two verses, and withall a Paronomasia or playing with the word" (423). Mere rhetoric, Berger charges; rhetoric, E.K. defends. Berger "speculates" within the exorbitancy of identifications within the mirror—voicing, variously, vicariously, the positions of Rosalind, of Colin, of E.K., and of Hobbinol. "How real—how genuine or authentic—are the love and grief that can be proportioned to the demands of poetry and displayed in the mirror of art?" (158), Berger queries. One answer suggests itself as the text places Berger's ethical stance, capturing it within the mirror. What, we may ask again, is the "place" of the *Januarye* eclogue within the "real"?

Alan Bray addresses the question, taking up the nineteenth-century misapprehension that the imitation of classical literature in the Renaissance functioned (as it could for the Victorians) as a sign "implying a tolerant attitude to homosexuality. . . . Apparently homosexual themes in Renaissance literature need to be treated with extreme caution," Bray argues.[7] Perhaps, he suggests, the extraordinary case of Christopher Marlowe (his supposed saying that St. John was "Our Saviour Christ's Alexis" [64]) does represent Marlowe's homosexual appropriation of Virgil's second eclogue, but more often classical imitations (as when Richard Barnfield writes to his Ganymede) are "literary exercises" (61) and nothing more—except to those readers who wanted to find in such poems justifications for their sexual tastes. They prove, Bray contends, nothing about their authors. Bray, then, would appear to agree with Berger; there is nothing real in the *Januarye* eclogue, it tells us nothing about Spenser himself, or his loves; it is all rhetorical play, exercises in a literariness at a remove from history.

What is shaky in Bray's argument is implicit in the title of the chapter in which he discusses these questions, "Society and the Individual," for those terms have already assumed an opposition that is, arguably, a post-Renaissance, Cartesian development, and whose use by Bray has the unfortunate effect of making an ideological argument by assuming as universal a quite particular historical (and liberal, bourgeois) construction of the "individual" subject.[8] This is something that Bray knows quite well since it helps him to explain the emergence of homosexual "individuals" in the early eighteenth century, and he cautions that the terms are not to be found in the Renaissance: "To talk of an individual in this period as being or not being 'a homosexual' is an anachronism and ruinously misleading" (16)—misleading, as I have argued elsewhere, even in the case of Christopher Marlowe.[9]

When Bray decides that Barnfield's commonplace book, "never intended for publication and . . . both robustly pornographic and entirely heterosexual" (61), offers the real truth about its author's sexual orientation, savoring of the "personal experience" (61) lacking in his literary exercises addressed to Ganymede and other Arcadian shepherds, he anachronistically assumes the opposition of homosexual and heterosexual, and he assumes that Barnfield must have been one or the other. The characterization of those entries as "robustly pornographic" (as opposed to the "delicate sensibility" [61] of the poems) as well as the categories of "entirely heterosexual" and "personal experience" need to be scrutinized for what Eve Kosofsky Sedgwick might call their "inadvertent reification" (86). For Bray, the secret status of the commonplace book assures the truth of Barnfield's heterosexuality; but this, too, is anachronistic. It assumes a modern "deployment of sexuality" (in Foucault's term)[10] to be in place, in which one can be sure that the deepest secret of the self is its sexuality, especially if, as in the case of Barnfield, it takes the excessive form that Bray calls pornographic. Yet to read the evidence about Barnfield this way rewrites him as a modern subject. It dismisses what might be called the "open secret" of Barnfield's published poems without asking how they found a "place" in the Elizabethan world.[11] For the answers to that question cannot be the ones that Bray offers: that its classical literariness necessarily assured that it would go unremarked (Erasmus suggests otherwise); nor that it could be read homosexually by those inclined in that direction. For, as Bray himself argues, one could not identify oneself as being so inclined. Or, to put the point—*Bray's point*—more radically, there were no homosexuals in Renaissance England.

Such, too, was the case in Virgil's Rome; if *homosexuality* is a term that signifies only in relation to the binary opposition homosexual/heterosexual, then the second eclogue does not operate within that system. Within the Roman sexual system, as Veyne has argued (following Foucault), what mattered was not the gender of the love object but his/her class and age; sexuality was congruent with power differences. So long as a man was the penetrator, he was a man; slave boys and women were the appropriate objects of his desire. Virgil's poem is not necessarily circumscribed by this system—Alexis is not a slave, but his master's favorite; Corydon, who may well be older, also appears to be of a lower class than Alexis, and his love seems to exceed the Roman norm of a passionless sexuality. Virgil's poem, translating the grotesquerie of Polyphemos's love for Galatea, opens itself towards the Erasmian dismissal of its disorderliness even as it uses that safeguard towards an extension of the limits of acceptability, an extension that may also return his poem to the orbit of the erotic system of ancient Greece, which, although similar to the Roman system, had not viewed slave boys as the preferred sexual objects. Rather, as Foucault has argued, the entire ethical system of Greek pederasty was directed at questions having to do with free-born boys.[12]

As Bray argues, differentials of class and age in a number of institutional sites—the family, the school, the apprentice system—also operate to define sexual spheres in Renaissance England in which homosexual acts could and did take place. Such acts do not prove their actors homosexual; likewise, texts like the *Januarye* eclogue (or Barnfield's classical pastorals) will never tell us whether their authors slept with boys. But they may, in the very exorbitancy that I have been reading, tell us about the "place" of homosexuality in Renaissance England; not least if, as Bray contends, it had no place, was not a site of recognition of sexual identity. Rather, Bray posits a *disconnection* between the stigmatization of homosexual acts (within the larger category of sodomy) and their enactment in places in which they went unseen and seen. This is, in effect, to describe the place of homosexuality as an open secret. If *sodomy* is the term most proximate to *homosexuality* in the period, it functions neither solely to designate sex between men, nor is it only (perhaps not even primarily) a sexual term. Designating a range of interlinked social and religious transgressions, it also leaves untouched, Bray argues, the ordinary social channels that permitted homosexual acts to be disseminated through all the differentials of power that mark the hierarchies of Renaissance society. "The individual could simply avoid making the connection; he could keep at two opposite poles the social pressures bearing down on him and his own discordant sexual behavior, and avoid recognising it for what it was" (67), Bray writes. But what *was* it? Bray's sentences, brilliant in suggesting the dehiscence that opens the place of homosexuality, has already foreclosed it by assuming an identity for that "it" which, as his argument suggests, cannot succumb to the later scheme in which homosexuality is a recognized and recognizable category.

The reading of *Januarye* that I have been offering may appear to have been an exercise in deconstructive undecidability, merely rhetorical play. I would contend, however, that it offers a way to read the (no) place of homosexuality in Renaissance culture—that the mirror effects of *Januarye* secure a place for homosexuality through such tactics of resemblance. How to move from the text, and these textual effects, into the world is in fact suggested by the *Shepheardes Calender,* not least by E.K.'s tactics of reading. For his gloss, on the margins, also opens up a relationship between the text and the world, opens it and covers it over as does his gloss on "pæderastice." That double play has the structure of the open secret. Who is Colin Clout? "Under which name this Poete secretly shadoweth himself" (422). Hobbinol? "a fained country name, whereby, it being so commune and usuall, seemeth to be hidden the person of some his very speciall and most familiar freend, whom he entirely and extraordinarily beloved, as peradventure shall be more largely declared hereafter" (422). "Rosalinde: is also a feigned name, which being wel ordered, wil bewray the very name of hys love and mistresse, whom by that name he coloureth" (423). E.K.'s directions for reading cannot be taken very straightforwardly (nor, for that matter, can "E.K.," whose initials remain to be deciphered). If Spenser "is" Colin Clout, for example, he also is figured as Immerito in the *Shepheardes Calender* and no "proper" name is ever delivered for the doubly named author of a yet anonymous text.[13] E.K.'s directions for reading Rosalind treat her name as an anagram—as if the name were itself disordered (or the name of disorderly love), and as if to find her would be the same as performing a play on the letter. In this teasing play between revelation and reveiling, the *Calender* dangles its secrets—the secret of an authorship maintained through a disappearing act in disseminative naming; of an eros that may never pass beyond the letter, and which yet opens a way (within a certain psychoanalytic framework, *the* way).[14] The open secret of this text is not homosexuality, as might well be the case if this were a Victorian imitation of a classical poem. It, rather, has no name "being so commune and usuall" and, at the same time, "very speciall and most familiar." Or, if it does have one, it could be called (following Sedgwick) homosociality. In this text, the name of the open secret is Hobbinol.

Spenser's name remains veiled in the *Calender*; E.K. and Rosalind have never been deciphered; but E.K.'s promise to declare hereafter the identity of Hobbinol is delivered in a gloss to *September*. "Colin cloute: Nowe I thinke no man doubteth but by Colin is ever meante the Authour selfe. Whose especiall good freend Hobbinoll sayth he is, or more rightly Mayster Gabriel Harvey: of whose speciall commendation, aswell in Poetrye as Rhetorike and other choyce learning, we have lately had a sufficient tryall in diverse his workes" (455). That revelation is prepared for from the start. E.K.'s dedicatory epistle to the *Calender* is addressed to Harvey, introducing the new poet to someone who scarcely needs such an introduction, "his most special good frend" (418), and that description is immediately applied to Hobbinol, as we have seen, in the gloss to *Januarye*: "his very speciall and most familiar freend" (422). Hobbinol, moreover, is a name that Harvey takes for himself at the close of the third of the *Three Proper, and wittie, familiar Letters* (632) that he exchanged with "Immerito" in a volume that appeared in 1580, a year after the publication of the *Calender*, another anonymous production in which Harvey's name is the open secret as soon as one gets past the title page and to the first letter addressed by Immerito to his "long approoved and singular good friende, Master *G.H.*" (611). And, if there were any doubt about who "Maister G.H. Fellow of Trinitie Hall in Cambridge" (635) is, as he is addressed in the first of the *Two Other, very commendable Letters* that accompanied the first three, a poem of Immerito's enclosed in that letter twice names "Harvey" explicitly, puns on his angelic first name, Gabriel, and ends by bidding farewell to "*Mi amabilissime / Harveie, meo cordi, meorum omnium longè charissime*" (638), "My sweetest Harvey, to me of all my friends by far the dearest."[15]

Within the *Shepheardes Calender*, Hobbinol is the shepherd suffering from unrequited love for Colin, and that fiction is maintained from *Januarye* to *Aprill,* where, in response to Thenot's question about the causes of his sorrow—lambs stolen by wolves? bagpipe broken? abandoned by a "lasse" (4)? weeping like the showers of April?—Hobbinol replies "Nor thys, nor that, so muche doeth make me mourne, / But for the ladde, whome long I lovd so deare" (9–10); to *June,* where Colin tells Hobbinol that his paradise is not for him; to *September,* and the line that E.K. glosses: "Colin he whilome my ioye" (177). But in the gloss, and in the surrounding apparatus that extends from the poem to other texts and into the world, Hobbinol is Gabriel Harvey, and the poet's special friendship for him is repeatedly announced. Indeed, in the farewell poem to Harvey (written when Immerito plans to leave England on a voyage to the Continent), Immerito's veil is almost dropped as well when he ventriloquizes Harvey's lament for his absent friend:

> Would Heaven my Edmund were here.
> He would have written me news, nor himself have been silent
> Regarding his love, and often, in his heart and with words
> Of the kindest, would bless me.[16]

The relationship between Hobbinol, in the eclogues of the *Calender,* and Harvey, in the margins, functions like the reverse mirror of *Januarye,* identifying (Hobbinol is Harvey), doubling (Harvey is Hobbinol), and reversing (the rejected lover is the special friend) all at the same time. This mirror extends into the world, Harvey taking Hobbinol for his own name in a letter to Immerito. What the eclogues structure as denial and refusal, the surrounding context figures as the acceptance of a special friendship. How is this (non)relationship to be read?

One answer lies within the eclogues themselves, and Hobbinol's role within the pastoral fiction; there he secures a literariness associated with that transformative place, and Colin's refusal of his advances also signals his frustrated attempts to pass beyond pastoral. From the start, Colin has broken the pipes of Pan, moved towards the urban Rosalind, to his devastation; and as late as *Colin Clouts Come Home Againe* (1595), his return to pastoral is a return to Hobbinol, as "The shepheards boy (best knowen by that name)" (1) reencounters the one who "lov'd this shepheard dearest in degree" (14). As late as that poem or the sixth book of *The Faerie Queene,* Rosalind still names what cannot be had. And those returns to pastoral and to Hobbinol remain returns to a refusal of Hobbinol. Colin continues to look elsewhere. This is how Hobbinol explains his plight to Thenot in *Aprill*: "the ladde, whome long I lovd so deare / Nowe loves a lasse" (10–11), and that love has made the writing of pastoral poetry impossible. "Lo *Colin,* here the place" (*June,* 1): so Hobbinol speaks to Colin, luring him to a "Paradise" (10) that Colin rejects as no longer possible. Hobbinol, throughout the *Calender,* is associated with "the place"—the literary, erotic, and sociohistorical place—from which Colin affirms his displacement.

This refusal reads doubly, however; within a duplicity that can be found in the *Calender,* one can begin to move towards the world which it mirrors in reverse. For however much Colin denies, he is a figure in a pastoral poem; the place from which Colin affirms his displacement is the place in which he affirms it. The poet embraces what his figure refuses. These denials are productive. They produce the poems as that double place from which aspirations—toward Rosalind, towards kinds of poetry other than pastoral—can be launched and denied at the same time. Rosalind refuses Colin; she has instead taken Menalcas (*June,* 102), the dark young man whom Virgil's Corydon scorned. Even as the poems glance beyond the confines of pastoral, they are returned within its limits, still turning on Virgilian tropes. But it is also within the confines of Virgilian pastoral that the genre be exorbitant, that it establish relationships with the world; it establishes them by denying them, and Hobbinol is within the eclogues the figure for that denial.

It has become commonplace in certain critical practices that are called New Historicist to argue that "love is not love" or that pastoral *otium* is really *negotium.*[17] This chapter shares with such work the desire to read texts into the world. But in describing the trick mirror that the *Shepheardes Calender* holds up to the world, in pursuing the reversed identification of Hobbinol and Harvey, it seems to me important not to allegorize and thematize the text so entirely that its sole function is to read the world at the expense of the text, to decide beforehand that the world is real and that the only reality that a text might have would be its ability to translate the world in terms that need to be translated back into the social, historical, or political. The literary and erotic translations performed in the *Calender* extend into the world, as the Hobbinol-Harvey identification would seem to guarantee. But it cannot be read as a simple act of translation. The name Hobbinol is carried beyond the confines of the *Shepheardes Calender*, even as the name Harvey appears on its borders. And the double structure within pastoral that I have been describing also extends into the "real" world. We can see it as congruent with the dehiscence that Bray describes, articulating the site of a (non)relationship and a (non)-recognition. We can see it, too, in the fact of double nomination, Harvey/Hobbinol, Immerito/Colin, and the space of (non)identification that it opens. These are structures of identification in a mirror, a productive site of replication.

If we look at the moment in *September* when the veil is dropped, and Harvey's name delivered, we find it in a gloss on Hobbinol's request that Diggon tell the tale of Roffynn; Hobbinol would hear the story since "Colin clout I wene be his selfe boye" (176)—that is, Colin is Roffynn's boy and not, as Hobbinol goes on to say, as he once was, his own: "(Ah for Colin he whilome my ioye)" (177). *September* is a particularly dark eclogue, glancing in Roffynn's tale and elsewhere at matters of state and church, but this particular identification is not all that hard to decipher. We can find "Roffynn" on the flyleaf to Harvey's copy of Jerome Turler's *The Traveiler*, as he records it as a gift from Spenser: "ex dono Edmundi Spenserii, Episcopi Roffensi Secretarii. 1578."[18] *Roffynn* anglicizes the Latin name of John Young, Bishop of Rochester, whose secretary Spenser became in the spring of 1578. If, elsewhere in the *Calender*, and throughout Spenser's poems, Hobbinol appears as the rival for Rosalind, here he is in a similar position with Roffynn; as Colin moves beyond the pastoral world, Hobbinol stays behind, representing what must be refused in order to advance. But advancement also occurs through what is represented by Hobbinol: a mode of high literariness that gives one credentials within the world—in this instance, the classicizing pastoral of the *Calender*—within the exorbitancy of humanistic pedagogy. The secrets of the *Calender* are the open secrets of a secretariat, and of aspirations that must veil themselves in this humble form.

Harvey's role in this worldliness is insisted upon as E.K. continues his gloss identifying Harvey in the *September* eclogue; he lists his recent publications "aswell in Poetrye as Rhetorike" and details Harvey's presentation of a copy of "his late Gratulationum Valdinensium" to Queen Elizabeth "at the worshipfull Maister Capells in Hertfordshire" (455). Harvey's attempts to use his rhetorical/literary skills to secure him a place in the world are perhaps the most spectacular example of the failure of the promises of humanistic pedagogy in the Elizabethan period. Uncannily, Spenser uses Hobbinol/Harvey as the name that secures failure by denying the very tools by which success can be achieved. Yet Harvey, probably not more than a couple of years Spenser's senior but, more importantly, already a Fellow at Pembroke when Spenser entered as sizar, a poor boy, in 1569, also functions as mentor and guide. The intimacy with his special friend writes the aspirations within the rhetorical/literary domain even as the name Hobbinol insists that such aspirers know their place: boys, secretaries to the great and powerful.

The trick mirrors of *Januarye* negotiate the place of the literary within the sociopolitical and the homoerotics of a textual economy that extends into the world and writes the world as much as the world writes the text. The veils of the *Calender* can be drawn only when they open upon an acceptable version of aspiration within the homosocial sphere, aspiration, that is, that knows its place—"A Shepeheards boye (no better doe him call)" (*Januarye,* 1). Immerito, the worthless one, attaches himself to his special friend Gabriel Harvey, hailing him as in his farewell poem as "a poet transcendent" ("egregium . . . Poetam," 637) addressed by "the lowliest poet" ("malus . . . Poeta," Gottfried, 256). The point of homeostasis in this differentiated and hierarchized relationship with angel Gabriel is their friendship; to this friend, the first line of the farewell poem insists, he is not unfriendly ("non inimicus Amicum," 637); no disorderly love, it secures the status quo. Within this mirror relation, Harvey/Hobbinol functions as an alter ego, so much so that E.K. can close his dedicatory epistle by urging Harvey to imitate the new poet and publish: "Now I trust M. Harvey, that upon sight of your speciall frends and fellow Poets doings, or els for envie of so many unworthy Quidams, which catch at the garlond, which to you alone is dewe, you will be perswaded to pluck out of the hateful darknesse, those so many excellent English poemes of yours, which lye hid, and bring them forth to eternall light" (419). And the letters exchanged between Immerito and G.H. continue this theme, referring again and again to their secret poems, and urging each other to make them public. This is a structure of emulation recommended by Erasmus and his followers as necessary to pedagogic success; the title page of the *Three Proper, and wittie, familiar Letters* proclaims the writers as "*two Universitie men.*"

Spenser's Familiar Letters

Yet, in the poem of farewell to Harvey, Edmund urges him to venture even further, beyond such pedagogic, humanistic, pastoral economies, towards the love that Harvey despises, what G.H. designates as Immerito's "womanly humor" (641): "A magnanimous spirit, I know, spurs you up to the summits / Of honor and inspires your poems with emotions more solemn / Than lighthearted love."[19] For the point seems to be that Harvey's misogyny (displayed at length in the three letters, as when he paraphrases "Arte Amandi" as "Arte Meretricandi" [641], or offers two accounts of earthquakes, one for women, another for men) is not requisite for their attachment, nor does the poet's desire for Rosalind mean the end of their extraordinary friendship. So, Immerito's final letter closes, urging Harvey to believe in "the eternall Memorie of our everlasting friendship, the inviolable Memorie of our unspotted friendshippe, the sacred Memorie of our vowed friendship. . . . Farewell most hartily, mine owne good *Master H.* and love me, as I love you, and thinke upon poore *Immerito,* as he thinketh uppon you" (638). This mirroring reciprocity defines a proper "unspotted" relationship between men, not the path of Harvey's aspirations (figured in the *Calender* as Hobbinol's rootedness), and one secured through the negations written as Rosalind's refusals and transferred from Colin to Hobbinol, from

Immerito to G.H. Letters of farewell, again and again. Harvey/Hobbinol confined to the margins—where the "real" enters the poem—and Harvey, in life, never making his way, confined to *his* marginalia.

The love of women does not interrupt this love. Thus, the *Shepheardes Calender* closes by dispatching Hobbinol as go-between to Rosalind: "Adieu good *Hobbinol,* that was so true, / Tell *Rosalind,* her *Colin* bids her adieu" (*December,* 155–56). These poems of farewell to Harvey/Hobbinol also write him into Colin/Immerito/ Spenser's position, structures of denial that ramify out into the world. Here, as they establish a relationship of nonrelationship *between men,* they do so as Hobbinol is asked to voice the farewell to Rosalind that he has so often received from Colin. In these (un)productive circles, the woman is drawn into the circuit of letters passing between men (Rosalind's name is never realized beyond such anagrammatization); she is infolded as that furthering negation that opens a movement towards the real.

So, too, in response to Immerito's question in the first of the *Three Proper, and wittie, familiar Letters,* asking why G.H. had not responded to his beloved's letters (612), G.H. replies—as Hobbinol—promising to reply in letters that are worthy of her: "By your own Venus, she is another dear little Rosalind; and not another but the same Hobbinol (with your kind permission as before) loves her deeply. O my Mistress Immerito, my most beautiful Collina Clout, countless greetings to you and farewell."[20] The *same* Hobbinol/Harvey (one and two at once) writes to Mrs. Immerito (the beloved whom Immerito has married), who is *not* Rosalind, within the folds of this letter to Immerito. But it is also within the letter that Immerito tells G.H. to remember their special friendship and love—"Continue with usuall writings" (638)—although he wishes for "a Reciprocall farewell from your owne sweete mouth" (636); and G.H. hopes to comply, wishing that "I may personally performe your request, and bestowe the sweetest Farewell, upon your sweetmouthed Mastershippe" (641).

These *proper familiar* letters exchanged between friends openly declare their secrets of translation and transference from the start, beginning with a *literal* scene of translation in the very first letter from Immerito to G.H. Immerito offers samples of his skills in translation, his efforts (under the tutelage of G.H.) to classicize his English verses and make their meters Latin: "Seeme they comparable to those two," he asks, "which I translated you *ex tempore* in bed, the last time we lay togither in Westminster?" (611).

Spenser slept with Harvey, and it is no secret. Indeed this is the open secret of a *proper* and *familiar* scene, exhibiting the very structure E.K. read in the name of Hobbinol in *Januarye,* "so commune and usuall," "very speciall and most familiar," for men habitually shared beds in the Elizabethan age. A secret written elsewhere too, for there is nothing to hide. So Roger Ascham, pausing to memorialize his student John Whitney, now dead, and to bid him farewell, recalls, in his book on double translation, this scene of instruction: "John Whitney, a young gentlemen, was my bedfellow, who, willing by good nature and provoked by mine advice, began to learn the Latin tongue."[21] The text chosen for this double translation "out of Latin into English and out of English into Latin again" was "Tully *De amicitia.*" A proper choice. The scene fulfills the dictates of Erasmian pedagogy to the letter, as the teacher incites the pupil to learn—by loving imitation within the specular relationship of similarity and simulation. The child "must be beguiled and not driven to learning," Erasmus writes in *De Pueris Instituendis.* "For a boy is often drawn to a subject first for his master's sake, and afterwards for its own. Learning, like many other things, wins our liking for the reason that it is offered to us by one we love" (Woodward, 203).

To that bedroom scene Harvey brings another. Judging some other efforts at translation, he recommends the use of models for imitation:

> Some *Gentlewooman,* I coulde name in England . . . might as well have brought forth all goodly faire children [as a poet might produce excellent poems] . . . had they at the tyme of their *Conception,* had in sight, the amiable and gallant beautifull Pictures of *Adonis, Cupido, Ganymedes,* or the like, which no doubt would have wrought such deepe impression of their fantasies, and imaginations, as their children, and perhappes their Childrens children too, myght have thanked them. (626)

"Nature has made the first years of our life prone to imitation," Erasmus writes (Woodward, 189); pedagogy is founded in simulation. But for Harvey, all conception is specular, for men and women alike are produced in the mirror, after the images of desire—Adonis, Cupid, Ganymede.

This is not only Harvey's fantasy; it is one shared by his culture. Consider the lines that open Shakespeare's first and third sonnets: "From fairest creatures we desire increase / That thereby beauties *Rose* might never die"; "Looke in thy glasse and tell the face thou vewest, / Now is the time that face should forme an other."[22] This is, indeed, the mirror stage, and not only of Colin Clout. For, as Lacan writes in his essay on the role of the mirror stage in the formation of the I, that initiation into an alienated and split subjectivity has a biological support instanced, for example, by the necessity for the maturation of the gonad of the pigeon that it see another member of its species—of either sex—or even that it see itself in a mirror. "Facts which inscribe themselves into an order of homeomorphic identification which would fold within itself the question of the notion of beauty as formative and as erogenic."[23]

The homeomorphic structures identified in this essay ramify within an order that Lacan calls "orthopedic" (94), the (non)support of an ideal projection—for which Lacan finds the "ancient term *imago*" (90) apt, and Spenser, the Virgilian *imago*—in which subjectivity is founded. The Lacanian insistence on the prematurity of human arrival, and its destiny within an imaginary scene, has its Erasmian correspondent: "Man, lacking instinct, can do little or nothing of innate power; scarce can he eat, or walk, or speak, unless he be guided thereto" (Woodward, 184); "a man ignorant of Letters is no man at all" (181). Imitation of the letter founds the human within a pedagogic apparatus, the "virage du *je* spéculaire en *je* social" (95), turning the specular I into the social I. Such destiny, as Derrida argues, is a *destinerrance,* a straying within a letter whose arrival is never guaranteed.[24] Within that spacing, which, for Elizabethans like Spenser and Harvey, takes the historically specific situation of the apparatuses of a homosocial pedagogy, the Spenserian career—in life, in letters—is launched. In it,

Hobbinol/Harvey serves—in life, in letters—as a marginal site, the "place" of the exorbitant *méconnaissance* that guarantees that institution.

Posting Sidneys

> Sunt enim Aulae quasi publica regnorum quaedam hospitia, in quibus improborum aeque ac proborum ingens est numerus: nullaque disciplina caveri potest, ne affatim sit voluptatum indies quae novae affluunt, atque viros in mulieres, mulieres in viros, homines in belluas, religiosos in cinaedos et scurras varie transformant.—Thomas Moffett, *Nobilis*[25]

The initial gesture of the Spenserian career, as no one needs to be told, is directed to Sir Philip Sidney, named on the title page of *The Shepheardes Calender,* and the addressee imagined for its initial poem ("To His Booke"). Equally familiar is the shift that occurs, as the poet who signs himself Immerito is supplanted by the initialed E.K., and "Mayster Gabriell Harvey, his verie special and singular good frend" (416) steps into Sidney's place. With Harvey and his double, Hobbinol, as I have been arguing, a further scenario of displacement is enacted, one that engages and disengages a career tied to the circulation of letters between men and to spheres of intimacy that *The Shepheardes Calender* opens and forecloses. Displaying and denying a special friendship, the *Calender* desituates its doubly named poet—shadowed as Colin to Hobbinol, Immerito to Sidney—to launch a career in letters "*under the shadow of his wing*" ("To His Booke," 7), Sidney's wing.

Spenser's letter to Sidney was repeatedly reposted, each subsequent edition of *The Shepheardes Calender*—in 1581, 1586, 1591, 1597, 1611, and on—reprinting the first, addressed Sidney, even beyond his death, beyond Spenser's too. Other letters were sent as well: the dedicatory sonnet of *The Faerie Queene* addressed to the Countess of Pembroke, acknowledging her brother as the one "who first my Muse did lift out of the flore" (413); a letter to the countess, dedicating *The Ruines of Time* to her and to the memory of her brother, "the Patron of my young Muses" (471); and, finally, *Astrophel,* appended to *Colin Clouts Come Home Againe.* The return of and as Colin Clout closes another circle; while the career had been launched under the name of Sidney, Spenser's name appears on the title page of *Colin Clouts Come Home Againe*; unannounced by any forewarning, the volume ends with elegies for Sidney. The friends who had urged him to show "thankefull remembrance" of Sidney lest he be tainted with "that fowle blot of unthankefulnesse" (*Ruines*, 471), as he publicly confessed, might have wondered at this belated and occluded gesture of final homage. *Astrophel* could easily have been overlooked in a cursory glance at the slim volume; the running head "Colin Clouts come home againe" runs over the poem, Sidney produced under another's name and title.

It is, perhaps, the belatedness of that final gesture, and the entirely secondary place of *Astrophel* in the volume that contains it, that lead the editors of the Spenser Variorum to ask the question I would reopen here: "How intimate was Spenser with Sidney?"[26] The editors of the Variorum answer by suggesting that one read the evidence, some of which I have been citing, against "the legend that Spenser and Sidney were united by '"friendship" in the deepest and tenderest sense of the word,'" as Alexander Grosart characterized their relationship in the early 1880s. Against that view, Francis T. Palgrave's opinion that the relationship was merely one of patronage is summarized in the Variorum, followed by T. P. Harrison's dismissive review of the tradition behind Grosart. Harrison is marshaled again, two pages later, to state the view the editors wish to endorse, that it would be as erroneous to think of the relationship merely as one of patronage as to follow Grosart. The relationship, Harrison avers, was a literary and intellectual one, though "the extent to which one influenced the other is, at present, impossible of exact definition" (7:490).

Between the two appearances of Harrison, the Variorum editors cannot resist another enjoinder: "Conclusions must rest almost altogether upon one's reading of the documentary references above" (7:488). Since Harrison's 1930 views are the up-to-date objectivity that the editors wish to promote, and since Harrison is given virtually the opening and closing words in the discussion of the relation between Sidney and Spenser, one has to ask why the editors needed to insist twice on the so-called "documentary references," especially since Harrison pointed readers to the "sane and unbiased discussion . . . of De Selincourt" (7:488), which the editors dutifully summarize a page later. Or, rather, two pages of it; the last of the three pages in De Selincourt to which Harrison alludes is suppressed in the summary. And no wonder: De Selincourt wrote to answer those who did not understand why Spenser "did not drop the pastoral cloak" to "speak in clearer accents" about his relationship with Sidney; his answer also was that one must read the text of *Astrophel*—but not quite as documentary evidence—to find that its "delicate reserve expresses far more," that Spenser "gives to the lay of *Astrophel* a lingering and tender pathos as potent and moving as the direct expression of personal regard" (p. xiv).

Between Grosart's unabashed declaration of the deep and tender meaning of friendship in the early 1880s and De Selincourt's 1912 rewriting of that relationship as one necessarily cloaked, an event had taken place, the trial of Oscar Wilde, that retroactively would require the rewriting of friendship as, in Harrison's phrase, the exchange of "literary ideas," untainted by "personal regard." De Selincourt rewrites, in a much more closed—more closeted—idiom the love that dare not speak its name, and that has done so, cloaked as the friendship of pastoral swains. The academic policing of the Variorum, with its ideal of a documentable literariness, of the translation of the literary into the historically factual, speaks beyond bias and for sanity, those by no means neutral terms that cloak homophobia and homosexual panic. (I should add here that these comments are not written in the supposition that I "know" the sexual orientations of any of the Spenserians named; the historic circumstances that make homosexuality visible also produce what Sedgwick terms an epistemology of the closet, the perils of revelation that lead gay men to cloak their homosexuality, and homophobic responses to homosexuality to attempt to render it invisible.) Spenser's worries about "that fowle blot of unthankefulnesse" (471) are nothing in comparison to the worry of the Variorum editors about what he might have expressed—and perhaps did.

Hence, our initial question returns: what if, in its displacements, the special friendship of Spenser and Harvey could be transported to the relationship with Sidney? How would one then read the destination of *Astrophel,* "*Made not to please the living but the dead*" (16). How, thus belatedly, to speak with the dead? How, in the words of the letter to the Countess of Pembroke, to replant "the seede of most entire love" "deepe sowed in my brest" "long sithens," those first buds and blossoms denied their blooming when Sidney was "cut off," but now "spired forth fruit" addressed to "that most noble Spirit" (471). The letter to the countess offers an answer to these questions; any letter to Sidney posted posthumously must address her, whom any address to Sidney "most speciallie concerneth," since she bears "his [Sidney's] goodly image living evermore, / In the divine resemblaunce of your face" (413), as Spenser declares in the dedicatory poem to *The Faerie Queene.* If, after Sidney's death, as Spenser writes in *The Ruines of Time,* he hears Sidney call, bidding him to "quicklie come to thee" (308), he can come by hearing Sidney's call in his sister's verse: "her to heare I feele my feeble spright / Robbed of sense, and ravished with ioy" (320–21). The final letter that Spenser would post to Sidney can be posted only by way of his sister and within the circuits of "divine resemblaunce": "Then will I sing: but who can better sing, / Than thine owne sister" (316–17).

To the pastoral cloak of tender friendship (to go no further in naming that relation) add another scene of displaced singing, this sending of the letter by receiving "deep harts sorrowing" (318), the robbery and ravishment of Sidney's sister, posting letters by her, as hers. Here, too, De Selincourt has something to say, about the so-called *Lay of Clorinda* that concludes *Astrophel.* The *Lay* is "commonly attributed to the Countess of Pembroke," De Selincourt writes: "But if she did write it, she had studied to some purpose the peculiarly Spenserian effects of rhythm and melody. The poem is, moreover, like the introductory elegy, woven into the plan of the volume, and not a separate work, standing by itself, like those that follow. It is more natural, therefore, to believe that Spenser wrote it in her name" (xxxv). It had been, for De Selincourt, in "rhythm and melody," "in verbal cadence, in melody of phrasing," more than in anything directly said, that Spenser's "delicate reserve" under the cloak of pastoral had conveyed his tenderness and "most intimate personal experience" (xiv). In the spurious name of the "natural," De Selincourt reserves to Spenser's hand the production of the entire elegy rather than perpetuate the "common" attribution that would assign the poem to Mary Sidney, a "common" error that also could be made in the name of "nature," for what more natural than a sister's love for her brother, or a woman's for a man? In the voice of Clorinda the poem comes closest to breaking its cover, under her cover. But what if the name covered the Countess of Pembroke? Or if Spenser could write his final letter to Sidney, as he claimed in *The Ruines of Time,* only by writing in his sister's hand? "Then will I sing: but who can better sing, / Than thine owne sister" (316–17)?

De Selincourt's attribution of the poem to Spenser received considerable support in the decades following, and views from the opening years of professional Spenser criticism are still cited in the most recent work on the poem.[27] But in the last decade, feminist scholarship, which has begun the important work of making visible writing by English women in the Renaissance, has wanted this poem to be part of the countess's corpus. In *Philip's Phoenix,* her recent biography of Mary Sidney, Margaret Hannay rehearses the arguments that have been made to keep the poem in Spenser's hands. She has an incontrovertible label with which to brand those who have advanced such claims: "sexist."[28] The justice of this charge does not, however, quite handle the issue. Directed at De Selincourt, for instance, it ignores what he was attempting to naturalize by keeping the poem entirely within the circuit of Spenser's correspondence with Sidney. The charge would be equally just, but quite different, in the case of those who follow the exemplary T. P. Harrison, who, in his anthology of pastoral elegies, declares that the *Lay* "seems also to be Spenser's," but on formal and thematic grounds (the *Lay* is seen to complete "the Astrophel-Adonis theme" and Clorinda is read as Spenser's way of paying "his respects to Sidney's illustrious sister").[29] The formal argument, like Harrison's insistence that the relationship to Sidney involved a meeting of "literary ideas," has a quite different agenda from De Selincourt's, and the label "sexist" blurs the differences. However variously just the charge of "sexism" is when turned against Spenserians, one must wonder too how it would read were it directed at Spenser. Is the circuit of the letter in *The Ruines of Time* a "sexist" imaginary? Is it realized in *Astrophel*? Who wrote *The Lay of Clorinda* and how might one give a definitive answer to that question seems caught up in the practice of Spenserian displacements that need themselves to be read. These literary matters are, as should be apparent by now, not simply literary either. The charge of sexism, which must itself be read, mobilizes questions of gender (and the gendered difference between a man's hand and a woman's) that must be read in relationship to questions of sexuality—in this case, a man's love for a man, a woman's love for a man.

"Arguments for Spenser's composition of the 'Lay' have been convincingly presented in P. W. Long, 'Spenseriana,' *MLN* 31 (1916), 79–92, and C. G. Osgood, 'Doleful Lay of Clorinda,' ibid., 35 (1920), 90ff.," Peter Sacks laconically notes.[30] "The question of authorship of Clorinda's 'dolefull lay' has recently been reopened," Richard McCoy admits in his *Rites of Knighthood.* "Spenserians have generally assigned the poem to Spenser . . . , a view I am still inclined to accept; but for an account of recent scholarship attributing the poem to Mary Sidney, see Josephine A. Roberts."[31] These footnotes cannot be understood fully without examining the readings of the poem they support, but even on their own terms they support a version of Hannay's charge of sexism. Sacks and McCoy look no further than the Variorum for their Spenserian authority; not only does this tie them to scholarship produced before 1943, but the Variorum, in its six pages of notes on authorship (7:500–505), is not quite as compendious as its title promises. Omitted is any reference to Frances Young's 1912 biography of Mary Sidney, which finds the poem "probably but not certainly written by Lady Pembroke,"[32] or to Walter G. Friedrich's 1934 Johns Hopkins dissertation (undoubtedly written under the supervision of those involved with producing the Variorum), which "came to the conclusion that the Lay was almost certainly written by the Countess."[33] That description of Friedrich's work I cite from Gary Waller's introduction to his 1977 edition of Mary

Sidney's poems, an item that obviously could not find its way into the Variorum, but that might have been consulted by Sacks or McCoy, the latter of whom seems to think that the question of authorship had been raised only by Roberts's 1984 essay. To go to, or to cling to, the Variorum as the repository of knowledge for such "tedious" matters of scholarship as attribution is to assume, as the Variorum does, that such questions are factual and decidable. Within an essentialist construction of gender, such historicist attitudes could be called sexist; more precisely to the point, however, is that the Variorum's inclusiveness operates in a dual manner. Work on Spenser before the end of the nineteenth century is generously surveyed in the spirit of antiquarianism; work after the foundation of English as a discipline is summarized only so long as it "counts" professionally. Young is excluded because she had no academic affiliation, Friedrich because his work was produced as a graduate student and was (and remains) unpublished. Quite different methodologies represented by the work of Sacks and McCoy—for the former, close reading informed by psychoanalysis and myth criticism, for the latter, an avowed New Historicism and cultural poetics—meet in the assumption that a certain form of historic knowledge can be gleaned from the Variorum, in Sacks's case because the kind of reading practice he espouses has no need of history, in McCoy's because the New Historicism he promotes comes down to questions of choice: he is "still inclined to accept" the traditional view of Spenserians. The volition expressed—a matter of "free choice"—affirms a liberalism that must not recognize its ties to a political tradition that assigned such rights to men; the professional allegiance affirmed similarly supports a configuration that still shapes English departments, both in terms of the number of tenured women in the profession or the ways in which graduate students are accorded second-class treatment. Waller's edition can be overlooked; it, after all, is a volume in the anything-but-prestigious Salzburg Studies in English Literature, a marginal production where, not surprisingly, the work of Mary Sidney can be published.[34] Hannay's allegation thus can be read in relation to these affirmations of traditional scholarship; two men produce strong readings of texts, and preferably their texts will be those written by men, supported by theories that bear the names of men (Freud and Frazier for Sacks, Greenblatt for McCoy), and that, for all their departures in the name of theory or a New Historicism, support the gendered foundations of knowledge that shape the profession.

When one looks at Long's 1916 essay, or Osgood's 1920 piece, it is easy enough to see how they could be accepted unquestioningly. Long appears to deal in entirely factual matters, Spenser's use of accidentals, particularly punctuation marks. Osgood picks up on Long's brief citation of verbal and syntactic parallels between *Astrophel* and the *Lay* to provide "a long list of these details" (91) that occupies four and a half of the six pages of his article. The very brevity of the pieces (Long's runs to three and a half pages) marks their scientificity and gives them the appearance of producing facts. Nothing like a reading of the poem is ventured; these are works of scholarship, Osgood's even offering the pathos of scholarship as the scenario in which he operates. Since he had not included the *Lay* in his 1907 concordance, the massive evidence assembled in his 1920 piece also provided an opportunity to correct himself. "Had I taken the trouble to index the poem, the Spenserian authorship would, I believe, have been at once apparent" (90). Indeed, since the knowledge that Osgood strives for has the quality of transparency, since the facts can be known, it is only the limits of labor, the spectacle of the rigors of scholarship in which the scholar always falls short, that kept him from the goal of immediately "apparent" truth.

Again, one could marshal the label *sexist* to describe this scientific dream with its teleological goal, or the notion of immediate and transparent knowledge that motivates these texts, although one would have to add that these protocols of knowledge also shape the investigations of "feminist" scholarship like Hannay's and Waller's in their arguments for authorship by the Countess of Pembroke. Insofar as attribution studies rest upon a juridical conception of knowledge that is implicated in the production of a gendered knowledge, or in the production of gender difference through and as the binarism that also governs the difference between scientific fact and mere opinion, between literary scholarship and literary criticism, between History and English as disciplines, the very basis of attribution must be called into question. These texts from the first decade of this century represent a moment in the legitimation of English as a discipline, and the production of knowledge eschews all the amateurism (and "femininity"?) that might make the discipline suspect. Contemporary feminist scholarship operates under similarly disabling conditions; when, for instance, it calls for a countercanon of writing by women, or the inclusion of that canon within the ones that prevail, or when it seeks to prove the existence of the woman's hand in *The Lay of Clorinda,* it operates within terms and strategies it should be seeking to dislodge. "The discussion has ostensibly proceeded along textual lines," Hannay remarks midway through her summary of attribution studies, "yet often turns on assumptions about gender" (65). The sentence is however as true of Hannay as it is of those she criticizes; if, for Spenserians, the question has been whether the *Lay* is "too Spenserian," Hannay offers an argument by default—it is not Spenserian enough and therefore can be attributed to the countess.

Such an argument resituates and repeats that made by Osgood; the poem, he claims, "is below the quality of even the poet's most perfunctory verse" (95). Since his three pages of parallels prove that the lines are Spenser's nonetheless, the failure in supposed quality must be Spenser's deliberate act (his "free choice") of self-impersonation. This is how, Osgood affirms, Spenser would write as a woman, producing "a qualification and cloaking of his natural tone to something more feminine and tenuous" (96); moreover, when one compares the poem to one certainly by the countess, it points, Osgood insists, "to her innocence of it." Had she written the *Lay,* he concludes, she would have displayed the cleverness requisite for "so close and skilful an imitation of Spenser as the poet seems to have made of himself" (96). This is sexist, surely, yet the argument also depends upon the assumption that Spenser's hand and Mary Sidney's can be distinguished (Osgood is not denying that the countess wrote, just that she couldn't have written this poem). To produce an account of stylistic difference, however much it is governed by gender distinctions, also results in producing a Spenser who "means to deceive" (96), who seeks to "cloak" his "natural" (that is to say male) "tone" and does so well enough to produce an entirely plausible imitation of himself—as a woman. If self-identity is "proved" by the assembly of echoes and self-citations (if that is how one knows Spenser wrote the *Lay*), that very proof of (gendered) identity displaces itself. If, that is, one has here the kind of gendered construction that Luce Irigaray has identified as the production of the feminine as simulative, and the implicit notion that the best and most convincing representation of or by a woman will be in a man's hands—that there is, in short, no space for feminine representation—the very definition of male selfsameness produces maleness as feminine duplication and duplicity. By the same logic, the poem undeniably by Mary Sidney, and not a duplicate, is, at one and the same time, outside the male simulative and, in being self-identical, a realization of what genuine maleness would be. This is, in fact, the logic of the scholar's identity; Osgood's pained confession that a failure of labor led him to be deceived by "Spenser" has been overcompensated for in the essay. Its pages of parallels are said to be a "tedious, though incomplete list" (95); they are, moreover, the work of "Mr. Richard M. Hewitt, of the Graduate College, Princeton" (91). The master has been supplemented by his graduate student's work, which he publishes (Hewitt is not the name under which the essay appears or is indexed); the *Concordance,* in which Osgood and Spenser (in a specular relation) have their identities confirmed, is the work of another's hand, work that is always to remain incomplete. The labors of self-simulation that produce the masculine are continually haunted by that male lack that goes under several names: woman (in the register of gender), graduate student (in the professional formation), and history (as telos and completion—history as the domain of a truth that would confirm identity, the possibility of wholeness that lies beyond the grasp of any hand).

What is the Spenserian mark? Long has an answer; it is the "device" that serves "as a trademark of Colin" since Spenser is himself "feigning himself in the shepherd Colin" (81). The device is a mark of punctuation, a characteristic use of the colon. Simulative identity is at work here too. Spenser displaces himself in his poetic identity; his poetic being takes form typographically; the typographic form serves as a trademark in the simulative economies of a capitalistic advertisement; the echo of *Colin* and *colon* produces its simulative mark within the stylistic register of a Spenserian assonance. I choose my poetic term carefully. We cannot suppose that "Lady Pembroke appropriated this trick of punctuation . . . which Spenser had made distinctively Colin's" (81), Long writes. Men and women both have colons, of course, but only a man, Long seems to think, can make use of another man's colon; in seeking the distinctive form of Spenser's style, the trick by which he makes himself Colin, Long produces this fantasy of anal penetration, a Spenserian poetics of assonance.

"The line of argument" that Long produces is, he admits, "superfluous"; all he does, he confesses, is "elaborate a little on the argument which Selincourt might readily have developed" (81). The supplementary logic of this elaboration seeks the distinctively Spenserian beneath the delicate cloak De Selincourt drew over the economies of male/male relationships; Long seeks to write as De Selincourt would have written. (In a parallel move, the final sentence of his piece declares that had the countess written the poem she would have "come measurably nearer imitating Spenser than did such passionate admirers of his verse as Shelley or Keats" [82].) The passionate construction of a male/male homosocial rests upon the "superfluous" organ (from the point of view of "nature" in its heterosexual construct) that men have for each other (but it is "art" that Long is talking about). Let me be clear here: I do not mean to suggest that Long is producing a gay affirmative reading of the Spenserian colon, nor that his argument reveals him to have been gay-identified. The cloaking of the secret that so vividly displays itself here depends rather upon the unavailability or unavowability to the homosocial imaginary of its relationship to homosexuality. In the drive of Long's essay to establish a masculinity that cannot be appropriated by a woman (a drive that could be situated historically in relation to the woman's movement coincident with Long's 1916 publication, the specter of suffragettes who might acquire the vote—the male voice—and who regularly were represented as mannish women, lesbians),[35] Long produces as normatively and exclusively male a homosexual foundation for the homosocial. He does this not to affirm the homosexual but the homosocial exclusion of women. It is only within the ruses of a self-simulative economy that will never produce the identification that Long seeks, that the mark—the colon—signifies in the ways I've been suggesting.

That this reading is not excessive can be seen in the uses to which Sacks and McCoy put their dependence on Long and Osgood. For both of them, the *Lay* must be Spenser's and must only stimulate the woman, since its work, as the end of *Astrophel,* is to establish a community—among men. At first, McCoy writes, Clorinda is as distracted as Stella is represented as being in *Astrophel*; "gradually, however, her song restores her to a sense of connection and community" (151). "Her song," of course, the footnote tells us, is Spenser's song for her, and she performs the woman's work of making a community, the community of poetic convention: "In *Astrophel* poetry enables the contributors to recover a communal order and preserve the memory and ideals of the dead hero" (152). The "contributors" are all male; the hero is an exemplary male and the order, facilitated by the represented female, is a transcendental masculinity that finds its highest expression in poetry-making, or in the myth-making that produced the heroic Sidney. (McCoy's New Historicist revision speaks these aims in large ways; *The Rites of Knighthood* extends the terrain of the New Historicism—chapters on Daniel and Spenser conclude a study devoted to historic figures, Dudley and Essex, with Sidney providing a leg in each camp. Subtitled *The Literature and Politics of Elizabethan Chivalry,* this foray into the codes and behavior of [would-be] aristocrats has very little to say about the queen who lends her name to the subtitle. The reclaiming of agency in the book is also the reclaiming of a male pathos. With its illustrations of knights in armor this is very much a boys' book.)

McCoy cites Sacks in the course of his discussion, and his argument is a similar one. For Sacks, Clorinda offers a "more adequate voice of mourning" (58) than any other heard in *Astrophel*; she serves as "an extraordinary example of Spenser's revisionary power" (60), one that "might well have satisfied even Sidney himself" (62; what fantasy is this?). Such is the "community" that she establishes, when, at the end of the poem, no longer isolated, she speaks in a "healthy" way, "with clear self-knowledge regarding the true motives of man's mourning" (62). How can this simulated woman speak this poetic truth about "man"—about men? By replacing Stella, Sacks claims, and thereby the "dangerous identifications" that Stella offers Astrophel. "The movement beyond Venus-Stella toward the sister, Clorinda, strongly suggests a deliberate purging or chastening of the maternal or erotic connection" (61). Clorinda offers a "healthy" cure for male anxiety about "the maternal or erotic"—a cure for castration anxiety, in a word: "It is in relation to this movement, together with the many castrative gestures, that the final consolation asserts its recovery of a figurative sexual power" (61). Figurative sex is a good thing for Sacks so long as the figures all lie in the hands of man. Sacks affirms male adequacy by disentangling the male from heterosexuality—from the mother or the female lover—and then by a *re*heterosexualization that takes place through the production of a female figure who serves to ventriloquize male wholeness. The psychic deformations that make real women the sign of male lack are thereby overcome in the entirely male poeticizing that produces a phantasmatic woman who serves only to solidify the "community" of men. Because Sacks argues within a "Freudian" ego-psychology paradigm of castration, gender difference and the possibility of overcoming oedipal dilemmas cannot escape a castration anxiety insuperable if always displaceable. Effectively, Sacks produces a homosocial "community" that dispenses with women but not with the figure of woman that guarantees that the community, however subject to "unhealthy" (that is, sexual) attachments to women and to the body—and therefore to the possibility of castration—can overcome that threat without being construed as a homosexual community. Woman is figuratively necessary, then, because she safeguards not only masculinity but also heterosexuality.

Although the arguments of Sacks and McCoy refuse any engagement with feminism, similar arguments can occur in discourses that write under that name. Gary Waller, for instance, rescues the *Lay* for Mary Sidney, following in the tracks of Friedrich. "Rescue" is his name for his project: "for want of a champion the Countess might have lain unrescued" (56). The same chivalric fantasy that McCoy indulges also provides Waller's plot; he is the knight in armor fighting on behalf of the defenseless woman. And she needs defending; "as he wryly indicated" (this is Waller describing Friedrich and making the view his own), "some of the 'Lay's' careless or strained lines are hardly up to Spenser's standard of competence" (56). What other critics had claimed as Spenser's mastery of simulation is now taken as the sign of female inadequacy, or, as Waller soon claims, as the sign of "deeply personal grief" (59). Tears are feminine, indeed, the personal is feminine; accomplished poets (that is, male poets) write the universal truth of "man" and are masterfully impersonal.

Hannay makes similar arguments. The *Lay,* she claims, is "the first and weakest" of Mary Sidney's poems (63; in the teleological arguments that write the poet's life, he always grows in strength, and Hannay absorbs this masculinist plot of poetic development); Spenser "took her poem, incorporated it gracefully into his own superior composition" (67; he rescued it, that is, and made it look better by making it part of his own work). No one, Hannay avers, could have been taken in by the duping that critics have argued, nor would Mary Sidney have stood for "such liberties with her own name" (65); besides, Spenser "would not have insulted the Countess of Pembroke, his patron in 1595, by writing an inferior piece in his own style and attributing it to her" (67). How then to account for the Spenserian style of the *Lay*? Perhaps, Hannay writes, "it was the result of cooperation between Spenser and the countess" (66). Certainly Hannay's argument, like Waller's, is itself a result of "cooperation" between "sexist" and "feminist" accounts. The assumptions upon which Waller and Hannay build are those of the critics they wish to refute. Mary Sidney is allowed to have the poem since its very inferiority is clear proof that only a woman could have written it. But, as should be clear by now, there is no clear proof about who wrote the *Lay,* at least not within the protocols of these arguments. Infinitely reversible, they are nonetheless governed by a binarism that produces woman simply as the imitation of man. Yet, were imitation to be destabilized and binarism refused, one could recognize a simulation that would explain why the attempts at stabilization can never succeed, and see that the difference between Spenser's hand and the countess's is entirely indeterminate; from this position of indeterminacy one thing that emerges is the impossibility of establishing the poem as either Spenser's or the countess's. This is not a position of indifference; it means, on the one hand, that the countess could have written a poem that can't be distinguished from Spenser; on the other hand, if this indicates that Spenser cannot be imagined as a self-identical or stylistically singular phenomenon, neither can the countess. Such arguments should trouble only an essentialist feminism or an essentialist masculinism, both attached to the high literary and the canonical and its professional reproduction.

The position that I want to argue is not that of joint authorship or cooperation, the view affirmed by the recent Yale edition of the minor poems; the evenhanded speculation that "perhaps the *Lay* was a joint endeavor"[36] rests upon formal grounds that have a gendered logic. "Together the two poems form contrasting parts of a complex whole, and their unity of idea is reinforced by common motifs, a shared verse form (the familiar sexain rhyming *ababcc*), and a numerological program" (565). The familiar sexain here is well named, since it is the familiar heterosexual organization of gender, male and female united in the idea—the spiritual form of unity that Sacks calls "man"—but otherwise opposed as "contrasting" principles. In this numerological program (fetched from a note in G. W. Pigman),[37] one plus one equals one, and man and woman can "share" a verse form that so handily translates alternating *a* and *b* into a single rhyming *c*. For the Yale editor, that *c* is divinity, the perfection that only a woman can articulate, and here in fact Oram joins many "feminist" readers of Renaissance women's writing by consigning their femininity to the safe terrain of a spirituality. "Readers trained to see God's hand in all events," Oram writes, introducing his discussion of *Astrophel*, best find it in the woman's hand. Exemplary and therefore self-abnegating woman that she is, whoever wrote her, Clorinda recognizes "the human self-centeredness of her grief, blessing her brother and bidding him farewell" (568). This is, then, a translation into theological terms of the consoling communal close that Sacks and McCoy found in the *Lay*. Oram need not decide who wrote the *Lay* if its truth lies in God's hands. (Interestingly, Hannay seems to think the *Lay* fails because in her reading of it it does not espouse the militant Protestantism that should reconcile Mary Sidney to her brother's death; the countess has imperfectly become what she finally does become in Hannay's biography, the pious writer and thereby the good writer—and the good woman).[38]

The notion that both Spenser and the countess could have written the poem, while it seems indifferent to the question of who wrote it, solves the dilemma by translating it into a Christian marriage, two hands joined in one. The position I am arguing is that the two hands cannot be distinguished one from another; that indistinction throws into question gendered difference and sexual difference, and no heterosexual plot of marriage will save it. For to refuse the normative differentiation that writes man and woman as an oppositional pair exposes the questionable assumption that there is only one form of desire, the one that seeks to unite that opposition. As my discussion earlier suggested, that sex/gender system does not seem to be the same as the one that finds the countess and her brother in a relationship of resemblance and imitation and that imagines any possibility of address to the dead Sidney as happening through the agency of his living simulation. Moreover, that economy of resemblance and displaced duplication governs Spenser's cloaked poetics and the mirror relationship that goes under the name of friendship.

The question of the hand that wrote the *Lay* has operated under the assumption that elsewhere the hands of Spenser and the countess—the hands of man and woman—are readily distinguishable. Yet the entire problem has arisen precisely because of the point in *Astrophel* when Clorinda's lay is announced as hers, for the gesture towards another singer, a singer other than the one whose words we have been reading, is so regularly the way in which Spenser displaces himself into other voices that there is no way of knowing at such a moment whether the cloak is being dropped or another veil is being placed over the text. Moreover, what is most problematic in the sentence I've just written to describe the situation is the appeal to Spenser in it. Who speaks *Astrophel*? In whose voice does it speak to the dead?

Astrophel opens with four stanzas printed in italics (the rest of the text is set in roman). This typeface can mark several different things: an italic hand, the hand of the humanist but also the woman's hand (the Countess of Pembroke's secretary, for instance, wrote her correspondence in italic, not the usual secretarial hand, because italic is the woman's hand; of course, it was because of his humanist training that he could write the woman's hand); italic can indicate something that is not in or part of the text, for example, something being cited, or a prefatory letter that comes before the text proper. These italic lines address a community of shepherds who, writing out of the "smart" of their love pains, have found a way to "*breed / Compassion in a countrey lasses hart*" (3–4). Is it that country lass who speaks here, having received the words spoken on the circuit of a desire that opens fellow feeling through the mutuality of wounding? The lines continue: "*Hearken ye gentle shepheards to my song, / And place my dolefull plaint your plaints emong*" (5–6). Before, the shepherds spoke only to lasses, and they received the words; now someone speaks, not to lasses, but to shepherds, "*to you whose softened hearts it may empierse*" (9). Is this a simple reversal, in which we hear a country lass returning the words, a circuit from man to woman to man? Or is the speaker a man in the place of a woman? Or speaking man to man? "*To you alone I sing*" (8) "*not to please the living but the dead*" (16), "*To you I sing and to none other*" (11). Who sings to Sidney? What community is this? In whose words? On what erotic trajectory? The questions about the authorship of the *Lay*—about the gender of the author—start in the opening lines of *Astrophel*.[39]

Or perhaps—since these questions of gender are above all questions of sexuality—they start in Nashe's claims about Harvey; that he wrote under the cover of the names of Spenser and Sidney—courting the latter "as he were another *Cyparissus* or *Ganymede*"—and defended himself against Nashe by employing the hand of a gentlewoman (the countess?) that Nashe claims is Harvey too, his female impersonation one more sign of his sodomitical designs.[40] Or perhaps they start on the title page of *The Shepheardes Calender,* and how it might have been understood. George Whetstone's elegy for the dead Sidney—one of the few such works that actually seems to deliver facts, not myth—has a marginal note beside a stanza about Sidney's pastoral verse, giving the referent to the allusion: "The last Shepherds calenders the reputed worke of S. Phil. Sydney a work of deepe learning, judgment & witte disguised in Shep. Rules."[41] We think we know how to dispose of such a misidentification, just as we think we know for sure that Spenserian authorship is definitively suspended after the *Lay,* whoever wrote it, when Thestylis starts singing.[42] What then should we make of the fact that Milton echoes lines from "The mourning Muse of Thestylis" in *Lycidas,* or draws on "An Elegie, or friends passion, for his Astrophill" in his "Ode on the Morning of Christ's Nativity," echoes them, one must assume, in the belief that Spenser's hand can be found in all the poems gathered in the *Astrophel* volume? What, moreover, is to be made of the name of the first of the mourners, Thestylis, which, as even the Variorum points out, is a name that could be taken by either sex? (Their further comment that "it was appropriate to [Lodowick] Bryskett after he had taken up a rustic life" [7:507] is a weird nonsequitur, an alignment of alienation from the center of power—the city and the court, with the indetermination of gender.) Bryskett, we think we know, authored the two poems that appear after the *Lay*; the Stationer's Register and the initials L.B. after "A pastorall Aeglogue" are our proof. Yet the poems show additions that must postdate their 1587 registration, and it could be asked whether L.B. signs more than the lines of Lycon that appear above them, and Lycon's role in the eclogue is to respond to verses spoken in that poem by Colin Clout. And if we think we know that we can discount the contemporary witness to Sidney's authorship of *The Shepheardes Calender,* what should we do with Thestylis when he identifies Stella's lament for Astrophel not only with Venus mourning her Adonis, but refers to it as "His noble sisters plaints" ("Mourning Muse," 130)?

"*Eccho* will our words report," Colin sings in "A pastorall Aeglogue" (33). What, then, is the "noblest plant" "pluckt untimely from the tree, / Whiles yet his yeares in flowre, did promise worthie frute" ("Mourning Muse," 8, 11–12), the trope of the flower that is said to formally unite *Astrophel* and the *Lay,* doing opening Thestylis's poem? Or, for that matter, how does it come to be in the letter to the countess prefacing *The Ruines of Time*? More proof of Spenser's hand everywhere? Or of the countess's? Echo rebounds within the *Astrophel* volume, perhaps nowhere more so than in the *Lay,* which starts by seeking the compassionate audience that *Astrophel* imagines only through its indetermination of its speaker's gender. Rather than finding one, it moves to speak to itself, and the echo of pastoral opens interiority as a path "lineally deriv'd" (64) from the dead; "O what is now of it become, aread" (65). What lines are to be read in this transmission, these letters from the dead? They are letters that "enfold . . . inward paine" (3), letters written on an "enriven heart" (4). Is not this the path of compassion that opens the italic lines of *Astrophel*? This divided and doubled path passes through the sister, who received a letter (signed by her brother, but made public only by her), that sent his "idle work" "only for you, to you," a letter doubled when that work was published, with one from the countess's secretary (written at whose dictate?), sending the work "done, as it was, for her; as it is, by her."[43] Sending it, as the countess did, in her own hand, when she wrote to Sir Edward Wotton, asking for the return of one of her manuscripts, one often taken to be the manuscript of the *Lay*:

> Cosen Wotton the first message this paper shall deliver is my best salutacon and ever welwishinge to yowr selfe from that wonted good affeccon still continued doe acknowledge yow worthy of the same regarde wherein yow are asseured to rest[.][44]

Whose affection circulates in this entirely circular sentence, hers or his? What or whose is this "same regarde" that seems at once self-identical, either his or hers, and yet delivered from and to "this paper"?

> For suche hath bin yowr merit not onlie towarde my self but in memory of that love to him which held yow a deere and speciall

> frende of his (who was to me as you know) I must and doe and ever will doe yow this right[.]

How is this relationship to Wotton written as a version of his special friendship to Sidney, of hers to him "who was to me as you know"? As he knows by knowing what he was to him? Is this not the structure that opens *Astrophel,* where a special love and a sister's love occupy a single line or single hand? A hand not writing heterosexual marriage, but an unspecified relation, avowed as known by another on the pulses of his special friendship represented to him by her as her relationship to him. If this scenario looks like the one that Sacks and McCoy take out of the countess's hand, how does it read in hers? As Hannay comments, the letter proceeds to configure the relation in the terms of the letters—written by whom?—prefacing *The Countesse of Pembrokes Arcadia*:

> Which downe the next is that these maie redeeme a certain Idle passion which longe since I left in yowr handes onlie being desyrous to review what the Image could be of those sadd tymes[.]

Whose desire to review and redeem is this? In whose hands was it, or is it? Is this "Idle passion" the text of those relations? A text that might be called, and is, in *Astrophel,* "An Elegie, or friends passion, for his Astrophill"?—a text that imagines Astrophill going to his death "attyrde . . . with her device" (163–64), cross-dressed as Pallas Athena?

> I very well know unworthy of the humour that then possest me and suche as I knowe no reason yow should yeld me any account of, Yet yf yowr care of these follies of suche a toy have chanced to keepe that which my self have lost, my earnest desire is that I maie againe see it, that by this bearer my honest Servant Ramsey safely seeled I maie receive it, asseuringe yow, I will when yow will store yow with other thinges better worth yowr keepinge[.]

The return of the letter, safely sealed, and the promise of another posting; a circuit of unknowingness, unworthiness, in which what has been lost has also been delivered, kept safe elsewhere—Wotton is stored with these letters which he is now asked to deliver up, or to deliver an account of. Yet for all the exchanges, overlaps, and identifications, what also circulates in these letters cannot be said except in the promises of keeping secret and a secret sharing. This letter, in the countess's hand, displays her hand as one—as the only one—that could write Sidney into the world of relations in which his name circulates, living and dead. It intimates not only that hers is the hand of the *Lay*, whoever wrote it, but of *Astrophel* or other letters planted in Arcadian soil.

Disclaiming and claiming identity, the determinations of the author's hand are never far from disguise. Such is the case, by now well known, about Spenser's hand; such, too, is the case with the countess. "What else is the awaking his musical instruments, the often and free changing of persons, his notable *prosopopœias*"[45]—what else is his, or hers? And if such is the case, there is no reason not to believe, as I do, that the countess wrote the *Lay of Clorinda*, to say the least. Such a belief—such a desire—can never be argued within the terms through which scholarship goes about its acts of attribution. But since those acts, as I've been arguing, are determined by structures of desire that must be scrutinized and resisted, it seems worthwhile to conclude by declaring a desire—in the name of the recognition of all that refuses the juridical determinations of a heterosexualized scholarly imperative—to claim in the name of the countess's authorship the special friendships, the passionate interchange between brother and sister, and the unspeakable desire to speak with and for the dead that demand to be heard.

'Play the Sodomits, or worse': The Elizabethan Theater

PART TWO

CHAPTER 4

The Transvestite Stage: More on the Case of Christopher Marlowe

FIFTY LINES INTO Marlowe's *Edward II,* Gaveston describes entertainments he thinks proper to his king. The work of "wanton poets, pleasant wits" (1.1.51),[1] they will provide "Italian masks by night" (55), while by day the spectacle will include pages dressed as "sylvan nymphs" (58) and satyr-like men:

> Sometime a lovely boy in Dian's shape,
> With hair that gilds the water as it glides,
> Crownets of pearl about his naked arms,
> And in his sportful hands an olive tree,
> To hide those parts which men delight to see,
> Shall bathe him in a spring (1.1.61–66)

to be spied by an Actaeon, who will "seem to die" (70). Such sights, he believes, "may draw the pliant king" (53). "The soliloquy," Sarah Munson Deats notes, "hints of a number of sexual perversions—transvestism (l. 60), homosexuality (l. 65), voyeurism (l. 67), and sadism (ll. 69–70)—although how many of these innuendos are deliberate is difficult to ascertain."[2] Hints? Innuendos? By only hearing "hints," Deats seeks to rescue Marlowe from what she nonetheless characterizes as "sexual perversions"; the lines seem calculated, however, flung out in the face of such a response, taunting it, provoking it. Not that Marlowe has anticipated the modern critic; rather, Deats's response is a familiar one, and we need look no further than the Elizabethan antitheatrical tracts to see that Gaveston's lines have been written to order, as it were. "There set they abroche straunge confortes of melody, to tickle the eare; costly apparel, to flatter the sight; effeminate gesture, to ravish the sence; and wanton speache, to whet desire too inordinate lust"; so writes Stephen Gosson in the first of those full-scale attacks on the stage, *The Schoole of Abuse* (32).[3] Theaters "effeminate the minde, as pricks unto vice" (29); they offer "wanton spectacles" (30), and they come armed like adders "that sting with pleasure, and kil with paine," or basilisks "that poyson, as well with the beame of their sighte, as with the breath of their mouth" (33).

Transvestism, homosexuality, voyeurism, sadism: these would seem to be Gosson's charges as well. Had Marlowe's play not been written some dozen years *after* his tract, one might suppose Gosson had it in mind; the relationship is not merely the reverse, however,[4] for as an "answer" to the antitheatricalists, Gaveston's speech rehearses and repeats, virtually embraces, their charges—along with others, that associated the court with profligacy, and Italy with vice. "*Bugeria* is an Italian word," the learned Justice Coke would write in his *Laws of England*;[5] sodomy was an Italian vice. Gaveston the Frenchman appears to be one of its Continental exponents.

Thanks to a number of literary critics, most notably Laura Levine and Stephen Orgel—in work variously indebted to Alan Bray's fundamental contributions to our understanding of male/male sexuality in the Renaissance—the task has begun of locating the antitheatrical, antisodomitical discourses apparently provoked by the spectacle of cross-dressing on the Elizabethan stage.[6] Orgel's and Levine's work needs to be distinguished from much that has been written by Renaissance scholars on the question of cross-dressing, which has examined gender rather than sexuality and has operated therefore under the presumption that there is only one form of sexuality, heterosexuality. This can lead, as it does in Deats, to an unthinking categorization of the perverse; so Valerie Traub has recently argued, and much that I say here runs parallel to the opening pages of her incisive inquiry, "Desire and the Difference It Makes."[7]

In a recent essay, Jean Howard lays out some debates within Shakespearean feminist criticism[8] around the question of whether a potential, liberation for women, can be glimpsed in cross-dressing. Howard tends towards a negative answer and provides, through the five plays she considers, a topology from less to more subversive; she concludes that the closest thing to a real possibility for female resistance to patriarchy can be found in the women who attended plays, middle-class housewives who were not staying at home as they were supposed to do. (Theater as an institution created by emerging capital interests was more progressive than the plays presented in it.[9]) Howard's account stays pretty safely within the dramatic diegesis, accepting as conventional that the boy actor plays and therefore can be taken as a woman: Howard's tacit assumption that there is only one form of sexuality is clearest in her discussion of the play that she finds most misogynist, the one in which cross-dressing holds out no prospect for women outside of patriarchal constraints, *Epicoene*; the play foregrounds the fact that the cross-dressed woman is a boy. Howard comments: "In this instance, male crossdressing becomes a way to appropriate and then erase the troubling figure of wife" (430). "This instance" finds Howard intimating that any recognition of the boy actor beneath the woman's clothes may "appropriate and then erase" women, and coming dangerously close to equating homosexuality and misogyny.[10] *As You Like It* is offered as the counterexample in which the boy's successful imitation of the woman, by exposing the fictiveness of gender difference, throws into question the hierarchization of men over women. Celebrating "the contamination of sexual kinds" (435) in the play, Howard nonetheless takes the constructedness of gender to reflect only upon relations between men and women.

As You Like It is assumed only to have such interests; by making such a claim, Howard remains within an *ideological* critical construction of dramatic convention, not the neutrality she supposes when she asserts that "the ideological import of crossdressing was mediated by all the conventions of dramatic narrative and Renaissance dramatic production" (418) or that "crossdressing motifs . . . are a staple of comic tradition with a long dramatic heritage" (429). Thus, while Howard admits that "sodomy haunts the fringes of" antitheatrical tracts (424), she treats cross-dressing in the plays solely as being about women, and declares that male "sexual perversion" is a "different" subject from female "sexual incontinence" (424). The only time Howard reveals she knows that the discourses of sodomy in the period could join these issues occurs in her discussion of Olivia's attraction to Viola, when she claims that Olivia is "punished" (432) for her sodomitical, lesbian dalliance. Who is punishing whom here?[11] "The Renaissance needed the idea of two genders" (423), Howard writes, but she does too. Following Kathleen McLuskie, Howard asserts that the convention of boys playing women was for the most part accepted unproblematically.[12] "Otherwise," she opines, "audience involvement with dramatic narratives premised on heterosexual love and masculine/feminine difference would have been minimal" (435). The audience here is presumptively heterosexual—something to be queried surely in an essay attending to the historicity of the sex/gender system, since heterosexuality is a modern regime; gender difference as Howard construes it is arguably the consequence of that modern sexual organization. But is that how it is in the Renaissance, in these plays? Marlowe would suggest otherwise, as do the plays Howard takes up. Howard reads Renaissance drama within the matrix of a compulsory and only minimally negotiable heterosexuality. It is worth considering whether a critical tradition, fully ideological, of reading Shakespeare's plays makes her account almost inevitable.

Levine and Orgel are far more alert to alternative sexual possibilities in the theater and the plays staged there than Howard is. Nonetheless, their considerations of what they term homosexuality are at times haunted by similarly normative views of (hetero)sexuality. Orgel, seeking to link sexuality and gender, treats boys and their sexual attractiveness as basically unproblematical, indeed, as preferable to women. Boys are *taken for* women, his title says; "women are only a cover for men" (17), and it is, he claims, anxiety about women that the antitheatricalists really voice, about an effeminization that the stage deflects in its transvestism. In making such arguments, boys become women, and what Orgel refers to several times as the "interchangeability" of the sexes (13, 22, 23) changes boys into women with the sexual threat removed. Homosexuality comes "unbreeched" in this essay—the boy is a fantasy of a return to a prior female state, a state before sex. Seeking to talk about homosexuality in the drama, Orgel's essay comes close to the suppositions found in Howard, a collapse of sexuality into questions of gender, a reading of all forms of sexuality as heterosexuality. In Orgel's account, boys make the best women.

Levine, on the other hand, takes the sexual anxieties in the antitheatrical tracts to be the locus of ontological anxieties about what she calls the self or person: "the idea that a man can be turned into a woman is a version of the more basic 'magical' idea that a given person can be turned into another person" (123). This self is male, and Levine's subject is a crisis in a masculinity that is presumptively heterosexual. This explains the trajectory of her essay. Starting from the ways in which the tracts imagine the possibility that the boy actor can become the woman he plays, Levine constructs a notion of homosexuality: "Why should men lose their human identity looking at women, but lose their male identity looking at plays?" (131), she asks, commenting on the passage from Gosson cited earlier; the answer to her question about the loss of male identity is that it presumes "a homosexual response on the part of the spectator" (131). This, offered as a "speculation" (132) about Gosson's tract, becomes a certainty in Levine's consideration of Stubbes. "It is at this point that homosexuality enters the discourse," she writes (134), and "this point" is the moment when Stubbes articulates the possibility that by putting on women's clothes, a man becomes a woman. The logical progression that Levine traces ("anti-theatrical tracts are moving all the time in this direction" [130]) finds its culmination in William Prynne's *Histriomastix,* where a man's desire for the boy beneath the woman's dress presumes a male spectator ravished by the spectacle, who thereby assumes a female position. Corresponding to the boy beneath the woman's attire is a woman trapped within the man, "tucked away somewhere inside his own body—is a woman herself" (134–35). This configuration Levine takes to be constitutive of homosexuality, a *failed* masculinity, "impotence" (137), and effeminization. This may well be the homophobic and misogynistic logic of attacks on cross-dressing, but Levine validates it as the truth of homosexuality. Prynne's *Histriomastix* is the endpoint of a logic that Levine labels pathological;[13] for her, with Prynne, a cultural discourse has become a "personal symptomology" (136). What Prynne's disease is Levine does not exactly say, but the drift seems clear enough: a man so threatened must be what he is describing.[14]

Levine's essay fails to pursue another path which it glimpses when it associates the unmoored and monstrously malleable "self" in these tracts with sodomy (135), but she does not engage Bray's point, that anyone could be a sodomite. Collapsing sodomy into cross-dressing and cross-gendered "effeminate" identity, Levine (like Orgel) decides what is in Bray's account undecidable, the difference between homo- and heterosexuality, and the decision is made on a heterosexual and heterosexist bias. Granted, the terrain here is enormously tricky precisely because those sexualities are undifferentiated in the period, because both boys and women are regarded as potential sexual objects for adult males. They are, as Orgel claims, sexually interchangeable, but this does not mean that one becomes the other, or, more to the point, that one would define homosexuality as that transformation. The boy is the locus of any number of crossings and differentials (questions of age and power status, for instance, of race, too, when the Indian boy of *A Midsummer Night's Dream* is considered) that cannot be decided by a simple mapping of male and female onto the boy's body, for these differentials cross the bodies of men and women differently, and the boy is not a locus of their resolution or identification. Nor is it the case (as Marlowe's example makes clear) that all homoeroticism in Renaissance drama is disposed of or legible through considerations of cross-dressing, as the work of Levine and Orgel implies. (Orgel proceeds to *Edward II* from considerations of cross-dressing as if the transition were a seamless one.) When effeminacy is taken as the transfer point from hetero- to homosexuality, Levine and Orgel lose sight of something they both know, that effeminacy was more easily associated with, and was a charge more often made about, men who displayed excessive attention to women than taken as an indication of same-sex attraction.[15] They do not consider, moreover, that the equation of boy and woman, as it is made in each of the examples, whether from the plays or the antitheatrical tracts, requires attention to a history of sexuality rather than the synchronic assumption of the structural identity of boys and women.

In short, the fact that there is no divide between hetero- and homosexuality does not mean that all sexuality is heterosexual (does not mean that the boy is really a cover for a girl or that homosexuality is a replay of heterosexuality without women). If that is presumed (if it is taken to be the case that cross-dressing reveals that male/male or female/female sexual attractions are really heterosexual, or would be if they could), the homosexuality that is allowed and recognized through cross-dressing is liable to be construed as failed (for Levine) or averted (for Orgel) heterosexuality. In the arguments of Levine or Orgel sexuality is collapsed through the assumptions of modern gender, the presumption that all sexuality is hetero and that same-sex relations are versions of male/female ones.[16] Orgel's claim that men are better women and Levine's that men are failed women are both misogynist and a consequence of the heterosexism that shapes their definitions of homosexuality.

The damaging supposition that homosexuality is a transvestite masquerade has been taken up by Craig Owens in an essay motivated in part by Elaine Showalter's attack on male feminists as critical cross-dressers.[17] As Owens eloquently argues, Showalter's essay uses the accusation to impugn the heterosexuality of the male critics whom she considers. Summoning up the verse from Deuteronomy beloved of antitheatricalists ("The woman shall not wear that which pertaineth unto a man, neither shall a man put on a woman's garment; for all that do so are abomination unto the Lord thy God," Deut. 22:5), Owens shows that in policing cross-dressing, Showalter also is insisting that men be men, women women, and that heterosexuality be the only sexuality. Homosexuality is taken as a threat of transvestite travesty, more broadly (since Showalter's essay is also antitheoretical), that cross-dressing might show that not only gender but also sexuality is constructed rather than natural or, as the biblical text affirms (it comes to the same thing), God-given. Chillingly, speaking for women, Showalter assumes the censorious position of the patriarchy and marshals energies against men's sexual relations with other men that are hard to distinguish from the ways in which women are policed under the regimes of compulsory heterosexuality.[18]

In an essay directed against her male colleagues on the Left for ignoring the political commitments of feminism, Lisa Jardine endorses Showalter, viewing as "worst of all" when such men incorporate feminism into their theoretical arsenal; the horror of this appropriation conjures for her as for Showalter the image of the cross-dressed man: "If the male critic wears a dress, maybe he can pretend that all those women facing him across the lecture hall are also 'travesties'—male critics in drag."[19] Jardine's views echo her treatment of cross-dressing in Renaissance texts in *Still Harping on Daughters,*[20] which, while important for positing a homosexual reading of the phenomenon, slips perilously from explaining the attitudes of antitheatrical polemicists to adopting them. Basing her account on what she takes to be the extreme instance of John Rainoldes' *Th'Overthrow of Stage-Playes* (1599), Jardine comes to endorse his views in her consideration of Renaissance stage practice. There, she claims, erotic titillation was caused by the slippage from female to male occasioned by the boy actor, most often when in drag but sometimes even when not. Jardine calls Rainoldes "hysterical" (9); thus coded female, he is said to display an "unhealthy interest" in what he decries. This sounds like Levine on Prynne, but Jardine goes further. Having thus characterized Rainoldes as (within her own definition of these things) "homosexual," Jardine also nonetheless accepts as true what he sees (it takes one to know one?), for she too finds that the plays display "unhealthy" examples of "misdirected" sexuality.

Jardine's arguments are positioned against feminist Shakespeareans, and the reason for exposing the homosexuality of Renaissance plays is to resist the notion that some genuine femininity can be found in these texts; for her, there are no women in Shakespeare, simply boys travestying the woman's part. (Transvestism is a travesty of women; homosexuality is the proper name for this.) Jardine's insistence on the constructedness of gender is an important point, as is her argument that what some feminist critics validate in Shakespeare as femininity (love, gentleness, compassion, and the like) is a constructed "female" docility within patriarchy. Jardine pursues this point through a homophobic argument, however, and homosexuality becomes responsible for the travesty of women. Along the way, her argument about constructedness disappears; by claiming that male transvestism produces this misrecognition, the possibility of natural, properly directed sex is resurrected.

Jardine insists that there is nothing for women in cross-dressed representations, that women take no pleasure in the performance of boy actors, but also that the femininity of these boys is appealing only to the man who sees beneath the clothing. That is what constitutes the "unhealthy interest" the figures provoke. A number of Jardine's examples in which women respond appreciatively would suggest otherwise, that the women who are represented as taking pleasure in cross-dressing may be responding sexually (even homosexually), but Jardine will have none of it. Jardine assumes that any woman in a Renaissance play really is a man, and she seems to assume that since men made them only men can get pleasure from them, that the only readers or spectators for these plays or texts are male ones. (Orgel attempts to answer this point by adducing the evidence of women in the theater audiences, but the women he describes seem entirely co-opted by patriarchal ideology.) The one moment (27–28) when Jardine allows for, as she calls her, the desires of "the girl reader" to be projected onto cross-dressed women, she quickly insists that "girls" soon learn that these fantasies are not for them. Policing feminism, Jardine disallows such, for her, lesbian identifications. In the name of showing up the constructedness of femininity, she reinforces the presumptions of heterosexuality.

For Jardine's claim is that transvestism produces "a sensuality which is independent of the sex of the desired figure" (24), that while the boy actor plays the female part, he has no female genital part to validate his performance. This free-floating eros (which, in arguments that really are in the service of construction, like Judith Butler's in *Gender Trouble,* goes to show that gender is not sutured onto biological sex, indeed that sex follows from gender) is sometimes called androgynous, problematic, or ambiguous by Jardine, but the problem for her lies precisely in the fact that these figures really are male; the "erotic interest which hovers somewhere between the heterosexual and the homosexual" (11) is suspect since it is, Jardine says, "gratuitous" (see 10, 21; Marlowe, not surprisingly, is Jardine's most flagrant example). That is, because it is detached from biological sex, it produces a sexuality unrelated to the bodies involved. *Androgynous* means this for Jardine: "female in persona but male in his sexuality" (12). Since boys play women on the Elizabethan stage, anything that looks like heterosexuality is really this "gratuitous" sexuality, and any erotic charge floats on the titillation provided by the boy beneath the woman's clothes. In these plays, then, the only titillation is that provided by boys and the only audience for it is men. Such representations, Jardine summarizes, produce "distorted sexual obsession" (13): hence, she notes, "Shakespeare uses male homosexual love to contribute to an atmosphere of distorted sexuality in *Troilus and Cressida*" (35 n. 31). Jardine would have things be undistorted, in a word, straight. "Dubious sex"—or, as Jardine says several times, the "sub-erotic" (see, for example, 14)—is added to and is the allure that poisons "legitimate sexual relations." "Sub-erotic" here is what is termed "gratuitous" elsewhere. The argument is that the stage plays only upon homosexual allure and that the misogyny of the representations is the consequence of this—that homosexuality is the route of misogyny: "perverted sexual activity is the inevitable accompaniment of female impersonation" (9). Jardine holds out for "legitimate sexual relations" between real men and women, holds out for a real that is not contaminated by representation.

Not surprisingly, then, Jardine responds to the lines from *Edward II* with which we began much as Deats did; Gaveston, she writes, "takes particular advantage of the latent sexual deviancy" (22) lurking in cross-dressing, the "particular advantage" lying, no doubt, for Jardine or for Deats, in the assumption that Marlowe was homosexual and Gaveston the spokesman for his desire. Gaveston's lines might appear to make such responses inescapable, especially when they insist on the male genitalia beneath the female disguise, "those parts which men delight to see" (1.1.65). Gaveston's image depends upon the disquieting equation of homosexuality, effeminization, and transvestism, but only the critic who thinks that the antitheatrical tracts tell the truth about Marlowe's text or homosexuality need read the lines as that pathologized truth. If there is a warrant for such an understanding of male/male sexuality, it lies not in Marlowe, but elsewhere in Renaissance drama, in Shakespeare, to go no further. It is thanks to Portia or Viola or Rosalind, the latter dressed up as Ganymede, that cross-dressing has come to seem the privileged locus of the representation of what gets called homosexuality in Renaissance drama. Gaveston's lines, responding to the logic of antitheatricality, anticipating its full working out in Prynne, also point forward to ways in which Shakespearean practice has been understood. Yet while Gaveston's cross-dressed theatricals suggest those affinities, and while the identification of boys and women is of fundamental importance in Elizabethan culture at large as well as in a number of Shakespeare's plays—though even there it is not the whole truth about male/male sexual relations—Gaveston's lines do not serve to represent homosexuality in *Edward II.* Gaveston rehearses one powerful way Marlowe's culture had for stigmatizing theatrical and sexual practices, defining in advance precisely the kind of theatricalization *Edward II* will not offer, the sexual sphere in which the play does not operate. Neither Gaveston nor Edward wears dresses. The familiar linking of boy and woman is disarmed, summoned up to be put aside.

For Gaveston's show is never put on in the play, and there is barely an indication that the "pliant king" requires the incitement that a cross-dressed boy might represent. Gaveston, in the initial lines of the play, does, to be sure, figure himself as Leander to the king's Hero (1.1.6–9), and, once, the king sees Gaveston in a mythological female position, as Danae, and in an image that could be selfreflexive (2.2.53). But if so, are both young men transvestite? The peers suggest as much when they cast the king and his minion as female, or when Lancaster compares Gaveston to "the Greekish strumpet" (2.5.15) Helen, or when Mortimer Junior describes the king's appearance on the battlefield as a show displaying (or seeking?) "women's favors" (2.2.185). Much more insistently, however, a different kind of male/male desire is voiced, as in Edward's letter summoning Gaveston to return from exile that Gaveston reads at the play's opening: "My father is deceased. Come, Gaveston, / And share the kingdom with thy dearest friend" (1.1.1–2). What follows (it might be termed Edward's play in contrast to the theatricals that Gaveston initially imagines or that the peers spy at times) is a sharing of the kingdom in which Gaveston sits beside his monarch, renamed to play parts that do not cross gender lines but transgress the limits of status and class: "I here create thee Lord High Chamberlain, / Chief Secretary to the state and me, / Earl of Cornwall, King and Lord of Man" (1.1.154–56). Before the first scene is over, the Bishop of Coventry has been sent to prison, and Gaveston receives "his house and goods" (203). No reverence is paid to his "robes," and Edward has him stripped: "Throw off his golden mitre, rend his stole, / And in the channel christen him anew" (187–88).

These transgressions, even in their sumptuary form, also provoke—and are provoked by—antitheatricalists. (Indeed, here one can follow what is most valuable in Jean Howard's work, the imbrication of questions of gender and class in her reading of antitheatrical tracts.) Gosson, for instance, is willing to imagine that some actors "are sober, discreete, properly learned honest housholders and Citizens well thought on amonge their neighbours at home"; the abusers are the "shadowes" of these good citizens and married men, "those hangebyes whome they succour with stipend" (40). Once again the boy actors, those apprentices hired by the adult males and brought into their households, inflame Gosson, but not because they wear dresses: these "hyerlings . . . which stand at reversion of vi.s by the weeke, iet under Gentlemens noses in sutes of silke, exercising themselves too prating on the stage, and common scoffing when they come abrode, where they look askance over the shoulder at every man, of whom the sunday before they begged an almes" (39).

Parallel charges are made in the play against Gaveston and the parts he plays in Edward's script. It is Edward's clothing Gaveston as a peer, in titles and silks to match, that enrages Mortimer to a Gosson-like response:

> . . . this I scorn, that one so basely born
> Should by his sovereign's favor grow so pert
> And riot it with the treasure of the realm.
> While soldiers mutiny for want of pay,
> He wears a lord's revenue on his back,
> And, Midas-like, he jets it in the court
> With base outlandish cullions at his heels,
> Whose proud fantastic liveries make such show,
> As if that Proteus, god of shapes, appeared. (1.4.402–10)

Mortimer charges Gaveston with a travesty of class, not gender, the theatricalization of social difference, not sexual difference. Indeed, sexual and social issues are explicitly separated, for Mortimer Junior responds, at this moment in the play, to his uncle, who counsels him not to oppose the king. "The mightiest kings have had their minions," the elder Mortimer assures him,

> Great Alexander loves Hephaestion;
> The conquering Hercules for Hylas wept,
> And for Patroclus stern Achilles drooped. (1.4.390–93)

"Uncle, his wanton humor grieves not me," Mortimer replies, proceeding to the lines just cited. This is an extraordinary moment in the play, precisely because it is usual to suppose that social and sexual irregularities are mutually causative and equally to be condemned. Mortimer's allowance of the sexual relation is as disarming as the flaunt delivered by Gaveston's transvestite theater, for Mortimer countenances what the antitheatricalists abhor, sexual behavior usually thought to be tantamount to social dissolution. Such connections can be seen when Gosson assumes that "wanton spectacles" make wanton spectators, in a mimetism in which the "right Comedie" (35), the real play, is played in the audience, as assignations are made among the riffraff who should be better employed. "Not that any filthynesse in deede, is committed within the compasse of that grounde," he claims (only theater takes place in the theater), "but that every wanton and his Paramour, every man and his Mistresse, every John and his Joan, every knave and his queane, are there first acquainted and cheapen the Merchandise in that place, which they pay for elsewhere" (35–36). A slightly later pamphleteer can see no difference between what occurs onstage or off: "they commit that filthiness openlie, which is horrible to be done in secret";[21] in *The Anatomie of Abuses,* Phillip Stubbes, in a passage crucial to critical discussions of cross-dressing, gives a name to the open secret of a debauchery without limits; it is sodomy.

> Marke the flocking and running to Theaters & curtens, daylie and hourely, night and daye, tyme and tyde to see Playes and Enterludes, where such wanton gestures, such bawdie speaches: such laughing and fleering: such kissing and bussing: such clipping and culling: Suche winckinge and glancinge of wanton eyes, and the like is used, as is wonderfull to behold. Than these goodly pageants being done, every mate sorts to his mate, every one bringes another homeward of their way verye freendly, and in their secret conclaves (covertly) they play the *Sodomits,* or worse.[22]

The Mortimers acknowledge, and justify, the "wanton" friendship of Edward and Gaveston; sodomy, which usually names a sexual relationship on the basis of its social transgressiveness is granted a scandalous affirmation.

When the Mortimers agree that kings have always had their minions, they depend upon terms that Edward uses to justify his relationship with Gaveston from the very opening of the play. More often than not, Edward calls him "friend," although he does also refer to Gaveston as his minion (for example, 1.4.30). What the peers defend when they seek to uncouple the relationship of king and minion from the social breakdown that the antitheatricalists regularly read in the debauch of "sodomy" is the privileged male/male relationship of "friendship" upon which they too depend; throughout the play, their allies against the king are referred to as *their* friends. Indeed, the recognition of their status that they seek from Edward is couched in the normative terms of male/

male sponsorship that friendship also covers, so much so that, railing against Gaveston, they vie explicitly for the king's "love"; the signs of royal favor they desire are exactly those conferred upon Gaveston, as the scene of renaming and promoting of the peers in act 1, scene 4, suggests, echoing as it does the opening scene in which Gaveston was raised from his "base" position. In this play anyone is capable of calling his ally (of whatever sex) "sweet" and the lubricant of "love" smooths the paths of friendship, clientage, and promotion. "If you love us, my lord," Mortimer Senior says, "hate Gaveston" (1.1.80). The peers, as much as the minion, want the king's love.

In his reading of *Edward II*,[23] Alan Bray has argued that the play is couched in the normative language of friendship, and that its "dark suggestions of sodomy" (9) inhere in such moments as the theatrical debauch of Gaveston's opening lines. It seems to me, however, that Bray's own arguments lead to quite different conclusions, for his point is that friendship and sodomy are always in danger of (mis)recognition since what both depend upon physically—sexually—cannot be distinguished. One switching point for the proper intimacy between men to be called sodomy rather than friendship was, as Bray argues, precisely the transgression of social hierarchies that friendship maintained, those transgressions of the kind for which Gaveston is accused when he usurps the privileges that the peers believe belong only to them. Edward may call Gaveston his friend, but what he makes of him (not, to repeat, putting him in a dress) makes both of them sodomites.

The sodomy inextricable from friendship in this play (and, Marlowe intimates, in all the privileged male/male relations that supposedly maintain social order) is not the sodomy that Bray reads by way of transvestism or that Orgel and Levine depend upon too. For part of the confusion, to cite Foucault again, of "that utterly confused category,"[24] is that sodomy can interfere with more than one form of social relation. When Levine, reading Stubbes, declares that "homosexuality enters the discourse," it is in terms of the production of "sodomy" in the cross-dressed theatricalization of gender. "Here," Levine comments on the passage cited above, "the dramatic metaphor is inextricable from the sexual act: they will 'play' the sodomite. . . . Stubbes makes sure we understand just what it is the spectator has seen on the stage" (134). The spectator, Levine argues, has seen gender travestied, and at home, in secret, the secret onstage is nakedly replayed. Yet, as Bray reminds us, part of the confusion of the category of sodomy lies in its refusal of boundaries, even those of gender. A "sodomite" need not be a man who sleeps with other men; the scandal of sexual acts that violate socially sanctioned forms of sexual behavior is produced only when the structures of the social hierarchy are seen to be violated. Thus, in *Homosexuality in Renaissance England*, when Bray claims, on the basis of the passage cited above, that "the Elizabethan and Jacobean theatre acquired a reputation for homosexuality, as Philip Stubbes graphically claimed" (54), one must qualify his remark, and precisely through his own arguments. For, as Bray contends, sodomy, as the allegation of certain forms of sexual debauch, became visible in the Elizabethan period only when supposed practitioners were charged with violations, usually religious or political, of the social order. Sodomy was coupled with the kind of social disturbance that the Mortimers mark in the "upstart" behavior of the "base" Gaveston. Yet, remarkably, what Marlowe allows them to voice is a scandalous acceptance of the friend, the minion, as a sexual partner. They can do this because what they want (to maintain their positions as peers of the realm) cannot be separated from the relationship that Edward and Gaveston have. Thus, the Mortimers give voice to the complicity of friendship and sodomy as sexual acts, and for the sake of maintaining male privilege and privileged male/male relations they mark the possibility of this sexual sphere. It is to be distinguished from the violation to relations of alliance secured through marriage and the exchange of women that can also be called sodomy. Indeed, in Stubbes, *sodomite* is not invariably used, as Levine's reading would suggest, to describe male/male sexual relations; in fact, the one other time Stubbes uses the same phrase, those "playing the vile *Sodomits* together" (H6v) are an adulterous man and woman. So little can Stubbes imagine the possibility of members of the same sex having sex together, that he proposes, as a solution to the incitement to lust that dancing is said to offer, that men should dance with men, women with women (N8v–O1r). Sodomy, for Stubbes, is a debauched playing that knows no limit—that has violated the proprieties of male/female married sex—or whose limit can only be gestured towards in a supplementary addition, "*Sodomits,* or worse."

"What is worse," Orgel writes, "is presumably the sodomized" (17). A long tradition, from antiquity on, could justify that supposition; masculinity has often been attached to the phallus, not the anus, penetrator and penetrated have been hierarchized, man and boy, master and servant. This assumption is particularly easy to make if it is assumed that the boy is wearing women's clothing, for then the hierarchy also involves one that structures invidiously the difference between man and woman in any number of western discourses. If Stubbes's "worse" points in this direction, it does so only insofar as it imagines all desire within this heterosexual hierarchy.

The relationship between Edward and Gaveston in Marlowe's play does not participate in the heterosexualized version of homosexuality that Levine or Orgel offers on Stubbes's model. This is the case not only because the play does not represent Gaveston and Edward in a transvestite relationship, but also because Gaveston has been raised from his lower-class position to be Edward's equal. Their relationship refuses the traditional hereditary social distinctions upon which the younger Mortimer insists, the hierarchies that ensured, as Bray argues, that sexual relations between men could go unnoticed in the period precisely because they were not "sodomitical" social transgressions. The sexual relation cannot go unnoticed in *Edward II,* and the radical move in the play lies in having the Mortimers contend that although Gaveston has not remained in his proper place, there is nothing improper in his sexual relationship with the king. What is "worse" for the Mortimers is not Orgel's "worse," the assumption of a subordinate position, but the failure of subordination. Stubbes's "worse" glances in this direction, too, for worst would be the refusal of all socially countenanced boundaries. Worse than playing the sodomite would be to be a sodomite. For Stubbes, this worse is virtually unthinkable, a being beyond any ontological category; to be a sodomite means to be damned,[25] a being without being. It is just such "being" that Edward and Gaveston have; they are not merely playing.

This "worse" is worst not least because it also dissolves the boundary between being and playing. Here Levine's insistence on ontological confusion is pertinent once we no longer assume the (ontological) certainty of gender difference that her argument supposes. Among the categorical confusions of the confused category "sodomy" is categorical confusion itself—as noted in the Preface, Stubbes calls a false argument a "Sodometrie" (B8r)—a denial of those socially constructed hierarchies that are taken to be natural, that social ordering that is thought to participate in and replicate the order of being. The king, in such a view, exists to maintain social order, yet Edward, from the first line of Marlowe's play, inviting Gaveston to share the kingdom, instigates a sodomitical order, one that alienates his peers and his wife, driving Queen Isabella and the younger Mortimer into an adulterous and rebellious embrace. If, as Foucault argues, *sodomy* is the word for everything illicit, all that lies outside the system of alliance that juridically guarantees marriage and inheritance, the prerogatives of blood, as the linchpin of social order and the maintenance of class distinctions, then what is remarkable in Marlowe's play is the way in which one normative system of alliance—friendship—is unleashed against another. From this clash emerges something like what Foucault calls sexuality, as opposed to alliance, and it is this that the Mortimers countenance when they allow the royal right to minions; it is upon that right that their claims also rest. In Marlowe's play, such a sphere is possible because it is the expression of the royal will, absolutist prerogative. Among the other things that Marlowe's play anticipates, it could be argued, are the debates that become rife under the rule of James I, the question of whether the king is king under law, or whether the king is above the law; within the Elizabethan context, Gaveston and Spencer represent versions of the "new men" who came to power, or the favorites Elizabeth raised, often from rather unpromising backgrounds.[26] The transgression of the legal system in *Edward II* starts with the king, and it begins in the first line of the play. It stops nowhere. The figure upon which all systems of relationship between men depend, whether conducted through women or not, is the figure who, in the very exercise of his prerogatives, violates the law that he is supposed to found. The site of legitimation and transgression at once, the king, from his opening words, announcing the death of his father and the refusal of the paternal law for the sake of friendship, institutes a sodomitical regime. In the extended sense of the term, as not only the ruination of the maintainence of male/male hierarchies through friendship, but also as the explosion of the marital tie, *sodomy* is the name for all behavior in the play. What the Mortimers countenance also defines their behavior, in the battlefield and in bed. When Mortimer and Isabella embrace as rebels they are Stubbes's adulterous couple, prototypical sodomites. But they are also rebels against a sodomitical king locked in the embrace of his minions.

Deats arrives at something like this conclusion by regarding all the characters in the play as androgynous—Isabella, she argues, is masculine in her Machiavellianism, feminine in her staged submissiveness, while Gaveston and the king continually exchange male and female behaviors.[27] Such a conclusion suggests the massive destabilizations through which the play unmoors any notion of being, but remains misguided in its attempt to gender those dislocations through the assumed distinctions of male and female, as misguided as the thesis of antitheatricalists and their commentators, who would line up a debased femininity with homosexuality. For what Marlowe intimates, insofar as it is possible to think of Isabella as a sodomite, is that the possibility for "strong" female behavior lies outside of marriage and its regularization of gender. As Stephen Greenblatt argues in his incisive essay on Marlowe in *Renaissance Self-Fashioning,* [28] Marlowe's reversals "fashion lines that echo in the void, that echo powerfully because there is nothing but a void" (221). Sodomy gives a name to that void; this calls into question Greenblatt's argument that Marlovian overturning, like weak deconstruction, pays continual homage to that which it opposes. Gender reversal, gender confusion, cross-dressing (topics that Greenblatt does not engage in that essay) can be such forms of limited overturning (Judith Butler's

Gender Trouble demonstrates that they need not be) when the Renaissance discourses that join boys and women are read through the framework of misogyny that lines boys up with a female sexuality that debases sexual and political hierarchies. In the relation of Edward and Gaveston, Marlowe's play interferes with these associations and, so doing, it does more than overturn. Sodomy may be a void, but it is central to the will, the locus of abyssal contradiction that Levine glimpses in her essay. The identity that Marlowe gives to the sodomite is a fully negativized one against which there is no positivity to be measured. With no ground to stand upon, Marlowe envisions the possibility of sexuality and sexual difference as a separate category. This is not a position easily assimilable to those who would find in Marlowe a spokesman for modern gay identity.[29] William Empson, with his usual genius, was closer to the point, when he argued that Marlowe believed that "the unmentionable sin for which the punishment was death was *the proper thing to do*"; Marlowe is defending sodomy, not an idealized friendship or some spiritual relationship or some self-integrative principle of identity; "a critic," Empson continues, "who muffles it up, from whatever kind intention, cannot be saying anything important about him."[30]

"Written in an age when moralists still debated the existence of feminine souls, [*Edward II*] is a remarkable achievement," Deats concludes ("Androgyny," 40). Indeed. But that achievement depends, precisely, on not assuming that Edward's relation with his lover is a version of his relation with his wife, and surely not from giving anyone a soul. Edward desires his relationship with Gaveston above all, and declares himself remarried to Isabella when she allows it too (1.4.334); indeed, it is at just that point that Edward marries Gaveston off to the woman named solely as Gloucester's niece. This is an undeniably misogynist moment in the play, but its animus is directed against marriage; relations between men secured through women occupy an entirely subordinate place in the play. Something like the misogyny that links boys and women in a transvestite theater can be seen when the queen and Gaveston wrangle over possession of Edward: "Villain, 'tis thou that robb'st me of my lord," the queen charges Gaveston; "Madam, 'tis you that rob me of my lord," he rejoins (1.4.160–61). An equation between queen and lover is made, an identification between "villain" (a class term as well as a moral one) and "madam." From such an equation homosexuality emerges in the arguments around cross-dressing. It is just such gender substitution that Edward refuses; when he loses Gaveston (indeed, even before he loses him), he replaces him with another man, not with his queen. The substitution of man for woman is irreversible. The possibility of having a lover and a wife makes those relations separate and supplementary. Hence, those repetitions that Greenblatt so acutely recognizes in Marlowe are not repetitions that replay the same. On the basis of the illicit, a defoundational site that cannot be read through or merely as a reflection of the licit, Marlowe's play negotiates difference—in gender and in sexuality—differently. Modern heterosexist presumptions are not in place.

Left alone, the queen wishes she had never married, or that crossing the sea from France to England (the very journey Gaveston takes as the play opens), "that charming Circes, walking on the waves, / Had changed my shape" (1.4.172–73). That Circean transformation, as many an antitheatricalist could quickly have pointed out, would have been the bestial metamorphosis that the boy actor accomplished. Isabella is, of course, played by a boy, but this allusion to shape-shifting, like Gaveston's initial spectacle of cross-dressing, is not an invitation to see the boy actor beneath the dress, or to collapse one sex into the other. Isabella's wish that she were a boy means that she is not to be taken as one.[31] Isabella sees her plot laid out in classical terms like those invoked by the Mortimers:

> Like frantic Juno will I fill the earth
> With ghastly murmur of my sighs and cries,
> For never doted Jove on Ganymede
> As much as he on cursèd Gaveston. (1.4.178–81)

She may claim the goddess of marriage as her avatar, but it is adultery she embraces. Like her husband, she refuses the boundaries of the licit. A sodomite, then, in Stubbes's sense of the term, but not a boy. Her "strength" *as a woman* lies in refusing the limits of marriage.

Isabella's reference to Jove and Ganymede recalls the opening scene of Marlowe's *Dido Queen of Carthage,* where the curtains of the discovery space are drawn to reveal "*Jupiter dandling Ganymede upon his knee*" (1.1.sd). With the exception of Simon Shepherd, Marlowe's critics have attempted to ignore that scene, treating it as an embarrassment, a joke, or a symptom of his "pathological" condition.[32] As Shepherd argues, however, that opening has everything to do with the play that follows: "*Dido* begins with the fact of Jupiter's sodomy and shows it to be truer to male sexual contact—with women—than moralist writings allowed."[33] In Shepherd's account, the predatory nature of the sodomitical relationship between Jupiter and Ganymede discloses a power relationship constitutive of masculinity and male desire, not its aberration, and not to be distanced from masculinity in its more usual form, as when, for example, Aeneas abandons Dido. Shepherd thus points to an overturning in the sexual sphere congruent with Greenblatt's arguments about race, religion, economy, and knowledge in *The Jew of Malta* or *Doctor Faustus.* Sodomy, Shepherd contends, founds masculinity; rather than its negation, it is its truth. This argument could be put beside Empson's crystalline remark that Marlowe insists on the *properness* of behaviors and beliefs stigmatized as fundamentally antisocial, for Shepherd also calls into question moralistic judgments and the stability of the ontological categories upon which they are supposed to rest. Valuably, Shepherd marshals sodomy against homophobic discourses, not least of all that to be found in much of the criticism of Marlowe (even, as we've seen in the case of Deats, when written by his admirers).

Insofar as Shepherd sees sodomy as a deconstitutive locus, his argument parallels the one I have been making about the work that sodomy, that confused category, can do. Shepherd also notes that *Dido* "refuses the sexual tease, the cross-gender scenes, which boys' plays are capable of" (201), that cross-dressing is not how

Marlowe represents male/male desire. For Shepherd, however, this refusal to disguise sodomy under some more acceptable form of sexual relation serves to expose the fundamental sameness of sexual experience. Paradoxically, Shepherd reads Marlowe's stance as achieving precisely the same purpose that cross-dressed scenes are taken to serve by critics who read boys and women as identical to each other. For Shepherd, the power relationship is the same one in both cases. Thus when he looks for instances of sodomy in Marlowe, he finds them in effeminized men, "bad kings" (199) like Henry III or Mycetes in *Tamburlaine,* or, more generally, in any man who displays "female" emotion, or any man put into the "feminine" position of being the object of the sexual gaze of another man. While such scenes deconstruct ontological differences between male and female, in Shepherd's reading of them, they nonetheless preserve the gendered structure of power relations. Hence, Shepherd can argue that sodomy is the truth of heterosexuality because he understands male/male relations as versions of the power differential in male/female ones, and because he writes the less empowered male into the female position.

How easily this view of homosexuality can become homophobic (rather than serving as a weapon against the homophobia and misogyny that conflate the position of women with the sodomite) is evident in a recent essay by David Lee Miller on "Hero and Leander."[34] Like Shepherd, Miller has a commitment to revealing the male oppression of women. For him this happens not only in Leander's treatment of Hero, but also in the narrator's investment in Leander. Miller shares Shepherd's supposition that for a man to look with desire at another places the one gazed upon in a female position. This view is not entirely supported by the poem; Leander may think Neptune has mistaken him for a woman when he attempts to embrace him, but he has not: the sea god thinks he is seizing Ganymede. (The difference between Leander and Neptune here parallels that between Gaveston and Edward II.) In Miller's view, Leander is represented as both masculine (with Hero) and feminine (with the narrator), the site of what then gets termed the "bisexuality" of the privileged masculine view of the poem (763). In other words, Miller takes the homosexual gaze of "Hero and Leander" to be the normative locus of male domination. Marlowe's poem becomes a piece of evidence for the timeless structure that psychoanalysis reveals; so doing, and fully within the grip of that discourse, Miller scapegoats homosexuality as the source of gender oppression (of the oppression of women; Miller never considers the discrimination against gay men rife in our culture, or against sodomites in Marlowe's). Shepherd, on the other hand, takes the same structure (of the gaze, of gender oppression) to be the site of a protofeminist intervention that Marlowe is performing. Rather than condemning Marlowe as a perpetrator, he sees him, from the vantage point of (his) sodomy, seeing through the structures of oppression.

In commendably seeking to forge an alliance between feminist and antihomophobic work, Shepherd's argument nonetheless runs the danger of supplying ammunition for Miller's argument or Jardine's similar one. For Shepherd also thinks that the traffic in women is a ruse for male desire for other men; embracing sodomy as the nasty secret of all male sexuality, whatever its object, Shepherd sees Edward as feminized: "Edward's language is gendered female when he talks of mythology and role-play"; he is "inconsistently masculine" (204). *Edward II,* he says, "centres the issue of sodomy" (204); "the sodomy" of Edward and his lovers, Shepherd argues, "is not so much an individual case-study of an anomaly but part of a debased form of human relations. . . . Masculinity is not privileged over sodomy: there is little pleasurable or reassuring differentiation between order and disorder, personal and social" (205). Masculinity, as Shepherd sees it, involves male competition and oppression; the peers, in his view, condemn Edward but condone male/male relations so long as power differentials are maintained. True enough: but, for Shepherd, for Edward to be a sodomite, he must be both male and female, and the sodomy the peers condemn in him is his effeminization.

This is, undoubtedly, a route of homophobia. But it is therefore important not to collapse all sexuality, as Shepherd does in marking Edward as "inconsistently masculine," into the same sexuality. Certainly, Shepherd is right to view sodomy as the "center" of the play, and one that decenters it; a center without a center, a void, sodomy ruins difference. But, as I have been arguing, it also allows for difference—sexual difference, gender difference—and allows for ways of conceiving sexual relations and gender construction that cannot be reduced to the normative structure of male/female relations under the modern regimes of heterosexuality.

The complexity in defining sexuality and gender in Marlowe lies in the ungroundedness—the undecidability—of these differences. By this, I don't mean to deny power differentials or to suppose some utopian state of egalitarianism can be found in Marlowe. Rather, I would recall Empson's fundamental insight: Marlowe affirms *as proper* what his society sees as warranting death: his unflinching representation of the death of Edward is one sign of this, a making manifest of sodomy as the ungrounded truth of the play. So doing, Marlowe glimpses the destruction of the social as constituted; what he is affirming is not something that can be taken into the social order, not its secret other, not its dark truth. This is what makes it difficult to use categorical terms which are themselves always under pressure, to treat male and female, masculinity and femininity, hetero- and homosexuality as ontologically pregiven rather than as in the process of a deconstitutive construction that also must be thought through in its historic specificity, for sodomy is not homosexuality *tout court*, nor are male/female relations of alliance the same as heterosexuality.

Further consideration of *Dido Queen of Carthage* will clarify these arguments. The play begins in a way that would seem to support Shepherd, since the relationship between Jupiter and Ganymede is explicitly positioned against women, against Juno: "Come, gentle Ganymede, and play with me. / I love thee well, say Juno what she will" (1.1.1–2). Jupiter titillates Ganymede with sadistic promises to rack his queen. By the end of their scene together, he also performs an action that is repeated throughout the play, giving gifts to the boy, a feather from the wings of the sleeping Mercury who lies at his feet, and, even more spectacularly, the "linkèd gems / My Juno ware upon her marriage day" (42–43). This is, explicitly, "theft" (45), and the point seems equally explicit. To legitimize the illicit relationship opposed by Juno, Jupiter marries his "sweet wag" (23), or, more accurately, appropriates a sign of marriage for their relationship. A moment later, Venus arrives, complaining that in toying with Ganymede, Jupiter has forgotten the plight of her son, pursued by avenging Juno. Venus accuses Jupiter of "playing with that female wanton boy" (51), Ganymede, when he should be attending to her "sweet boy" (74), Aeneas.

The movement of this opening scene, brief as it is, is extraordinarily slippery. It begins in a misogyny that structures the relationship between Jupiter and Ganymede as an opposition to Juno—an opposition to women, but, more particularly, to his wife, to marriage and the goddess who represents that social institution. It slides into a misogyny based on the appropriation of the relationship between Jupiter and his wife. Venus castigates this simulated marriage, and in her scorn for the "female . . . boy," she redirects Jupiter to *her* boy, to a proper male/male relationship rather than the improper one. Venus is a moralist at this moment, and she is also the voice of antitheatricality, attacking the cross-dressed boy who has been turned into a woman, or has been given the attributes of a woman. Antitheatricalists, following Tertullian, regularly term the theater a court of Venus; here, in a typically Marlovian twist, Venus has their voice. Indeed, as she calls Jupiter to attend to the claims of empire, she echoes the final pages of Gosson's *School of Abuse,* which argue that rather than wasting their time in the theater, young men should be training in arms and entering military careers.

There is, in the opening lines of the play, a route from sodomy to masculinity, but it is not the direct one in which male/female relations are seamlessly superimposed on male/male ones. The route from one male/male relation (Jupiter and Ganymede's) to another (Jupiter and Aeneas's) is structured by Venus's antitheatrical response to the relationship between Jupiter and Ganymede, and it passes through and is mobilized by the misogyny that is attached to male/male relationships in which one male plays the part of a woman. Perverse moralist, Venus is not staking out a claim for marriage, for she opposes Juno, but she is insisting on male/male relations (the promotion of Aeneas's career) that follow from maintaining gender propriety in the sexual sphere. Thus, the movement in this brief scene suggests both the similarity of male/male and male/female relations and their difference. If Ganymede can be dressed in female attire, it is because of the differences in age and power between the god and his boy; these provide the transfer point so that their relationship parodies Jove's marriage to Juno. But this is also a transformation of the relationship as originally conceived, where Jupiter's relationship to Ganymede represents an antithesis to his marriage to Juno, not its simulation.

The play that follows never recovers that oppositional moment; rather, its structuring effect leads to the representation of male/female relations caught up within simulation. Dido repeatedly invests her relationship to Aeneas with all the signs of her former marriage. If this theatricalization initially stays within the proprieties of gender—in their first meeting, she clothes him in the garb of Sichaeus (2.1.80)—later, when she actually renames him Sichaeus, she simultaneously gives him the jewels and the wedding ring that Sichaeus had given her (3.4.58–63). This crossgendering culminates when she crowns Aeneas in her place, and retiring within, sends him into the streets of Carthage to be king in her place (4.4.35–92). These are scenes of a displaced crossdressing, versions of the scene between Jupiter and Ganymede excoriated by Venus. Played out between a man and a woman they effectively challenge what either gender can be under the heterosexual regime of a Venus. If they look like the cross-dressed relation of Jupiter and Ganymede, it would appear that the parody is already installed in "natural" relations.

As in the *Aeneid,* Aeneas enters the walls of Carthage by passing through a picture gallery; the image of heroic masculinity that he represents is reenacted throughout the play—in his refusal of the relation with Dido and, with that, a defense against women and against effeminization. The simulation of marriage is disallowed, not in order to defend the proprieties of marriage (Venus opposes Juno), but to expose marriage as a deforming institution, for men *and* for women. When Venus lures Jupiter to aid her son, Jupiter warmly responds in his vision of "bright Ascanius, beauty's better work" (1.1.96), as if the refusal of marriage could lead back to his original idyll with Ganymede. Similarly, when Aeneas looks at the image of Priam on the walls of Carthage, and believes it is really Priam that he sees, his son knows better: "Sweet father, leave to weep. This is not he, / For were he Priam he would smile at me" (2.1.35–36). Ascanius casts the true relationship with Priam as a version of the relation of Ganymede and Jupiter. Jupiter dreams of a futurity modeled like Ascanius's recognition on an irrecoverable past. Such futurity is thought of in a pedophiliac vein, Ascanius as a replacement for, or a version of, Ganymede, an attempt in history to recapture the moment upon which the curtains opened as the play began, a moment as immediately lost, the primal moment that unravels as the opening scene proceeds:

> What is't, sweet wag, I should deny thy youth,
> Whose face reflects such pleasure to mine eyes,
> As I, exhaled with thy fire-darting beams,
> Have oft driven back the horses of the night,
> Whenas they would have haled thee from my sight.
> (1.1.23–27)

So Jupiter describes the initial idyll, that refusal of temporality that also marks Ganymede's original mythic status: a mortal who achieves eternal youth without ever having to die. The very violation of the conditions of human being here is the deontological ground of an impossibility unthinkable within the licit, not even thinkable as the miming (il)licit of cross-dressing.

These opening lines glance at a desire that echoes throughout the play in the substitution of Cupid for Ascanius; over and again, Dido plays with the boy as Jupiter had with Ganymede. That attempted replay of Jupiter's part is as impossible for her as it is for him to recapture the lost idyll, and for similar reasons: just as Venus voices a redirection of male/male desire through the route of its abuse as the abuse of women, so Dido, as a woman limited by the possibilities of marriage or its simulation, is incapable of taking on Jupiter's role. Her attempt at simulation is her undoing. The original relationship between Jupiter and Ganymede, like the sodomy in *Edward II,* initiates simulations—it is the groundless ground upon which simulation thrives; thereby it opens difference.

This is clearest when Dido crowns Aeneas and gives him her throne; acting like Jupiter, she constitutes him *as* Jupiter: "Now looks Aeneas like immortal Jove," she says, "O where is Ganymede to hold his cup / And Mercury to fly for what he calls?" (4.4.45–47). Dido's self-abandonment implicitly includes an acknowledgment of just what makes her abandonment inevitable, the difference between her relationship with Aeneas and Jupiter's hold on him as the vehicle of his desire. Aeneas attempts in this scene, as elsewhere in the play, to refuse what Dido offers; "O keep them still" (44), she insists, referring to crown and sceptre, and by extension, everything with which she has invested him. The nature of Aeneas's resistance is registered a scene earlier, in his first attempt to abandon Dido. To Achates' call that

> This is no life for men-at-arms to live,
> Where dalliance doth consume a soldier's strength,
> And wanton motions of alluring eyes
> Effeminate our minds, inured to war (4.3.33–36)

—lines that recall both Gosson's charge that theater effeminates the mind as well as his call to arms—Aeneas responds, "I may not dure this female drudgery" (55). Effeminization, not his reconstitution as Jupiter, lies at the hands of Dido. In the hands of Jupiter, Aeneas abandons his desire for Dido. The heroism he embraces is not allowed to recover a sodomy untarnished by the ways in which it is deformed by the pursuit of his proper career. Made to serve Jupiter's sodomitical vision, he comes closest to avowing it as his own when Ascanius is restored to him—and he is reprimanded by Mercury for doing so: "Spendst thou thy time about this little boy, / And givest not ear unto the charge I bring?" (5.1.51–52). Aeneas is not allowed any desire except to heed the imperial call; he is positioned at the crossroads of the conflicting desires of Dido (to undo marriage, to be Jupiter) and of Jupiter (to undo marriage, to be Jupiter without Juno and attached to Ganymede or his historical avatars). As the site where these impossible desires cross, Aeneas embodies a hollowed-out heroic masculinity.

In the highly charged final scene between Dido and Aeneas, Marlowe allows Virgil's Latin text into his own, has Aeneas say, "*Italiam non sponte sequor*" (5.1.140), "I do not pursue Italy of my own volition." Aeneas speaks Latin in response to Dido's Latin, and at the end of the play, concluding her suicide speech, Dido speaks Virgil's lines again, to foretell unremitting war between Carthage and Rome. "Live, false Aeneas! Truest Dido dies!" she continues, ending in Virgil's Latin: "*Sic, sic juvat ire sub umbras*" (5.1.312–13), "Thus, thus, I am pleased to go beneath the shades." Dido's truth is that she has been spoken by the Virgilian text. Marlowe, having rewritten that text so that it begins with the scene between Jupiter and Ganymede, and ends with a series of imitative suicides that follow Dido's, claims, citing Virgil, that his text coincides with his source. In his rewriting, Juno's ire is caused by her husband's relation with Ganymede (see 3.2.40), and Dido's by Aeneas's role in furthering Jupiter's pedophiliac empire. If, as Shepherd argues, sodomy structures heterosexuality, it does so insofar as Dido's desire—as woman's desire—simulates it. This simulation is oppositional even as it is imitative. Like Isabella, Dido plays the sodomite, cloaking adultery in the (cross-dressed) trappings of marriage. Her illicit desire cannot be made licit, and not least because relations between men and women are seen as and represented as leading to the effeminization of men. But her relationship cannot be the sodomitical one of male/male relations either, for her gender under the presumptive sexual regimes of Juno and of Venus bars her from that.

Aeneas's abandonment of Dido, and his desire for her, are written into Marlowe's delegitimation of heterosexual relations as a deforming of masculinity, of men's relations with women and with other men. Aeneas's misogyny, which is also an antitheatricality, and an opposition to cross-dressed relationships (he speaks not only with Gosson's voice, but also with his mother's), serves a desire that is also not Aeneas's own, not a function of his volition, but of the cultural impossibility of desire as constructed within the protoheterosexism of empire-building. This does not justify Aeneas's abandonment of Dido—despicable from any angle—but it does register his impossible position, for he also has been abandoned by women, and first of all by Venus, who nonetheless propels his career. (One need not read this as merely a misogynist instance supposedly showing what women do to men but also as displaying what the institutional possibilities for women—marriage, adultery, motherhood—do to both women and men.) At the end of the play Aeneas is able to leave Carthage thanks to Iarbas, the man who hopes to marry Dido once his rival is out of the way, and Iarbas's suicide is one of those that Marlowe adds to the plot. A rivalry between men for a woman translates into an alliance of heterosexuality and misogyny. The sodomitical order is also a misogynistic one, but it, not heterosexuality, lends Dido's voice its power—and its pathos. She, unlike Aeneas, but like Jupiter, is a site of volition. A true Marlovian hero, her situation is even more untenable than that of Edward II. She is the locus of a double negation, structured by heterosexual and homosexual misogyny, and the implacable hate that she voices, to her own undoing, is the oppositional ground on which she stands, one that depends upon the identity and difference of these doubled and divided desires. What she wants even Jupiter barely can have (he loses it almost as soon as he starts talking; it is an irrecoverable past). In this play, there can be no marriages, not even the one simulated by Jupiter and Ganymede. (Jupiter's gift-giving only provokes Ganymede to ask for more.) Aeneas, too, is doubly divided and undone; the false life which is his truth comes from occupying a position between Jupiter and Dido, between sodomitical desire and a heterosexuality that simulates it and opposes it, as cross-dressing does too, and that is destructured by misogyny. Neither desire is his own, and the pursuit of fame and glory, a soldier's life in the service of empire, rests upon the doubled negations that lead him to say of himself, what I do is not of my volition.

"The definition of gender is shaped by the project of empire," Shepherd astutely writes (195). Aeneas, the empire builder, is sent on his way by a misogyny that is doubly structured, by sodomy and by heterosexual relations (between men and women and as they restructure male/male relations and mark the impossibility of sodomy), a structure of identity and difference that produces man and woman as opposing categories, neither of them self-identical nor identical to each other. There is no place in this structure for the "female . . . boy." The play rehearses antitheatrical arguments and endorses them as the grounds for its scandalously improper

proper, sodomy that is not assimilable to heterosexuality or to heterosexist homophobia. Aeneas is not effeminized and, despite himself, he resists Dido's simulations. His pursuit of empire serves Jove's and Venus's designs, but it is not propelled by his own sodomitical desires. If sodomy is the secret of Aeneas's heterosexist misogyny, as Shepherd contends, it is a secret precisely because its articulation could only repeat Venus's response to the initial scene of the play, the homophobia that sees sodomy as a travesty and as a transvestite version of heterosexuality. In this play, written to be performed by boys, and arising out of an educational system whose summit was the kind of familiar translation of Latin that Marlowe reveals in the play (a pedagogy that is also pedophiliac in its structure),[35] Marlowe aligns a number of all-male institutions—the school, the acting companies, the military—that constitutionally depend on not recognizing their propinquity to the unmentionable sin. That sin is more than mentioned in the play; it opens it and structures what follows. But if sodomy is the truth in the play, the truth of empire, it can be recognized within the licit only as the illicit, as the dirty secret. Here again, what Empson says of *Edward II* is true, that Marlowe sees the illicit as the proper thing to do, even gives it its own authorizing voice in Virgil's Latin text. That improper proper, in quite different ways, structures the relationship of Dido and Aeneas as the site where false and true meet and divide, the restructured difference between heterosexuality and homosexuality.

The play's project is radically conceived, not least in its deformations of the institutional and textual sites upon which it rests. As in *Edward II,* more than overturning is involved as the play drives towards a truth that undermines categorical oppositions even as it regrounds them in a volition that can never be made legitimate. The situation here is like the one that Jonathan Crewe argues for in an analysis of the relationship between *Tamburlaine* and antitheatricality. "The issue of Tamburlaine's cultural egregiousness," Crewe writes, just those qualities that the antitheatricalists fasten on, and akin to the monstrosity of desire revealed in *Edward II* or *Dido Queen of Carthage,* "is continuously renegotiated within the play, and in being so, seemingly brings within the realm of the negotiable most of the constitutive categories of Elizabethan cultural and political order" (327).

Dido Queen of Carthage takes on a number of those categories, most crucially the question of the construction of gender in its relationship to theater and to the imperial project. Effectively, it rewrites Gosson's *School of Abuse,* even as it appears to echo it. Posing itself against cross-dressing, it aligns the career of the empire builder with the heterosexist misogyny that founds masculinity on the resistance to effeminization—the effect of woman on man—and against this it offers the scandal of sodomy as the possibility of a difference unthinkable within the discourse of the licit. The play offers a reading of the conjunction of a cultural and a political order, theater and empire, that structures Gosson's tract, and destructures its premises: that theater effeminates the mind; that military exploits are properly masculine.

These are also the premises of a poem that Gosson wrote "in prayse of the Translator" Thomas Nicholas's *The Conquest of the Weast India* (1578), a translation of the account of the conquest of Mexico originally told by Francisco López de Gómara, Cortés's secretary and apologist.[36] Gosson's poem opens by putting behind the example of the poet who once "trod awry / And song in verse the force of fyry love" (1–2), Gosson himself, at one time a playwright;[37] in his stead is the poet celebrating "endlesse glory" (12), Gosson himself, who sees "manly prowesse" (34) reflected in the image of Cortés "that English Gentlemen may vew at will" (33) in Nicholas's translation. Marlowe's *Dido* deconstructs this simulated masculinity, showing it to arise from what is supposedly left behind in Gosson's poem. Gosson's poem depends upon a familiar elision, in which the exploitation of gold produces shining fame and glory (precisely the elision broken in *Tamburlaine* or *The Jew of Malta*). Nicholas's Gómara depends upon this equation, too, as when Cortés rallies his troops with the promise of "Golde, Silver, Pretious stones, Pearles, and other commoditie, and besides thys, the greatest honour that ever any nation did obtaine" (135). Cortés continues his ideological justification, predictably, with something else "besides all this," the abolishment of idolatry. (We could recall the antitheatricalists here, too, and their conviction that theaters were not only the court of Venus but the devil's palace as well.) And then, like Stubbes, there is a further supplement to this supplementary logic, "many other grievous sinnes so much here used, for the foulenesse whereof I name them not" (135). Human sacrifice and cannibalism are the unnameable here, but also the unmentionable vice finally mentioned in the closing pages of the book. Not only have the Indians become Christians, Gómara writes, but "through great punishmente they have left off the horrible sinne of Sodomy, although it was a great griefe to put away their number of wives" (402).

This is a nonsequitur whose logic we have seen, the conflation of promiscuous debauch (as native polygamy is characterized) and sodomy. It is precisely that equation that Marlowe also deconstructs in refusing to give grounds for the criticism that invidiously defines homosexuality as an overindulgence in female pleasures (a feminization that is a form of transvestism) and, so doing, makes the violence against women that is constitutive of heterosexist masculinity a homosexual act. The workings of empire in just these terms can be found in those cross-dressed Indians that appear in Prynne's *Histriomastix*, berdaches who, in Orgel's reading of Prynne's ambiguous syntax ("Nobody's Perfect," 16), although dressed as women, apparently take the active part in sodomizing their partners. Actors and Indians are discursively produced in remarkably similar ways (Gosson's antitheatricality and militarism are consistent colonialist gestures); the man who really desires the man beneath the woman's clothes is so effeminized that he assumes the position of "the passive beastly Sodomites" in the sex act that Prynne recounts, one performed it appears by the already cross-dressed "Male-Priests of Venus" (209). For Prynne, at such a moment, *nature* has been violated or, even worse, when a man lusts after another man dressed as a woman, nature has been simulated, "reducing" sodomy "as neere to naturall lewdnesse as they could devise" (211). Everywhere, Prynne clings desperately to the possibility of separating the natural from the unnatural. He does this not merely to protect heterosexual masculinity from an undermining from which it might never recover, but also to ensure the invisibility of sexual relations between men that do not take a transvestite form. This is perfectly clear from an episode that Alan Bray recounts in Prynne's edition of the diary of Archbishop Laud. "He tried to read into it the sodomitical sin one would expect of the papist in heart that Prynne presented him as being," Bray comments, "but when he came to [Laud's] dream of sleeping with the Duke of Buckingham he merely transcribed it. Its meaning was too obvious to do otherwise" ("Homosexuality and the Signs of Male Friendship," 7). That is, as Bray argues, friendship entailed shared beds, and Prynne does not notice—cannot afford to notice—the relationship between that sexual act ("in a dream the Duke of Buckingham seemed to me to ascend into my bed, where he carried him with much love towards me" [4]) and the one he calls sodomy. The pathological logic of the tracts lies in the refusal to recognize the connection between this unseen sexuality and the excoriated "unnatural" sex that mimes heterosex. Marlowe's work makes these connections visible, striking a blow at a mimetology that cannot be grounded in nature.

The pathology that constitutes homosexuality within the discourses of the licit—that constitutes it as a simulation of heterosexuality—was realized in assaults on sodomy in the New World, as when, in a scene we will consider in Chapter 6, Balboa fed forty so-called sodomitical Panamanians to his voracious dogs as a way of cleansing a corrupt cross-dressed Indian court. The animus against the sodomite as foreigner—against the court, too, as it is marshaled (and disabled) in Gaveston's opening soliloquy—can be recalled. But also that "extreme" (in fact normative) instance upon which Jardine rests her case, the antitheatricalist John Rainoldes, fulminating against cross-dressers as male whores, even more detestable than female whores, he writes, as is shown by the fact that male whores are called "dogges," for they are the "occasions whereby men are transformed into dogges." The solution he offers is what Balboa enacted in order "to cut off all incitements to that beastlie filthiness, or rather more then beastlie."[38] What constitutes this proper masculinity? Richard Eden tells the Duke of Northumberland in his letter prefacing his 1553 translation of Sebastian Munster: it would be the honor spent in conquering new lands, not that wasted "in soft beddes at home, among the teares & weping of women."[39]

Prynne's "pathology" is no personal aberration, nor is it merely the final working out of a discourse; its pathology is the protonationalist logic of empire that produces proper masculinity by defending against women and effeminization, against bestiality and Indians, and hence (within this misogynist and racist logic) against sodomy. Therefore, and perhaps not so strangely, Prynne's career parallels the course of English history. Having had his ears cropped, having been branded, having suffered imprisonment under Charles I, he was released in 1640. Jonas Barish tells the rest of the story of his "compulsive" behavior: "with his sentence nullified, he promptly returned to the attack, first against Laud, then against the Independents, then against the Army, finally against the Cromwell government. The return of the monarchy at last met with his approval. Instead of denouncing it he welcomed it back from exile, and for his loyalty was rewarded with the post of the Keeper of the Tower Records, in which fortress of sanctity he ultimately died."[40] Prynne finds his place, at last, in the Restoration. The English history that he is finally in sync with is also theatrical history, for with the return of the Stuarts, the theaters were opened again, but with women playing the parts of women. Prynne had his ears cropped for a remark about female actresses that had been taken as an assault on Henrietta Maria and court theatricals, but much as Prynne abominated theater, he desired a nature in which the difference between the sexes was maintained. The Restoration theater aimed at such a mimetism. Under the new regime, the stage replayed a new social decorum; nonetheless, this stage had transvestism too, with women actresses dressed as men, assuring, on the one hand that, despite appearances, all desire (including a woman's desire for a woman) was heterosexual, on the other still promoting Prynne's denunciation that all actresses were whores, presumably not least so when they "naturally" sought to rise out of their subordinate place and mime male form.

The histories that intersect with and finally coincide with Prynne's career must be read within the history of sexuality; for with the Restoration, for the first time, the terms that I have been using, *homosexual* and *heterosexual,* attempting to move between modern vocabularies of sex and gender and those of the Renaissance, seem the right ones; heterosexual seems correct not least because it is at this time that a recognizable homosexual subculture becomes visible in the molly houses, where men dressed as women enjoyed each other's company. *Molly* derives from the Latin *mulier*, itself thought to derive from *mollies,* the softness and pliability of women. In this guise, homosexuality founds itself upon charges of feminization and transfers the misogyny that structures male/female relations to find an identity for itself that parodies the supposition upon which an emergent heterosexuality battens. For as the emerging sexual regimes installed man and woman as the opposite sexes, the molly embodied an opposition that deformed that supposition, a transvestite embrace of the orders it opposed, and which opposed it in the raids and pogroms unleashed by the Reforming Society, the police, and the courts.[41] This situation fulfills the dream of *Histriomastix,* and these persecutions are of an entirely different kind from the attacks on sodomites. Heterosexuality and homosexuality emerge as oppositional and simulative categories; the men in dresses who had sex in the molly houses called their bedding wedding. The dark shadow of the sodomite, the sphere of an illicit that had no proper name to deform and upon which Marlowe had operated to think sexual difference otherwise, is not this new, incipiently modern, regime of sexual difference.

It has been my assumption throughout this chapter that Marlowe's radical rethinking of the possibility of being a sodomite was not widely shared in his time, that the deconstructive energies he bequeaths are not assimilable to the subsequent discourses of sexual difference. But by this I do not mean to suggest Marlowe's singularity save in the value he attached to what his culture so vehemently opposed. Hence, it is possible, imperative, to recognize in Marlowe a site of political resistance. To recognize too that this could have literary consequences. A rereading of Elizabethan drama through what Marlowe makes available might be undertaken, and even Shakespeare would be implicated. Such work has begun, as in Joseph Porter's recent book on Mercutio,[42] and it, along with Alan Bray's recent essay, suggests that the representation of friendship in Shakespeare (Hamlet and Horatio, Macbeth and Banquo, Brutus and Cassius, and the list goes on) needs to be rethought, from the ground up. That ground might well be the sonnets, and it is about time that criticism followed Sedgwick's reading of them in *Between Men.* Against arguments that take such cross-dressed figures as Julia, Portia, Viola, or Rosalind as the privileged locus of homosexuality, one might read, as constituted otherwise, the relations between friends:

Between Antonio and Bassanio, to see that Portia's success, described ably by Karen Newman as her position as woman-on-top,[43] however much it denaturalizes gender, also is fueled by the misogyny that shapes her as the dark lady, that her power as boy is directed against and serves to police Antonio and Bassanio and to separate them; that the boy-girl figures a triumph for the patriarchy, that however much it has been deformed by installing a woman in the father's place it ensures that when s/he saves Antonio and defeats Shylock the two acts form a single gesture—unleashing energies that are racist and homophobic, that secure in his/her transgressive body the acceptable limits of marriage and homosociality under regimes of alliance close to those of heterosexual privilege; at the end of the play, Portia is in the father's place and the wife's, but not the friend's.

Between Sebastian and Antonio, to see that the pathos, for instance, that Greenblatt evinces as he contemplates "poor Antonio" barred from the happy heterosexual ending, which, Greenblatt has also argued, is not *really* heterosexual since we can never forget that Viola is a boy ("if poor Antonio is left out in the cold, Orsino does in a sense get his Cesario")[44] is really on one count misogynist, on both counts homophobic, and not an occasion for liberal tears but for anger.

But one might also see that Rosalind/Ganymede, unlike Portia/Balthasar (all cross-dressing is not the same, even in Shakespeare), sustains a differentiated identity that produces the boy as a sex that is neither male nor female and thus as a site for male/male (those two beardless boys, Orlando and Ganymede), female/female (those two dark ladies, Phebe and Rosalind), and male/female desires that are not collapsed one into the other; when the epilogue refuses to settle the question of the gender of its speaker, it can only suggest, as Valerie Traub argues, that the marriages in the play are a great deal more iffy than is usually supposed.

Against the boys dressed as women married to Caius and Slender at the end of *Merry Wives,* one might want to think, as Beth Pittenger does, about the pages,[45] the traffic in boys in that play, and a scene of pederastic pedagogy played out before a Quickly who has nothing to do with marriage, a quean who plays the fairy queen—Elizabeth I?—in the final masque.

One might want to take up the notion of "notorious identity" that Linda Charnes reads in *Troilus and Cressida* and to rethink it, not least by the ways in which the relation of Achilles and Patroclus is not simply a reaction to male/female relations, and to look again at the scene in which Patroclus is accused of acting the parts of the Greek heroes in travesties that are not transvestite—which as simulations without an original cannot merely be the product of homophobic homosexuality.[46]

One might want to think about the substitutive logic of a play about lieutenants that lands Cassio in bed with Iago, his leg flung across him.

Finally, one might want to think about Shakespeare's play about the economies of empire and gender, to ponder not only Prospero's relation to the transvestite Ariel, but also his horror at, and inability to punish, that conspiratorial pair separated in *Twelfth Night* but rejoined in *The Tempest,* Antonio and Sebastian.

The route to such rethinking is not through cross-dressing as it has been understood; the way to understand these relations lies in the discourse of sodomy, and Marlowe provides leverage upon such relations. One might see, then, that what cross-dressing in Shakespeare defends itself against is not only effeminization but something even more threatening, something that can resist assimilation to the logic of heterosexual simulation.

CHAPTER 5

ALTHOUGH THE RESPONSE to him has not been unanimous, most critics in this century have found it all but impossible to resist the attractions of the prince.[1] Phyllis Rackin, for instance, in a recent book on Shakespeare's history plays admirably aiming to decry their exclusions of women and the lower classes, and insistent on deploring the making of history coincident with the recording of the deeds of upper-class men, finds herself, not once, but three times in the space of fifty pages, describing Hal as the mirror of all Christian kings.[2] This is the Chorus's view of him at the opening of the second act of *Henry V*,[3] and Rackin's reiterations seem to find it inescapable, perhaps because the mirror is ineluctably seductive, as more than a page of Christopher Pye's *The Regal Phantasm* brilliantly argues.[4] That post–World War II critics, following J. Dover Wilson's *Fortunes of Falstaff* (1943), read the second tetralogy as a morality play and fastened on Hal as the embodiment of virtues indistinguishable from Englishness is, of course, well known. Such opinions shape the introductory pages to the Arden editions of the two parts of *Henry IV* that A. R. Humphreys produced, which locate Hal as the midpoint between the dangerous claims of Falstaff and Hotspur, taking from each what is best, "combining and transcending" them.[5] While Humphreys stresses the national import of the prince's career, he also endorses the New Critical reading of Cleanth Brooks and Robert Heilman, who found that trajectory coincident with the path of maturity. That view, buttressed with impressive footnote support that suggests that virtually everyone writing in *Shakespeare Quarterly* for the past thirty years has been saying the same thing, is the theme of the introduction to the edition of the play prepared by David Bevington for the new Oxford series. "Undoubtedly Hal needs to mature, to come to age, to learn the language of his countrymen, to put away childish things," Bevington writes, concluding a page later, "we admire the Prince for his victory" at Shrewsbury and, a bit further on, "we accept the rejection [of Falstaff] as necessary. . . . Falstaff is the sleeping child we will have to punish, the silly dying father we are destined to replace."[6]

"We admire . . . we accept . . . we are destined": the marks of identification couldn't be clearer. Hal's story mirrors "our" oedipal drama.

> "Who does not all along see," wrote Upton in the mid-eighteenth century, "that when prince Henry comes to be king he will assume a character suitable to his dignity?" My point is not to dispute this interpretation of the prince as, in Maynard Mack's words, "an ideal image of the potentialities of the English character," but to observe that such an ideal image involves as its positive condition the constant production of its own radical subversion and the powerful containment of that subversion.

I'm quoting, as the signature phrasing of subversion and containment makes clear, Stephen Greenblatt,[7] whose demystifications of the workings of power subscribe nonetheless to its idealization and here at least to espousing a New Historicism that can be written as the latest word in a production of the prince that finds its origin in the beginnings of Shakespeare criticism, and draws support from yet one more statement of the traditional view of the prince as "ideal image." Greenblatt never forgets that Hal is the master of illusions, but this, he claims, only furthers "our pleasure," for ultimately there is no difference between the prince and his play: "The play operates in the manner of its central character, charming us with its visions of breadth and solidarity, 'redeeming' itself in the end by betraying our hopes, and earning with this betrayal our slightly anxious admiration" (47). So much so that even when the ideality of *1 Henry IV* has been retroactively stripped by the plays that follow, the allure of the prince, now King Henry V, Greenblatt argues, is all the more inescapable, the spectators (the critics) "dazzled by their own imaginary identification with the conqueror" (63).

"Imaginary identification": Hal as the nation, as the mature individual, as the dazzling fabricator, English essence, American construct, in any event, ego ideal, mirror for any critic, despite her reservations. Greenblatt's phrase is more exact perhaps than he means it to be, for he points not simply to a literary, imaginative captation by the captivating prince, but rather to a specular structure that entrances the ego, Pye's regal phantasm, an imaginary locus of identification that founds the ego in its desire for sovereignty—he points to ego erotics, in a word. Hence, it might prove all but impossible not to join the critical chorus. That is not my aim here, but I also do not want to deny the powerful effects of the character to which these testimonies, written from quite different vantage points, nonetheless attest, but to ask further what that allure might be, and to put pressure on its various normalizations as an inevitability—whether understood as a desired moral rectitude, an achieved national purpose, or even the workings of a theatrical illusion coincident with the workings of power—above all, with the power of Shakespeare. For, to accept these, however uneasily, is to succumb to an ideological effect: "imaginary identification." Hal's sovereignty reflects a sovereign subject; between him and his admiring critic there is a trajectory of desired identification.

While critical responses testify to Hal's desirability, what allows that to go unnoticed—to go without saying—is that the criticism describes a Hal remarkable for his lack of desire. These are history plays, after all, and when desire enters, in the person of Princess Katharine, it does so to secure the patriarchal trajectory. Yet, oddly enough, that ending to *Henry V* hardly has been read as the point of Hal's arrival: it is, rather, for him to replace his father, to secure the throne, and this means the defeat of Hotspur and the rejection of Falstaff, the reconciliation with the dying king and with the Lord Chief Justice that brings *2 Henry IV* to its conclusion. The marriage made at the end of the second tetralogy appears to have another logic than that which produces the mature national character who is the locus of critical desire. Or, rather, the plain soldier wooing that ends *Henry V* seems to perform a desire for Kate at some distance from the conquest of France that is the king's proper goal, and thus also as somehow not part of the achieved character of Hal. However mature, perfect, and complete he has become, or perhaps because he has arrived at such perfection, nothing ought to be leading him to marriage except the exigencies of politics (marriage in the period being a juridical institution for the conveyance of title and property, and for monarchs a matter of national, not personal, interest). One must therefore pause over what form of "maturity" Hal might represent when heterosexual relations seem exiguous or supplementary to it.

Putting the case this way, I do not mean that the appeal of the character is in any simple sense homoerotic. For one thing, modern regimes of sexuality are only imperfectly, incipiently to be found in the text. The celebration of Hal's maturity serves moreover as a site of nonrecognition of any sexual interest in the character, more crucially, as I will be arguing, of a complicity between criticism and the reinforcement of a misogynist heterosexuality always in danger of homophobia. To recognize that the critics' attachment to Hal goes hand in hand with the patriarchal effacement of women will not settle the question of desire that I want to open here. Which is to say that to find the locus in the plays for the desire for Hal, it is not to Katharine's pained language lesson—in which she, in any event, learns an English "we" already know—nor to the wooing scene, where even her resistance only registers further her submission to an implacability that, the critics tell us, Hal has by then come to embody, that I would turn. I'd suggest we look elsewhere, to Henry IV's description of his wayward son in *Richard II*, act 5, scene 3, for example (his first thoughts after becoming king), or to the fantasy that he indulges in the opening scene of *1 Henry IV*, where mention of Hotspur triggers what the king apparently has forgotten, attending to rebels on his every border, the rebellious son who threatens never to inherit his throne. What we might see, I'd suggest, is a version of desire that might trouble the oedipal resolution usually read into the arrival in the father's place.

Henry's wish—that "some night-tripping fairy had exchang'd" (1.1.86) children, so that Hotspur might be his Harry—not only conditions the plot of replacement brought to a close at Shrewsbury, it casts that wish of exchange in terms familiar from *A Midsummer Night's Dream*; the victory of Oberon over Titania in their fight over the Indian boy, a changeling, supports the paternal fantasy in *1 Henry IV* in which a son who is the very mirror of the father can be produced simply by the desire for a simulacrum. Faeries, not wives, deliver such children; insofar as *1 Henry IV* fulfills the king's desire, Hal occupies the imaginary terrain described by Theseus as the paternal power of duplication, the ability to figure or disfigure the wax impression of the child.[8] It is a version of that fantasy of paternal parthenogenesis, I'd suggest, that the critics indulge as well. To say that such a view effectively participates in the suppression, the effacement, of women is an understatement, as is more than revealed when Hal speaks, as he does once, about his mother. To the Hostess's announcement that "there is a nobleman of the court" come from his father, Hal responds: "Give him as much as will make him a royal man, and send him back again to my mother" (2.4.286–87). The destiny of the royal coin, stamped as the father—an image of Hal's destiny within the fantasy of sovereign reproduction—is Hal's dead mother. Hal produces the nobleman as an image of himself and chillingly hurls him into his mother's grave. Hal expresses his utter contempt for the waiting lord as this loathing for his dead mother.

This is what preferment looks like at Hal's hands, and it is suggestive about the place women (the dead mother and the Hostess) and aspirants (like the waiting lord) occupy in the play. If such a moment has gone unnoticed in the criticism of the play, however, it is because there is a voice that represents the acceptance of such ferocity. Uncannily, it sounds much like the paternal voice desiring the prince's arrival, and we hear it in the first words addressed to Hal in *1 Henry IV*: "I prithee sweet wag, when thou art king. . . . Marry then sweet wag, when thou art king" (1.2.16, 23). The speaker of this repeated refrain, no one needs to be told, is Falstaff, and Hal's arrival in a kingship tainted by usurpation, one in which the apparentness of the heir apparent will never be fully abrogated (in which counterfeiting will always haunt the legitimacy of the royal man), is Falstaff's theme—as it is Greenblatt's too. Serving this legitimizing function, Falstaff is not the infantilism or the bad father the prince leaves behind, as Bevington and so many others have claimed; for Hal's ultimate self-sufficiency is a self-love that incorporates Falstaff's desire, in much the same way as he acquires the mantle of Hotspur's honor. Contra Humphreys, I would not mystify this process as a "transcending" or a taking of the best from them; nor do I mean to restate a thematics of subversion/containment in which Hal "produces" and contains the waiting nobleman, the dead mother, the rebel, or the loving and discardable companion. Rather, following Pye, I pursue here the indeterminacy of "specular snares" (84), imaginary identifications that can work in more than one direction.

For if the desire for Hal—for his arrival as king—is one the critics voice along with the king and the prince's boon companion, it is complicated not merely by the similarity of these supposedly antithetical desires, but also by a shared trajectory. The antithesis is set up when the king sees "riot and dishonour stain" (1.1.84) his son's face, sees Falstaff as the blot on his character, the mark made where the paternal impression should be. But, at the moment of his arrival, when Hal replaces his father and discards his companion, the antithesis collapses, and Hal sends the stain packing along with his father.

> My father is gone wild into his grave,
> For in his tomb lie my affections;
> And with his spirits sadly I survive
> To mock the expectation of the world,
> To frustrate prophecies, and to raze out
> Rotten opinion, who hath writ me down
> After my seeming. (*2 Henry IV*, 5.2.123–29)

Becoming his father, Hal does not only banish Falstaff (as he promised in their rehearsal of this scene in Part I), he casts his dead father as his former wildness, even as the producer of his disreputable past, his rot and the "rotten opinion" that has so written him. The usurping, illegitimate, "wild" father is erased, razed, and rewritten. Harry replaces Harry here (5.2.49) as he had replaced another Harry at the end of part one ("Harry to Harry shall, hot horse to horse, / Meet" [4.1.122–23]), and the Lord Chief Justice, *chosen* as father now in place of both the king and Falstaff, is the father only of the newest self-simulation, the artificial paternity that the king first dreamed. Hal is still bent, as he was in his first soliloquy in Part I, on the mockery of expectation and the falsifications that are coincident with his truth.

In his first soliloquy, and in the fulfillment of his promise to the king that he will prove himself the king's true son by taking upon himself the form of Hotspur's honor, Hal composes this image of himself. The promise he makes to his father in act 3, scene 2, answers the paternal desire, for Henry sees himself in Hotspur (another mirror in which two Harrys meet), and one trick of the play (it answers fully to the double, duplicitous nature of the king) is for him to come at the end to be both his father's proper son and the very image of the rebel—an image as razed as the paternal image is at the end of Part II.

> I will redeem all this on Percy's head,
> And in the closing of some glorious day
> Be bold to tell you that I am your son,
> When I will wear a garment all of blood,
> And stain my favours in a bloody mask,
> Which, wash'd away, shall scour my shame with it.
> (3.2.132–37)

Hal's promised redemption involves a restaining and scouring that produces not exactly himself but, as he goes on to say, an exchange like the one his father dreamed: "I shall make this northern youth exchange / His glorious deeds for my indignities" (145–46). This shameless deed rewrites Harry's brow as unspotted only by casting the northern youth as the locus of his glory; that the lines also promise to "engross" (148) these deeds—in a metaphor that makes Hotspur a piece of real estate that Hal comes to (dis)possess and in which he comes to be written (an engrossing hand is the one that writes such a legal document of property exchange)[9]—implicates this rewriting in the one that Part II brings to a close, when Hal's gross companion is cast off, leaving engrossing Hal once again supposedly unstained.

The rewriting here—the staining and erasing—aims at legitimizing the illegitimate. This is a political project, to be sure, but that in no way guarantees—the opposite in fact—that it will not be played out in a bodily register. Hal can engross, but unlike his fat companion his body fails to serve as the register of what he has done. Falstaff's *gross* body is not Hal's *engrossed* one, and the "base contagious clouds" (1.2.193), "the foul and ugly mists / Of vapours" (197–98) which figure Falstaff's flatulent body[10] suggest an anality—sodomy, in a word—that Hal's anal economies seek to overcome, a mode of disembodiment that will keep Hal as thin as the blank sheet of paper on which he comes to be inscribed, as in the production of his perfection attested to by the admiring bishops at the opening of *Henry V.*[11] Thus, too, the new stain on his brow can be scoured away, and with it gone he becomes the now unstained northern youth, all honor, no rebellion. This "now" accomplishes the retroactive rewriting of the past. Riot and rebellion wear the unmarked face and trim body of the perfect prince. To be engrossed by this image is to cooperate in this fantasy—a fantasy, it needs to be said, which is not that of lacking desire, but of masking fully a rapacity that is as self-producing as it is self-consuming. Hal has designs on Falstaff and Hotspur; only by engrossing them can he be unspotted. What criticism has called Hal's maturity is this process of economization; the life and honor that he takes from Falstaff and Hotspur make him an ego ideal.

If we are to understand how Hal at these moments of betrayal (to pick up Greenblatt's remarks), of merciless calculation, still can charm, we must come to terms with the ego erotics of the play. Here, our critical guide might be William Empson who, fifty years ago, in a few pages in *Some Versions of Pastoral* that have never received the critical attention that they deserve,[12] noted the register of desire that I believe must be taken into account. The prince has been cast in the part of the fair young man of the sonnets, Empson writes, and "Harry has no qualities that are obviously not

W.H.'s."[13] Falstaff's desire, even what is made of the father's desire, are, in this light, not to be distinguished from the desire of the sonneteer, always ready to take upon himself the faults of the faultless young man. "Henry's soliloquy [at the end of act 1, scene 2] demands from us just the sonnets' mood of bitter complaisance; the young man must still be praised and loved, however he betrays his intimates, because we see him all shining with the virtues of success" (104). In his soliloquy Hal makes up to the audience by promising to cast off his bad company (by the end of Part II, as we've seen, his father makes up part of that disreputable crew). As Empson observes, Hal gives one twist further to the dynamics upon which the male/male relations in the sonnets depend: it is the prince, speaking in the position of the young man, who proclaims his own perfection and dumps his faults upon those who love and desire him. "We have the central theme of all the sonnets of apology," Empson concludes, "the only difference, though it is a big one, is that this man says it about himself" (105). How complicated one's investment in this might be is suggested when Empson takes up the modern Sir Walter Raleigh's opinion that Hal speaks the poet's success too: "he has made low friends only to get local colour out of them, and now drops them with a bang because he has made money and grand friends. It is possible enough," Empson reflects, "though I don't know why it was thought pleasant" (103). Empson points to an unpleasantness here fully coincident with the pleasure critics take (and not just the Oxford professor) in the prince, to the complex cross-identifications involved. For if Shakespeare plays out his abjection with the young man through Falstaff, he plays out too the success that is so achieved: identification with the prince.

That unpleasantness is given voice, for instance, in Falstaff's repeated claims that the prince has corrupted him. For the truth he points to is that no one in the play is innocent, that predation is endemic. From their first scene together, Falstaff stands to be abused. It's often said that we desire Falstaff's resurgence (given in his resurrection at the end of Part I, half-promised in the epilogue to Part II), but it is his condition throughout the play, and if we desire his repeated comebacks it is because it is on his desire that ours floats. (Falstaff teaches us to see the prince as a sweet wag.) That desire is, importantly, the desire to take abuse. If we accept his banishment, it is then because we take it up as our position, because we have been accepting it all along, and because it is part of the way in which we need never give up desiring Hal. This is more or less what Hal tells us in his first soliloquy, positioning the audience to assume the stance of the sonneteer. It also suggests, to return to the psychoanalytic terms glanced at already, the nature of the ego formation involved. For Hal's imaginary self-control mirrors a desire for self-punishment rooted in that specular structure of turning around (an autoerotics) that Jean Laplanche identifies as the origin of sexuality and of the ego. This is a masochism which, in the political register, signals an abjection coincident with the fantasy of empowerment.[14] Imaginary identification. If Shakespeare is on both sides of the exchanges between Hal and his companion, "we" are too.

These fantasies guarantee Hal's desirability to the extent that it remains possible to believe that he does not desire, that attachment to him puts "us" in the position of the one who will not be cast off because we are so busily casting ourselves off, and thereby identifying with—producing—the self-denying prince as the very index to our own abjection. Empson's firmly intertextual reading, in which Hal's first soliloquy is shown to be a tissue of citations from the sonnets, demonstrates that there is hardly a line in which the prince praises himself that does not recall the terms in which the young man is praised. Empson juxtaposes his reading of Hal's character not only with that of such other seemers as Angelo, but especially against the young man of sonnet 94, who appears not to deliver the hurt that lies in his power, and whose corruption stains everyone but his unscathed though scathingly revealed seeming self. Empson has no difficulty saying that Falstaff loves the prince or, even, having allied Falstaff and the sonneteer, from placing Shakespeare in Falstaff's position. He takes as one piece of evidence a brief exchange in the tavern:

> PRINCE. Sirrah, do I owe you a thousand pound?
> FALSTAFF. A thousand pound, Hal? A million, thy love is worth a million, thou owest me thy love. (*1 Henry IV*, 3.3.134–36)

What the love that dares speak its name here might be—and how it might be related to the desire that animates critical response to Hal, the love "we" expect from Hal for loving him (even to our loss, much as Falstaff is still expecting the thousand pounds at the end of Part II)—remains however to be said. This declaration of love is protected from being read at face value: Falstaff is once again being shamed, caught out this time lying to the Hostess and defrauding her. As Empson says, "the more serious Falstaff's expression of love becomes the more comic it is, whether as hopeless or as hypocrisy" (109); his love can always look like a form of rapacity. Yet when Hal saves the Hostess from Falstaff and from his claim that she runs a bawdy house, he does so only by revealing that it was he who picked Falstaff's pocket. Hal's "saving" of the Hostess is of course entirely suspect (in Part II she will be sent off to jail), but the declaration of love is shielded by putting a woman between the two men, by having Hal save his reputation (he can produce the truth even as he incriminates himself) by saving hers.

The Hostess plays a part here, as she did when she delivered Hal's message to the waiting lord. Placed between men, she is nonetheless outside their circuit of relations, though it would not be quite right to say that she is where the predations end: her lines about Falstaff in *Henry V* recast his death scene as the death of Socrates, a rebound of her voice that suggests a productive role and not her total effacement. Nonetheless, the complex trajectories of Falstaff's declaration of love cannot fail to remind one of the structure of the sonnets. Indeed, we might notice now that the royal desire for simulation participates in that project too. For, from the moment (at sonnet 17) that the possibility is abandoned that the young man might, through marriage, be the source of an ever fresh supply of duplicate young men, the sonnets seek to propagate the young man through the writing of his perfected image—the image declared perfect despite all the faults and failures revealed. Henry IV never specifies what stains his son's brow; although he characterizes him as a "young wanton, and effeminate boy" in *Richard II,*[15] little afterwards would suggest that Hal is spending himself in the company of women (no bawdy houses for him, nor does the king ever think about a marriage for his son). Hal's "loose companions" (5.3.7) even in *Richard II* are highway robbers and tavern companions, a low-life that appears as exclusively male as the public world of court and battlefield. These are the sites of struggle for Hal and in them the plays seem to occupy the terrain of sonnets 18 through 126, with its production of an image of perfection and the tainted rebounds of that desire—the desire that I've suggested rebounds upon king, rebel, and tavern companion. That rebounds too on the admiring critics.

That criticism has not followed Empson is thus perfectly understandable, since it would require seeing how it seeks to legitimize relations between men that might otherwise be suspect. But, as I've been arguing, this legitimization is itself suspect and on more than one count. For if one had to give a name to what Empson (not mistakenly) calls love, it would have to be sodomy: the terms *stain, riot,* and *rebellion* suggest that, as does the deployment of the patriarchal exchange of women as a virtual cover for male/male relations (patriarchy is written within the register of the sonnets' fantasies of duplicative inscription).[16] If one must suspect the critics who ignore that the mature Hal they idolize is one who seems ultimately bent only on having (sexual) relations with himself, and who comes to that position of narcissistic self-possession through the route of his relations with Falstaff (with Hotspur too as I will further suggest), one can also understand the role women play between men. The Hostess has provided one example, but we might attend now to what Christopher Pye notices, that Hal's exchanges over the body of Princess Katharine, at the end of *Henry V,* take, as he puts it, a notably homoerotic turn.

> BURGUNDY. . . . maids, well summered, and warm kept, are like flies at Bartholomew-tide, blind, though they have their eyes; and then they will endure handling. . . .
> KING HENRY. This moral ties me over to time and a hot summer; and so I shall catch the fly, your cousin, in the latter end, and she must be blind too. (5.2.325–32)

As Hal and Burgundy banter, the king's winning of Katharine is figured as his conquest, making him, Pye writes, "the passive victim of a homoerotic capture" (32), taken "in the latter end" by the blind fly Katharine that refigures the blind boy Cupid. Thus, by the close of the tetralogy, Hal's marriage is written not merely within the homosocial bantering with Burgundy, but as so dangerous to male relations as to require a "homoerotic" rewriting. Pye argues that this exchange serves to further secure the glamor of the sovereign, and he notes its extension (in the final lines of the Chorus) to Shakespeare's project itself when he is figured as "our bending author," the author in the pose of a serviceable passivity, like that of Falstaff or the sonneteer, that promotes the prince. For the prince also to be bending suggestively embodies the route of imaginary identification: the prince gives up his male powers when the woman mounts him, a sovereign submission that might model "ours" as we submit to him.

As Pye remarks, there are various ways to understand this scene, and the simplest, to recall that the French princess is played by a boy, is least useful. He suggests instead that Shakespeare cannot write about sovereignty without thinking about the woman on the throne, and that the exchange is an instance of the endless play of being/having the phallus brought to a crisis by the gender of Elizabeth I. The scene imitates these instabilities, reenacting them across the supposedly determinate lines of gender (that queens and the French princess transgress), even of class (when our bending author produces greatness). Pye rests his case upon the historic specificity of the female monarch and her role in upsetting gender; yet, as Barbara Correll has persuasively argued, these exchanges characterize the ways in which class aspiration is written in the sixteenth century, from Erasmus on, whether the ruler is male or female.[17] The inordinate desires of subjects upon their sovereign mask themselves beneath a submissiveness coded as female, even as sovereigns are taught to the tune of their humanist pedagogues to restrain their own desires, to submit to their teachers. Women become the site for the production of male anxiety.

Such exchanges write men into the place of women, a ruse of (dis)empowerment. This might serve to give pause to Pye's characterization of the remarks about Katharine as evidence of a homoeroticism within homosocial exchange. For the lines are more ambiguous, and it is not clear whether the king imagines himself taken *a tergo* or whether that is how he imagines having Katharine. Only when it is assumed that anal sex marks the difference between hetero- and homosexuality can the banter be read simply as homoerotic. Rather, the sexual fantasy is sodomitical, since, either way, nonprocreative sex is involved. The image taints the marriage and, insofar as women are defined solely through that institution, taints the princess too. But it also suggests the scandalous grounds upon which it might be possible to say that Katharine is not being excluded entirely from male/male relations at the end of the play. Katharine is allowed into the charmed circle of sovereignty—she is a princess after all—on just those terms through which sovereignty is constructed in the play. For what is jokingly allowed here comes from a king whose sovereignty we must recall is itself mockery, as Hal himself says when he promises to "mock . . . expectation" at the moment of his arrival in *2 Henry IV* (5.2.126), and as the Chorus insists just before the decisive victory at Agincourt (*Henry V*, 4 Chor.54), making it a mocking show even before it is represented as that triumph.[18] The exchange intimates that phallic investment is not necessarily male, not even necessarily—insofar as the phallus and pen can be elided—in the hands of the sovereign but held by those who write his sovereignty and who, so doing, put themselves in his place. Falstaff's love does this for Hal; but this is yet another way of saying that Shakespeare is in that position too. Gender difference is transgressed in the exchange with Burgundy through anal sexual relations. Undeniably, the scene is misogynistic—Katharine is not in on the joke, not there at all. But the joke is also on marriage and legitimate patriarchal exchange. Read from the prospect of sodomy, it suggests how little Hal's "mature" arrival has to do with modern heterosexuality; to call these desires homoerotic is thus to erect a divide between homo- and heterosexuality that the lines will not support. A woman is put between men here, as the Hostess was in *1 Henry IV*, as if to guarantee that only on her body could such desires become sexual ones. The homoerotic can thus be read as if within the heteroerotic; it is this reading of the sodomitical sexual representation that legitimizes Hal's desire, or "our" desire for him. We can succumb to him without having to bend over.

Such a reading secures Hal for the domain that Michael Warner terms "Homo-Narcissism; or, Heterosexuality";[19] it places the prince within the modern "understanding of gender as simple alterity" (190), the supposition that narcissism is equivalent to homosexuality, and that "our" ego ideals could not possibly have anything to do with that. It is such an understanding that allows critics to admire Hal and think they know what they're seeing. Warner's brilliant reading of the social imperatives derived from Freud's reading of narcissism sheds light on twentieth-century readings of the play. We have begun to see what in the sociality that the second tetralogy represents enables this move of (blind) identification, but also that this is not all that can be read. Although there is more to be said about the role women play to secure these (mis)recognitions, or the place that gender occupies in the complex sociality represented (and the relations of these to modern identifications), we need also to complicate our understanding of the relation of gender and class. Here it is worth recalling Empson's solution to the dilemma of the class status of the young man of the sonnets. Is the youth an aristocrat or a boy actor? Empson answers that either way he is an arriviste, that his social status remains indeterminate. He represents a site of crossing between a declining old aristocracy and the emerging new class. The latter includes those humanists whose writings Correll explores and, by the late sixteenth century, the new men of the Elizabethan age, among them those with pretensions to high literariness (Shakespeare is one of them too, at least in his published poems). As Empson suggests, it is along these lines that Shakespeare can identify with the young man or with Hal; for Hal's ambiguous position as legitimate illegitimate monarch answers to the class negotiation in the sonnets—a negotiation of class difference which structures desire as well as the sonneteer's abjection. All of this can be applied mutatis mutandis to Falstaff, whose fall from every claim to aristocratic distinction, save that which his knighthood confers, is the obverse image of Hal's successful negotiation of his squalid origins as son of a usurper.

It is thanks to the mirror effects of these class negotiations that critics find a place for identification. For what joins the classes together is bourgeoisification. When Warwick explains to Henry IV that Hal's "gross" entanglements are simply a lesson in hatred—

> The Prince but studies his companions
> Like a strange tongue, wherein, to gain the language,
> 'Tis needful that the most immodest word
> Be look'd upon and learnt; which once attain'd,
> Your Highness knows, comes to no further use
> But to be known and hated. So, like gross terms,
> The Prince will, in the perfectness of time,
> Cast off his followers. (*2 Henry IV*, 4.4.68–75)

—he speaks within the language of humanist pedagogy, that system of self-restraint whose workings Norbert Elias studied, restraints that mask predation. Katharine's language lessons leads to this too. Even Henry IV is cast in this mold when he laments the hard work of parental "engrossments" (4.5.79) that produce thankless children, and imagines the achievement of the throne as an act of labor that his son abuses when he seeks to take the crown from him, as if its value lay in its gold. In *2 Henry IV* Hal's arrival is written into the economies of an emerging middle class intent upon drawing the social distinctions of Warwick's speech, or the domestication of woman drilled into Katharine, the installation of habits of thrift that differentially mark class and gender. These are the economies of Hal's first soliloquy and of his every move thereafter, leading him to the evacuation and engrossment of Falstaff; they serve to make him a bourgeois ego ideal. Hence the aptness of the "unpleasant" truth of Sir Walter Raleigh's comment, for Shakespeare participates in these economies too: the second tetralogy was written at the same time that Shakespeare was claiming arms for himself and buying New Place, home of a decayed aristocratic family. Hal's arrival is the dreamed-of success of the arriviste, masked as the prerogatives of a chastened sovereign self that rewrites desire as self-abnegation, and who casts off his "bad" self in the person of his abjected others. The artifice of paternal image duplication fashions a middle-class ego ideal: the making of self through such mystified labor.

These unequally shared domains of restraint open up the possibility of a public sphere and, as Warner argues, these are the voices (of teachers, of leaders) that Freud's narcissistic subject internalizes to pursue an ego development (the teleological narrative that Shakespeare's critics call maturity) that involves leaving behind the narcissistic ego investments of homosexuality for the "genuineness" of heterosexuality. Shakespeare writes well before these modern regimes are in place; yet the negotiations around Hal and the path he pursues are capable retroactively of taking on the charge of this modern heterosexual male subjectivity.

In short, what entrances criticism in Hal is that homo-narcissism whose other name will come to be heterosexuality; what I've been suggesting is that this is a misrecognition that the second tetralogy only potentially, partially promotes; it would be equally mistaken to say that Hal is offered up to homosexual desire. Rather, the plays forever transgress even as they seem to be producing the boundaries between illegitimate and legitimate male/male relations. Their project is to produce Hal as the legitimate son of his father; but bypassing biology as the means to do so, this legitimizing project is, as we have seen, wholly allied to the artifices of image-production, the simulations of paternity based on the production of similitude; this is the economy of a narcissistic image production—the production of an ego ideal—but not simply of the uninflected sameness that has come, in the wake of Freud, to define narcissism, especially in its invidious doubling with homosexuality as the institutions of psychoanalysis have (continually) written it. This is the case in the Henry IV plays, first because the image, as we have seen, is riven by its imperfections and by the willed nature of the production of perfection, with all the exchanges of tainting involved; second, because the production of the image is riven by the insupportable line between legitimate and illegitimate, true selves and false ones, grossness and engrossing, life and riot, rule and rebellion. It's on this divided terrain that an image is erected—call it Hal—that both allows and masks its desires and sends them along the rebounding trajectories of identification and difference that I've been tracing.

Empson speaks (before the fact, as it were) to what the critics have (mis)read in Hal when he comments on Hal's promise in his opening soliloquy to pay the debt he never promised: "this *debt* looks like an echo of the debt to nature there was so much doubt about W.H.'s method of paying; it has turned into a debt to society" (105). Such a debt so paid solidifies bonds between men and enhances a male imaginary from which women have been banished. This "solution" occupies the terrain of the ordinary "homosocial," always perilously close to becoming its abjected other, the "homosexual." Negotiating these paired terms under the modern regimes of sexuality, as Sedgwick has taught us, is extraordinarily difficult; but such too (but differently) is the case in Elizabethan England. For if, on the one hand, I've been implying a degree of homophobia in the critical construction (let us say insofar as the sexuality that I've been adducing is continually unnoted, insofar as a certain infantilism is said to be surpassed in Hal's mature arrival), the production of these critical desires could be mistaken as my claim to their "latent homosexuality" (since the critical terms are all fetched from the ego psychology that becomes commonplace Freudianism, this would be how my argument would be read in those terms). Yet that is not what I'm arguing at all; rather, that the critics' admiration for Hal also involves the policing of homosexuality.[20]

Thus, while it is certainly fair enough to invoke the term *homosocial* to describe male/male relations in the plays, relations between homosociality and the modern regimes of hetero- and homosexualities cannot be presumed. The importation of the term *homosexuality* would seriously misconstrue the place of sexuality, if only because it obscures what Alan Bray has shown, that much in the ordinary transactions between men in the period, in their negotiations of the social hierarchies, took place sexually.[21] How unremarkable that fact was can be seen of course in *Henry V* when one of the king's betrayers turns out also to have been his bedfellow: their physical intimacy was supposed to have kept

Scroop ever from turning traitor to the king. His crime is not what he did in bed. Thus, while Hal is forever casting off his companions, it is not bedfellows per se that are called into question. Hence there is no reason not to suppose that Hal and Falstaff were bedfellows too. In what situation, after all, does Falstaff ask his first question—"Now, Hal, what time of day is it, lad" (*1 Henry IV*, 1.2.1)? If he is just waking up, what is Hal doing? What should be made of the fact that the next time we see Falstaff asleep (at the end of act 2, scene 4), Hal is in . . . his pockets? Is this attraction to his sleeping companion what the critics claim, a sign of infantilism? What *is* Hal talking about when he charges Falstaff with being an exorbitant "bed-presser" (2.4.238)?

There is no absolutely definitive way to answer such questions, but not because the plays give evidence for the modern supposition that a line can be drawn between homosocial and homosexual relations. That Hal has a bedfellow in *Henry V* is publicly announced as the scene opens (2.2.8); with whom a man sleeps in the climb for power is not private knowledge, nor has sex been cordoned to the area of the private as in the modern fantasmatic.[22] We do not know whether Hal sleeps with Falstaff, though, and this points to one way in which the plays police male/male sexual behavior. For if, on the one hand, it would be unremarkable for men to be sleeping with each other, it would be unspeakable if the wrong men were, if the sex between men was not conducive to maintaining social hierarchies and distinctions. Hal, we know, is stained with riot, and the king fears he might join the rebels. His blot is embodied in Falstaff, his rebellion in Hotspur: they wear two of the faces of what the period calls sodomy. The very fact that Hal's misdeeds are never specified, and that his riots are allied to Hotspur's rebellion but supposed to be enacted in his relations with Falstaff, places his "shame" on that unspeakable terrain. It is arguably that "shame" that Hal scours when he dispatches Hotspur. Yet the defeat of Hotspur at the end of Part I importantly marks Hal's path towards "maturity"; it is a Hotspur-like Hal who voices his plain soldier wooing. This suggests that it is around Hotspur that the play negotiates what is allowable in relationships between men. Hotspur serves as the site for the production of a misogyny and an incipient homophobia—an incipient heterosexuality—that serves both purposes.

To see this, we might follow Rackin's account of the Welsh scene in Part I (act 3, scene 1). Mortimer, behind whom the rebels rally, does not succeed, and his incapacity is displayed, Rackin argues, by his attachment to Glendower's Welsh-speaking daughter; his *effeminacy*, she claims, marks him: "the seductive allure of a world that is feminine, effeminating, and also theatrical . . . disrupt[s] the historical narrative with a fleeting glimpse of all that must be excluded to preserve its coherence" (173). Rackin pits theater against history here, an argument rendered questionable certainly by the work of Greenblatt or Pye, and inimical to the imaginary terrains of sovereignty as I have been tracing them. She produces this analysis by taking what Hotspur says in the scene as the play's truth. It is he who rails at Glendower's magical illusions and mocks his daughter's song and Mortimer's attachment. Rackin's "must be," like other critics' insistence on the inevitability that Hal's career represents, shows her succumbing to an ideological argument and reproducing it uncritically. The work Hotspur does is most explicit in his relation to his wife (something Rackin fails to consider), as when he demands that she be as accommodating with him as the Welsh woman is with her husband Mortimer. Lady Percy submits unwillingly, and the play represents this, much as Rackin (or Hotspur) would deny it.[23] The "fleeting glimpse" in the Welsh scene is historically consequential, not least for the history of sexuality, for the domestication attempted here is the gendered support of the production of the sovereign male subject: it is part of the bourgeoisification that the play represents. Rather than the exclusion of women, the scene depicts the invidious terms upon which women may be included in the production of the sovereign male subject, and even marks a certain impossibility in producing accommodating women for that project. This doesn't make Shakespeare a protofeminist, but it does give grounds for a feminism that might seek to do more than tell one more time the story of women's exclusion from culture, the story of a time-out-of-mind patriarchy whose every retelling only makes it seem all the more impervious to change.

> HOTSPUR. Come, Kate, I'll have your song too.
> LADY PERCY. Not mine, in good sooth.
> HOTSPUR. Not yours, in good sooth! Heart, you swear like a comfit-maker's wife—"Not you, in good sooth!" and "As true as I live!", and "As God shall mend me!", and "As sure as day!" (3.1.239–44)

Hotspur's Kate is his closest way to the throne (she is Mortimer's sister); like the French princess she anticipates, and not only in name, she is the route to legitimize illegitimacy (his rebellion, in this case); she too receives a language lesson. In all these ways, Lady Percy is in the quintessential place of exchange allotted to women within patriarchal structures of alliance. Hotspur would have Lady Percy assume the position of bourgeois domesticated sexual object, but he also would have her speak as a lady, no gross terms in her mouth. He polices her gender by attempting to declass her, hearing a candy-maker's wife's speech in her refusal. His attempt backfires, however, and *he* produces more of the very speech he meant to censor, and at the prompting of her language. This reflects upon his attempt to silence her and reduce her to her sexual part; it also anticipates Warwick's lines on Hal's education in hatred. The repression of the woman here, like the casting off of gross male company there, produces sites of proper male relations: with women and with men. Gender difference is made into a class difference. Rather than simply establishing lines of exclusion and inclusion, however, such scenes rebound within the specular structures of abjection requisite to the illusory production of a sovereign subject. Kate's abjection suggests limits to male empowerment, its insecure bases.

The scene that Hotspur plays with Kate has many echoes in *1 Henry IV.* Consider, for instance, Hal's attempt to turn the tapster Francis into the single word "anon." Hal practices on Francis his own reduction—the prince's economizing that leads him to live for and in the "anon" of his arrival—and thus what in his design looks like repudiation and exclusion (and thus serves as a rehearsal for the big scene with Falstaff) also shows dependency, a threatening and necessary cross-class relation. Hal relies upon Francis's love for him as much as Hotspur does on Kate's. Hotspur puts Kate among the candy-makers; Francis proffers Hal a penny's worth of candy as the sign of his love. Hal pays Francis back as he pays Falstaff for his love. It was Francis's love gift that got Hal going (to see how far he could betray it and yet remain loved); so too Hotspur depends upon his wife, not only to connect him to Mortimer, but also to legitimize his male/male relations. For "proper" masculinity is displayed in the contempt for women that Hotspur voices, and in the repudiation of the effeminacy that unmans Mortimer. (Rackin's charge of effeminacy is what Hotspur guards against and deflects elsewhere.) No wonder that the intensely theatrical Hotspur is so resistant to Glendower in this scene: we need only recall how earlier (1.3.92–111) he had imagined the meeting of Mortimer and Glendower as a heroic encounter of single-handed combat, a description that appears to have been fetched from the *Iliad.* In that scene too Hotspur explains his refusal to behave as a vassal should, why he has not given up his prisoners to the king. His answer lies in his scabrous description of the courtier who arrived on the battlefield speaking "holiday and lady terms" (1.3.45), talking "like a waiting-gentlewoman" (54), perfumed and taking snuff. (Glendower may not be so directly effeminized, but he does insist that he has been properly schooled at court.) Describing the feminized courtier, Hotspur reports himself "pester'd with a popinjay" (49). This is a phrase that the author of *Hic Mulier,* that tract on the monstrosity of the man-woman, recalls when a voice is introduced in that tract defending the transgression of gender difference that women attempt donning male attire.[24] The woman become man, the man become woman: how threateningly reversible this might be is suggested by the echoes to Hotspur's line about the popinjay in *1 Henry IV,* Hal's naming Francis a parrot, for instance, but especially Lady Percy calling *Hotspur* a paraquito (2.3.86).

We can see what Hotspur was policing in Kate: with her reduced to her sexual part, by attempting to turn gender difference into the supposedly more manageable regimes of class, there could be no equivocation about the masculinity he achieves on the battlefield. It is only with Kate in her proper place that Hotspur's claims on Mortimer will not look like the Welsh woman's desire. Consider, after all, that Hotspur's pedagogic scene with Kate echoes Northumberland's earlier schooling of his son's tongue when Hotspur ranted in what his father termed a "woman's mood" (1.3.234). Hotspur's sole cry then was "Mortimer," the word he would have trained a bird—a parrot—to repeat in the king's ears (1.3.221); in his "woman's mood" Hotspur anticipates Glendower's daughter—his single English word is the burden of her incomprehensible Welsh. What the father attempts with his son, Hotspur exacts with his wife. When she calls him a paraquito, she speaks with his father's voice.

These representations of Hotspur serve at least two functions in the play. As the site of a contradiction in the production of "proper" masculinity, Hotspur is at once the locus of a normative misogyny defended against women and effeminization—this is the masculinity founded in the exchange of women that solidifies ties between men; but Hotspur also is a rebel, and hence the site upon which these norms may rebound, so that rebellion wears the face of femininity and theatricality. We see what Hotspur desires when he tells his wife the terms upon which he will accept her love: "When I am a-horseback, I will swear / I love thee infinitely" (2.3.102–3). Kate ends that scene forced to agree to her subordination to his militarism and male camaraderie, and marking her enforcement. Hotspur's masculinity—emblematized by his devotion to his horse—is secured by the supplementary addition of a wife that assures that the all-male rebel world in which he thrives could not be tainted by the effeminacy of a perfumed courtier or of a man who loves his wife too much. But what secures him is also what threatens to make his heroism a sham and his masculinity a performance guarding against what it is always in danger of revealing.

Hotspur is both a rebel in the play, and also the locus of the chivalric honor that Hal fetches from him. Because he serves this double function, he is the site at once of the production of misogyny and the locus of its rebound, male effeminacy. Hal ideally derives chivalric masculinity from Hotspur (it's the mask of masculinity he dons); the possibility that such charged male/male desires might place one man in a feminine position rests upon Hotspur so that, ideally, Hal is not tainted even as he assumes the glamor of the rebel hero. But the ideality that Hal embodies is founded in simulation, and like Hotspur he too may be pestered by a popinjay. Attempted exclusions (of women, of the lower classes, of the gross in language and body) threaten their returns. Parallel pedagogies, played out in the paternal, marital, and class registers, attempt reductions that rebound upon the teachers, failures to seal off and cordon what would be controlled. Women are policed so that effeminacy can be avoided, so that "proper" male/male relations can be secured that are not tainted. The taint lies in playing the woman's part with another man. Through Hotspur, as the voice of a misogyny that is incipiently homophobic, but also as the site upon which charges of effeminacy threaten to lodge, the play polices male/male relations in the very character that it also abjects. It is for that reason that Rackin's claim that women are excluded is complicitous with the mechanism that produces "proper" masculinity, and this helps explain why she finds Hal a mirror of perfection. For Hal would appear exempt from the perils that attend Hotspur's masculinity.

Harry reproduces Harry in a mirror effect, however, and the point of crossing is erotic attraction. While Hotspur, in his woman's mood—playing out in the sexual sphere what counts as rebellion in the political sphere—suffers no womanish man to compromise his masculinity, it is in the throes of such hypermasculinity that he wishes to meet Harry on the battlefield, Harry to Harry, hot horse to horse (the slight asymmetry in Hotspur's phrase perhaps registers his attempt to maintain his advantage in the relation):

> Come, let me taste my horse,
> Who is to bear me like a thunderbolt
> Against the bosom of the Prince of Wales.
> Harry to Harry shall, hot horse to horse,
> Meet and ne'er part till one drop down a corse. (4.1.119–23)

Hotspur responds here to Vernon's heavily eroticized depiction of Hal, vaulting "like feather'd Mercury" (106), his thighs tightly clenching the horse beneath, throned as Hotspur would be on his roan, the male horse he straddles. This is an image of Harry-as-Hotspur fully to be achieved when his rival lies dead at his feet, when Hal will have the potency of a feather, the pen that can rewrite this masculinity as chivalric honor without the taint of rebellion, that can engross aristocratic glamor to cover the calculations of the arriviste, that can absorb the misogynist masculinity transferred from the older orders of patriarchal alliance to the incipient new bourgeois sphere. From Hotspur, Hal seeks a proper masculinity, a sexuality that will permit relations with men not tainted with effeminacy.

As Empson suggests, some of this supposed achievement is marred immediately when Falstaff wounds the dead Hotspur in his thigh, delivering a counterfeit death blow that suggests that Hal cannot take from Hotspur what he most desires. The thigh wound is a sexual wound, and that Falstaff can deliver it suggests what defeating Hotspur was defending against sexually, and where the charge of male/male erotics lies. From Hotspur's misogynistic relation to women, Hal inherits a masculinity that cannot secure itself, for what is being policed in and by Hotspur can also be applied to relations between men. To this point one could adduce Empson's brilliant recognition that the eulogies spoken over Hotspur and Falstaff are capable of being transferred one to the other. In this counterfeit relationship, the masculinity that Hal achieves by killing and robbing Hotspur of his accomplishments is one that secures itself as proper male/male admiration, an incipient heterosexuality, a homo-narcissism that guards against any possibility that Hal's relations with men—with Falstaff—might be sexual. Killing Hotspur, Hal has become a real man, a man's man, insofar as Hotspur's relations with women and men are normative; he has defeated the man who hates women and womanish men, and could not possibly be *that* man. From Hotspur, Hal acquires what criticism will come to see as his heterosexual credentials, a way to view male/male relations as the escape from the danger of effeminization, and a way to regard male/male sexual relations *as* effeminizing. Those male/male relations constitute the homo-narcissism that secures heterosexuality. The emulative relationship with Hotspur is that mirror of male/male admiration supposedly free of the taint of sodomy. It's in this mirror that the critics look.

As Empson suggests, Hotspur's lines imagining his hot encounter with Hal seem very Marlovian; indeed, it's not difficult to think of Hotspur *as* Marlowe. As Empson remarks, Shakespeare outdoes Marlowe, parodies him to ward off the Marlovian effect. The usually "more homosexual" Marlowe (44) is gone one better, however, and the excess of the representation threatens to get out of hand. In a word, that excess—meant as a critique of Hotspur, and as an exposure of his masculinity parallel to the one offered in Hal's mocking lines in act 2, scene 4, where Hotspur's bravado is a performance for his admiring wife—threatens to reveal an incipiently homophobic defense erected against the attractions of the figure. Ideally, Hal should be untainted, but Falstaff rises up to reveal the counterfeiting. To the critics who embrace the ideal Hal, Shakespeare bequeaths the legacy of the possibility of reading Hotspur as the embodiment of a homosexuality that is destructive, misogynist, and a defense against the womanized man, the legacy of homophobia.[25]

How far such understandings might be from the sexual orders of the play is suggested by a casual remark the Hostess makes about Falstaff in *2 Henry IV,* that "he will spare neither man, woman, nor child" (2.1.16–17), that he is "a man queller, and a woman queller" (51–52; hence Hal's gift to him of the page boy who presciently promises to tickle the Hostess's catastrophe [59]). Falstaff's sexual tastes are those possible for any man.[26] Hotspur, after all, virtually admits that to his wife when he tells her that his horse is his preferred partner, or when he expresses his desire for the shining prince. His wife likewise reveals that Hotspur's dreams are of such battlefield encounters. It's for these reasons that Hotspur's sexual relations seem only incipiently heterosexual. What Warner characterizes as the long history of the patriarchal subordination of women is pertinent to the regime that Hotspur inhabits. But that long history is always, and differently in any historical period, in relation to the history of sexuality. From the vantage point of the regimes of modernity, hetero- and homosexuality produce gender difference—the difference in object choice—as the basis for a supposedly immutable difference grounded in the gender so circularly produced. This gender exclusivity however follows upon the supposed differentiation of sexualities. In the Elizabethan sex/gender system that can be read from an indifference of sexual objects, the situation is far less stable. The possibilities of crossing gender policed through the stigmatized and stigmatizing figure of Hotspur, transferred to Hal as constitutive of his sexual ideality—of his becoming the ideal that criticism has found inescapable—is also capable of another reading.

If in his defeat of Hotspur Hal becomes the phallus, it is, to borrow a sentence from Judith Butler,[27] only to reveal that the phallus is always already plastic. It can be had only as a fantasmatic endowment, and as we've seen, by the end of the tetralogy even Katharine might have it. Hal's nervous banter with Burgundy could be read beside his exchanges with Poins in Part II, the only other scene in the tetralogy in which a marriage is proposed for Hal, the marriage with Poins's sister that Falstaff claims that the prince's other companion has in mind. Hal's rejection of Nell constitutes a refusal to legitimize his relation with Poins through marriage with his sister: "Do you use me thus, Ned? Must I marry your sister?" (2.2.131), a rebuff delivered to the man he knows down to the peach stockings he wears. Between them, the terms of their illegitimate relation are offered as they joke about the bastard children Hal imagines Poins has sired. Poins calls this idle talk (2.2.29), and Hal's imagining of his companion's sexual prowess is perhaps as fantastic as the endless tales of conquest Portia plans to tell once she has donned a codpiece—tales that will assure the attractions of male companions. Hal's refusal of Poins's sister as the means to legitimize their relationship is answered by the installment of the fantasized woman between men. When Hal has the scepter, he will still be in the same position, threatened by the woman nonetheless necessary to secure his illusory power.

1 Henry IV anticipates these regimes in an imagined theatrical scene. Between Hal's play with Francis and the paternal play with Falstaff, a brief drama is conjured up, one in which Hal's "damned brawn shall play Dame Mortimer" (2.4.107–8). Dame Mortimer is Hotspur's wife, but also the effeminized Mortimer (Rackin's reading is thus Hal's defensive one). For a moment Hal entertains the possibility that his "damned brawn," the hulk of flesh called Falstaff, might play Dame Mortimer, the woman, the feminized man to Hal's Hotspur. Hal imagines Hotspur and his wife in the same reductive mode that he does Francis, all reduced to a trim reckoning. But to see that even this scene participates in complex routings of identification and difference that exceed Hal's economizing, we should note that Falstaff is made into a trial Kate only *after* Hal has (parrotlike) imitated her voice:

> "O my sweet Harry", says she, "how many hast thou killed today?" "Give my roan horse a drench", says he, and answers, "Some fourteen", an hour after; "a trifle, a trifle". I prithee call in Falstaff; I'll play Percy, and that damned brawn shall play Dame Mortimer his wife. (2.4.103–8)

This deflection of cross-gender identification has not been noticed by critics who have all too easily read Falstaff *as* a woman—on the basis on his "gross" body. Not only would one want to caution against the potential misogyny and homophobia of this connection, one would want to add that the size of the body is as much an index to class negotiations as it might be to gender and sexuality.[28] Hal's new regime of trim reckonings (the predations of the engrossing arriviste that write themselves as civilized restraint) would cut the body down to size; it is mobilized against decaying aristocratic corpulence—the fat body that will come to be the body of the malnourished poor—and the woman's body. As Empson argues, the point at which the eulogies for Falstaff and Hotspur cross comes when Hal summons up the *weight* of their bodies. Critics who repeat Hal's agendas in act 2, scene 4, as the truth of Falstaff's "female" body—rather than seeing it as a reflex against his own identification as a woman—or who associate Falstaff's loquacity with the female tongue, are once again in Hotspur's position in act 3, scene 1, policing Kate.[29] Hal's imagined scenario with Falstaff is no more benign; he recoils from the possibility of crossing gender, and attempts to put Falstaff where he was a moment before. It is that recoil that must be read if we are to interrupt the route from such grossness to femininity that has been understood as a "normal" connection or even as one that psychoanalysis makes available as the truth (infantile Falstaff now seems to be the mother's body).[30]

Yet, it has to be seen what such connections serve in the play and what insidious argument is thereby repeated by the critics—the effacing of male/male relations into misogynist heterosexuality. We are here once again on that difficult terrain of the Elizabethan sex/gender system. It is true that Falstaff claims his womb undoes him, that he compares himself to a sow that has overwhelmed her children, true too that Falstaff is the sole adult male in any Shakespeare play to don drag. Feminization, as in Hal's fantasy play with the brawn as Dame Mortimer, may be part of the casting off of the character, the slurring together of an abjected femininity whether male or female, but it also represents the attempt to distinguish male and female as sexual objects. It is just that distinction belied by Falstaff when he fails to know the difference between men and women. Falstaff's "femininity" is not written within the misogynist masculinity of a protoheterosexuality and homophobia. I do not mean to idealize Falstaff's sexual capacities or to suggest that his relations to the Hostess can be shielded from misogyny—he makes her a site of continual demands and is always defrauding her. Yet there are differences between his relations with the Hostess, for example, and Hal's use of her as a screen between them in the scene discussed earlier; the latter seems determined by what Hal acquires from Hotspur, the potential for a rigidified gender exclusivity to be contrasted with Falstaff's inclusiveness. Critics like Patricia Parker call Falstaff a woman in order not to have to think about his sexual relations with men; even a critic as alert as Valerie Traub falls into the heterosexualizing of homosexuality in her discussion. It is the presumed difference between those sexualities that Falstaff's body breaches.

Hal first casts Falstaff as Dame Mortimer as part of his attempt to cast him off. When Falstaff arrives, Hal attempts to shame the cowardly liar, the monstrous bed-presser. Falstaff catches Hal out—his truth that he robbed Falstaff makes the difference between lying and truth-telling moot. And to the charge of bed-pressing, the fat knight has a devastating response, pointing to skinny Hal's pitiful endowment: "you starveling, you eel-skin, you dried neat's-tongue, you bull's-pizzle, you stockfish . . . you tailor's-yard, you sheath, you bow-case, you vile standing tuck!" (2.4.240–44). His thinness, in these charges, as David Bevington glosses these lines in his edition, carries the accusation of "genital emaciation." Falstaff points to the phallus Hal lacks just as at the end of the play he will mock the one Hal has from Hotspur. The old bed-presser knows where to get the prince—like Katharine perhaps, in the latter end. He takes him, in fact, where Hal virtually admits his pleasure lies in their very first exchange. To Falstaff's irrelevant question about the time of day, Hal replies that the time would be of interest to his fat companion only were the "blessed sun himself" to appear like a "fair hot wench in flame-coloured taffeta" (1.2.9–10). Hal, we know, thinks he is the blessed sun, and in this line the sun is male; Hal imagines himself as cross-dressed.[31] Hal places this imaginary woman between himself and Falstaff, this imaginary locus of self-identification between them. It looks as if the only desire Hal can acknowledge is male/female desire. It looks as if that is how he acknowledges his relation with Falstaff. Hotspur has a wife he can despise so that Hal can have a bedfellow in this way. What way? The lines intimate the kind of sexual pleasure Hal does have and why Hotspur must be produced as a voice protesting against feminization.

This is where I take my critical pleasures, slim as they are, in Hal, in imagining that he, like the young man in sonnet 20, whose *body* seems to be cross-dressed, has a prick that is of no matter to the sonneteer. Like the master/mistress, Hal can be used elsewhere and otherwise. If this seems too crude a supposition, one can point to the ways in which their status difference, which should place Hal on top, is crossed by the age difference that has made Falstaff Hal's tutor and mentor. These crossings of age and status are the sexual locus for the rebound that Hal attempted to control with Francis (in Part II Hal and Poins appear *as* Francis, and Falstaff has no trouble recognizing the two serving lads), or that Hotspur tried with his wife. They are bound to fail. In the short run, perhaps not: new regimes of class and gender are at work in the play, and women and the underclasses do not immediately benefit from them. But, in the long run, the regimes just opening in the play are those we now can hope are coming to an end. But it is up to critics not to go on talking about the repression, subordination of women or of the lower classes, as if that project ever was fully effective. Above all, for the purposes at hand, it is crucial not to act as if these plays operate within the sphere of the modern phantasm of sexual difference, with its suppositions of rigid differences in gender and the impermeability of homo- and heterosexualities. And it is certainly most crucial that the male/male relations in the play not be read through the axes of heterosexism or its blinding double, homo-narcissism.

What is at stake comes as close to being made explicit as is possible in that scene in which Hal confronts a former bedfellow and attempts to cast off the treasonous "English monsters" (*Henry V*, 2.2.85); Pye has argued brilliantly for the constitutive relationship between treason and sovereignty. There is a sexual register here as well, for the monstrosity of the treasonous bedfellow is a way of naming sodomy. In the next scene Falstaff's death will be reported. What Hal's sexual relation with his bedfellows was is all but spelled out in the lines spoken to Lord Scroop, the last treasonous bedfellow (unless Kate inherits that part); Scroop knew "the very bottom of my soul" (97), Hal declares; he held the "key" to Hal's treasure and "almost might'st have coin'd me into gold / Would'st thou have practis'd on me for thy use" (98–99). The description returns us once more to the sonnets—

> So am I as the rich whose blessed key,
> Can bring him to his sweet up-locked treasure,
> The which he will not ev'ry hower survay,
> For blunting the fine point of seldome pleasure.
> Therefore are feasts so sollemne and so rare,
> Since sildom comming in the long yeare set (sonnet 52, 1–6)

—to the very lines that echo Hal's first soliloquy or his father's later ministrations on the economies of royal image production. In *Henry V* Hal is still attempting to cast off the revolting male lover who makes the king a queen. In such ways, the misogyny of the second tetralogy is complicit with homophobia. In such ways, the endorsement of Hal as the very locus of an ideality repeats these desires, the foundations of modern heterosexuality. But only a heterosexist criticism need read Shakespeare this way.

'THEY ARE ALL SODOMITES':

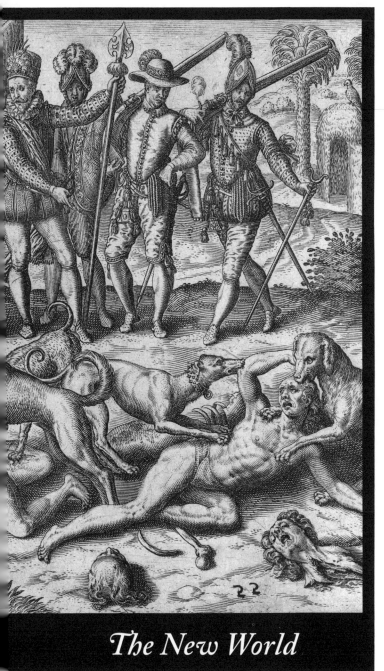

PART THREE

The New World

CHAPTER 6

Dis-covering America

To THOSE WHO KNOW Jonathan Katz's groundbreaking *Gay American History* or Walter Williams's *The Spirit and the Flesh,* the topic of this chapter will not be unfamiliar: the systematic persecution of so-called sodomitical Indians in the New World "discovered" by Europe in the Renaissance, and the transportation to the Americas of habits of thought and prejudice endemic in Europe.[1] After the deplorable decision of the U.S. Supreme Court in *Bowers v. Hardwick,* with its appeals to sodomy laws enrolled in English statute books in the sixteenth century, and to a time-out-of-mind hatred of homosexuality, the recovery of the history of sodomy in the New World is of signal importance as one way of resisting modes of thinking which, every day, seem to be growing more widespread, and which the decision of the Supreme Court can be said to have licensed. I take therefore as an originary moment in the history of the making of America not the act of "discovery" or of successful colonization or declaration of nationhood which the U.S. calendar celebrates (Columbus Day, Thanksgiving, Independence Day)—and whose very duplications suggest that we don't quite know when or where America starts, that the justices' appeal to "fundamental" principles may cover a multiplicity that cannot be reduced to a single origin—but what happened two days before Vasco Núñez de Balboa first laid eyes on the Pacific Ocean. In a Panamanian village, after killing the leader of the Indians of Quarequa and six hundred of his warriors, Balboa fed to his dogs forty more Indians accused of sodomitical practices.

The earliest account of these events of October 1513 that I know appears in Pietro Martire d'Anghiera's *De Orbo Novo,* first published in 1516. I will be citing the 1555 English translation of Peter Martyr's *Decades* (as the name and title are anglicized) as one way of immediately suggesting that these events cannot be thought of solely as episodes in Spanish-American history; I have no interest in perpetuating the black legend that seeks to exculpate northern Europeans from the atrocities of the Spanish, and which is fueled with protonationalist and racist energies.[2] As we will see, Richard Eden, the translator, not only makes Peter Martyr's text English but cannot resist endorsing Balboa's final act of carnage. To read the scene, I will also be glancing occasionally at an illustration of it that appeared in 1594 in the fourth volume of Theodore De Bry's *America,* a huge publishing venture that widely disseminated colonial texts, and whose illustrations engraved them in the European mind. The illustration accompanies a mid-sixteenth-century Italian text, as it happens: the story of Balboa is told again and again, and it knows no national borders.[3] It reminds us that translated texts fill the pages of Hakluyt and Purchas. They communicate with the history of English colonization.

Here is the scene in Peter Martyr:

> [Balboa] founde the house of this kynge infected with most abhominable and unnaturall lechery. For he founde the kynges brother and many other younge men in womens apparell, smoth & effeminately decked, which by the report of such as dwelte abowte hym, he abused with preposterous venus. Of these abowte the number of fortie, he commaunded to bee gyven for a pray to his dogges. (89v)

A number of elements in this description, starting with the designation of "abhominable and unnaturall lechery," make it clear that sodomy is its subject even though the term is never used. The crime of "preposterous venus" says this in a highly condensed way.[4] "Preposterous" means a confusion of before and behind ("venus," of course, refers to sexual acts); the cross-dressed Indians have confused gender and the supposed "natural" procreative sexuality that follows from it. The designation "unnaturall" and the judgment that such acts are not merely abominable but represent an infection in danger of spreading are familiar ways of representing sodomy. To halt a reading of the text by pointing out that sodomy is in question does not take stock of the excessiveness of this representation, its confusion of questions of gender and sexuality (cross-dressing and sodomy are by no means the same thing). In simple narrative terms, moreover, Balboa has already established his power by the slaughter of the "king" of Quarequa and his warriors that precedes the further act of carnage in which these men are fed as "pray to his dogges." If Balboa needs to remove the king's brother in order to make his position absolutely secure, it's more than a bit odd that the king's brother must be depicted as a cross-dresser. But what this does—it is not something that can be found in the previous description of the battle scene—is infuse Balboa's acts with moral purpose. It's as if he's righting a wrong against the prerogatives of gender. (In this context, it is worth noting that many sixteenth-century narratives make this point quite explicitly when they report that Indian women are offended by the sodomites in their midst.)[5] But if the elimination of the king's brother and his minions is done for the sake of women—for the sake of the proprieties and prerogatives of gender—it is also obviously fueled with misogyny, as the disgust at effeminacy implies. Yet that disgust is displaced upon the cross-dressed/sodomitical body and its making preposterous the act of Venus.

Furthermore, one must notice that what Balboa knows about the king's brother he does thanks to native informants. If the king's brother's manliness is discredited—no warrior, he stays at home with his cross-dressed minions—his political abilities also are impugned. And this seems to be an opinion about him shared by the native informants. Balboa is thereby represented as serving the interests of those he has conquered. This is reflected too in the aftermath of the slaughter of the forty Panamanians, as the Indians accommodate Balboa by handing over more sexual offenders, delivering up "al such as they knewe to bee infected with that pestilence" in order to be rid of such "contagious beastes" (90r). "This stinkynge abhomination," Peter Martyr explains, "hadde not yet entered amonge the people, but was exercised onely by the noble men and gentelmen. But the people lyftinge up theyr handes and eyes toward heaven, gave tokens that god was grevously offended with such vyle deedes" (90r). It is at this point that Richard Eden cannot resist a comment; in the margin of the text beside these lines, he writes: "I wolde all men were of this opinion." The slaughter of sodomites is thus mobilized as a kind of quasi-democratic device since the behavior of the king's brother and his cross-dressed companions is now taken as a sign of the corruptions of those in power in Quarequa—or in Europe, Eden implies. The narrative strategy here is, of course, a ruse of power: for if Balboa eliminates the native rulers and their courtiers, he also supplants them. At the same time, he is represented as the liberator of the oppressed. Political oppression, however, has been translated into sexual oppression, the abuse of "preposterous venus," and that is the wrong he is said to right. Those Indians who decry the sodomitical "infection" of cross-dressing and male/male sexual relations are "good" Indians in this narrative, and not merely in their accommodating behavior: they provide a belief that Eden endorses. They have been made the site upon which European values can be foisted, but also an exemplary mirror in which Europeans might find themselves.

In the battle that precedes the slaughter of the forty Panamanian sodomites there are no "good" Indians, and all of the natives of Quarequa are described as animals, their slaughter explicitly an act of butchery; they were, Martyr writes, with perfect equanimity, "hewed . . . in pieses as the butchers doo flesshe . . . , from one an arme, from an other a legge, from hym a buttocke, from an other a shulder, and from sume the necke from the bodye at one stroke" (89v). This carnage serves as a foreground for what follows, much as it does in the De Bry illustration with its *disjecta membra* lying before the supine Indian bodies being eaten alive. After the sodomites are fed to the dogs, there are two kinds of

Indians in the text, sodomitical ones, and noble savages. As the latter lift their hands to heaven, it's as if they're proto-Christians, at the very least testifying to the universality of the Judeo-Christian condemnation of "unnatural" sexuality. Serving as a mirror of European belief, this split representation of Indians permits the covering over of divisions within the invading troops. Balboa himself is no noble or gentleman—though that is the status he strives to achieve in his conquests, and the De Bry illustration portrays him and his followers as a group of courtiers. The representation of the Indians (which, of course, starts with believing that they are ruled by a king, and that their society is divided along European class/status lines) helps to dissimulate Balboa's power grab within Spanish society. In this post facto rewriting, Balboa is not only the righter of sexual wrongs, the restorer of proper gender, he's also the universal liberator of the underclasses.

The slaughter of "sodomites," from such a vantage point, does not tell us anything about the sexual practices of these Indians; it functions only as a spectacle for Europe and its ruses of power. The De Bry illustration makes this all but explicit in its staging of the scene—Spanish spectators standing erect around their captain, as they watch the Indians being devoured. But such mirror effects are enormously complicated. Although Balboa's elevation is predicated on his replacing the native powers, when natives are made to voice European beliefs about corrupt sexuality the truth they utter is one about the corruptions of those in power, about nobles and gentlemen, the very courtier Balboa seeks to become. The mirror that the natives hold up suggests, in the doubleness of native construction, divisions within the Europeans. Moreover, although the natives hand over more "sodomites" to Balboa, this does not necessarily reveal anything about their attitudes towards sexual practices; it does suggest, however, that the natives also are divided. Such moments of accommodation are not at all untypical of responses to invasion; the history of native peoples in the New World is not one of simple pastoral contentment, and one mode of resistance developed in the face of warfare and invasions has been to seem to go along with the demands of the conquerors. Nothing in Peter Martyr will tell us why the natives at this moment accede to the Spanish, but there is no reason simply to write the episode off as one of co-optation and victimization, nor to assume that the natives shared European beliefs about sodomy.[6] But there is no reason either to assume that they simply and uncomplicatedly embraced it. Sexuality is never simply a set of acts unconnected to questions of power. The Indians can be imagined to be using European beliefs as a way to work their way into the European system, or represented as if that is what they are doing, but this also is a way to accomplish what they conceivably want—the elimination of certain members of their own society.

To read the episode this way allows one to notice certain things: that two nonhomogeneous forces meet here that get simplified if Spaniards and Indians are thought of each as self-identical and as entirely oppositional; that the account of sexuality which seems to exceed the requirements of the narrative nonetheless supplies ideological justifications that are elsewhere lacking in the account. These cross-dressed bodies are the locus of identity and difference, a site for crossings between Spaniards and Indians, and for divisions between and among them. The differentials involve class, race, and gender, all in uneasy relation to each other, sites capable of ideological mobilization, but also of resistance (one must think through what effects of identification the narrative attempts, and how the unities supposed may be broken). What the scene offers is not the truth of a naked body—which is what the De Bry illustration seems to deliver—but a site the text names well as preposterous.[7] After the fact of massive slaughter, this additional slaughter retrospectively justifies it. Post facto, preposterously, the body of the sodomite takes on the status of an origin, serving as the cause and justification for what was done to the Indians, but its originary status is troubled not merely by being presented as an aftereffect but also because, cross-dressed, it is a double body and the only truth it testifies to is the preposterous nature of colonial accounts, that the ideological production of the text will never justify the atrocities of the European invasion of the New World.[8]

These complicities between colonial representations and the sodomitical body can be further illustrated by turning briefly to a story about the origins of sodomy that circulates widely in the period; I cite from the version offered by Pedro da Cieza in 1553 as it is quoted in Garcilaso de la Vega's *Royal Commentaries of the Incas* (1609), the fullest of the several accounts to which Garcilaso alludes.[9] The story, presented as one "which the natives have received as a tradition" (561), is set in Peru, and involves the arrival of giants who ravage the countryside, indulging in cannibalism on a wide scale, but who find themselves sexually frustrated in their attempts on native women: "After some years the giants were still in this region, and as they had no women of their own and the Indian women were too small for them, or else because the vice was habitual to them and inspired by the demon, they practiced the unspeakable and horrible sin of sodomy, committing it openly and in public without fear of God or personal shame" (562–63). The truth of the account is credited: Cieza reports the finding of the bones of the giants.

Cieza, and Garcilaso after him, offer accounts of sexual practices in Peru which divide the native body. The Incas are said to have suppressed sodomy—they are the "good" Indians of the Balboa account whom the Spaniards replaced. But, in offering this story about the native origins of sodomy, sodomy is something that comes from the outside, and is not native at all. While this could be a story about the Incan invasions of Peru (they bring sodomy to Peru as the act that needs to be discovered and extirpated), in many respects it seems more like a story about the Spanish invasion, and not only because these Incan beliefs may be Spanish ones—these giants come from overseas, and they arrive without any women in their company. Moreover, while it is certainly possible that native mythologies included a belief in ancient giants, the story seems fetched from Genesis. And, of course, as it is told, the supposed native tradition is inflected with Christian values, so much so that at the end of the story of the giants they are burnt by an avenging angel sent by God (the very punishment ordered for sodomites in many European legal codes). Is this story about native tradition one that the natives tell about the Spaniards, whose concepts have forever altered the native understanding of their own myths and practices? Or is it a story that the Spaniards tell as if it were a native account, in order to produce "good" Indians who "properly" abominate sodomy? Or is it a story that the natives tell to the Spaniards as if it were traditional, accommodating their beliefs to Spanish ones, but keeping in reserve their own story under the cover of this acceptable one? By the time this story is told, can one separate native and Christian beliefs?[10]

Clearly not, but what can be recognized is that this story depends upon the complicities that these questions raise. Repeatedly told and elaborated, it retrospectively—preposterously—locates an origin that is a divided and doubled one. Yet, for all the ways in which the story doubly articulates native and Spanish beliefs, what it also bespeaks is the inassimilable nature of sodomy. Its origins lie neither with the Spaniards nor with the Indians, but with a race of giants. The sexual practices of male with male are seen as a response to the impossibility of male/female intercourse (an explanation that could justify such practices *among the Spanish* and which obscures the fact that in European culture of the time men found boys as well as women possible sexual objects). Precisely because the story is about what cannot be assimilated, about something that cannot be stabilized, it is capable of being told in the double register of "native" tradition and Spanish Christian belief. Yet, however extravagant the story is, it is also down to earth, its truth testified to by the empirical evidence of the bones that remain to be seen. And another fact about Puerto Viejo that Garcilaso quotes from Cieza: the wells of pitch found in the region which could be used " 'to tar all the ships one wished with it.' . . . Thus far Pedro de Cieza, whose history we have followed to show the Indian tradition about the giants, and the well of pitch at the same place, for it too is remarkable" (563). Remarkable and, it seems, natural—the coincidence of the tar pits and the giants is clinching evidence, a naturalization that serves the Spanish conquerors. (But *what* is naturalized, the outlandishness or the ordinariness of such sexual behavior?)

A similar coincidence, the slippages around sodomy that write colonial accounts, also can be found in two accounts of origin that frame Peter Martyr's telling of the slaughter of the Panamanian sodomites. As the Spaniards advance with their guns, the Indians flee in panic, certain that the Spaniards are one with the violent forces of nature: "as soone as they harde the noyse of the hargabusies, they beleved that owre menne caryed thunder and lyghtenynge about with them" (89v). After they deliver up the sodomites, the accommodating Indians report themselves relieved, convinced that the practices of the Indians they have handed over were the source of natural violence, "affirmynge this to bee the cause of theyr soo many thunderinges, lyghtnynge, and tempestes wherwith they are soo often troubeled" (90r). Spaniards and native sodomites are identified here as originating forces. The account serves the narrative, of course, both the desire to represent the forces of civilization as one with the providential control of nature (the Indians are made to voice a naive belief which it is in the interest of the Spaniards to believe they believe), as well as the aim of the narrative to represent the bodies of sodomites as the subversion of everything that retrospectively can be called nature. Within the space of a page in Peter Martyr's account, these two origins—this ignorance and knowledge—come to coincide. The natives mouth European beliefs in a mimetology that undermines them even as they produce them. In such ways colonial texts produce the sodomitical body as the body that needs to be effaced. Yet, as this exemplary account begins to suggest, that body also founds an ineffaceable site of disruption.

It punctuates the scene of discovery, October 7, 1513, Balboa's first sight of the Pacific, two days after the episode in Quarequa with which we began:

> he behelde with woonderinge eyes the toppes of the hygh mountaynes shewed unto hym by the guydes of *Quarequa*, from the whiche he myght see the other sea soo longe looked for, and never seene before of any man commynge owte of owre worlde. Approchinge therefore to the toppes of the mountaynes, he commaunded his armye to stey, and went him selfe alone to the toppe, as it were to take the fyrst possession therof. (90v)

The scene is staged through the familiar ideological structures which have written such events: an individual, a hero, a great man, fulfills everyone's dream. "Fyrst possession" is a spiritual event—a matter simply of seeing, and, as the narrative continues, Balboa falls to his knees in prayer, performing a "spirituall sacrifice," humbling himself in thanks for what his God has given him.

How staged this scene of possession is, how euphemized its presentation of self-conquest and humiliation, is suggested even in Peter Martyr's account. Balboa is there alone only because he has refused to allow his soldiers to accompany him. The spirituality, the providential history constructed in Balboa's prayer, the transcendental event—the mountaintop communication with God—is belied (and supported) by the troops and by quite other notions of possession and victory. He is there because he has been led, not by God, but by "the guydes of *Quarequa,*" and they are our guides, too, leading us back to the scenes of carnage this arrival seeks to efface, and not least to that other scene, staged in the De Bry illustration, the excessive, supplementary (and, for the purposes of Peter Martyr's narrative, absolutely necessary) slaughter of sodomitical Indians. Balboa's self-sacrifice euphemizes that scene of slaughter: the forty sacrificed as "pray" there have become here Balboa's prayer. It is on the bodies of those who are equated with animals that this European man can rise up to his spiritual heights. The connection can be brought down a peg when we hear the last thing that Balboa thanks his God for, that so great a victory has been given to "a man but of smaule witte and knowleage, of lyttle experience and base parentage" (90v). The—literal—dividing of the Indian body is requisite for covering over of European divisions, for the construction, eminently deconstructable, of the unified European body. Preposterously, the guides of Quarequa lead the narrative back to the (de)foundational scene to which we have been attending, and to the work that the sodomitical body performs in this account.

It does so not least because there is no such thing as *the* sodomitical body. The characterization of the cross-dressed Indians as sodomites has already voided any possibility of reading that body on its own terms. Rather, its crossings, its refusals of gender and class difference, are what is made to tell, and what may be made to speak against the prejudicial designs of the account. But any attempt to read cross-dressing on its own terms would fall prey to—and be enabled by—the same conditions of non-self-identity. For there is no such thing as the singular cross-dressed body, nor does it carry with it a univocal meaning.

This can be seen in the various attempts to consign it, and not merely in the Renaissance texts I have been considering. Contemporary and more sympathetic readings like that offered by Walter Williams have sought in the special status accorded by some tribes to cross-dressing a transhistorical locus for the affirmation of alternative sexual practices. This interpretation has been resisted in a variety of ways: by a gay-affirmative historian, for instance, whose misogyny leads him to reject cross-gender identification, but who also points to cross-dressing as a native practice of humiliating captured warriors;[11] by a feminist anthropologist, whose reading of male cross-dressing as an attempt to encroach upon female powers and prerogatives is fueled by homophobia but also by a sense that the crossing of gender divisions varies within native cultures and in ways not easily homologized with our own.[12] Without denying the value of affirming solidarity between gay identity and those persecuted for what have been seen as sexual transgressions, and certainly with no desire to endorse the misogyny or homophobia that has marked the refusal of such affirmations, it nonetheless has to be recognized that *all* these accounts offer projections upon native bodies, but that each suggests, too, insofar as they offer historical and anthropological evidence that can be credited, further revelations that cross-dressed bodies are not of themselves singular. Cross-dressing does not mean the same thing from one native situation to another, or even within the same tribe; to believe otherwise is to homogenize all natives into the figure of the Indian, and to once more give in to the ethnocentricity that has invented the category of people without history.

As a most telling instance of the dangers of such readings, consider this episode in structuralist anthropology, an essay in Pierre Clastres's *Society Against the State* called "The Bow and the Basket," recently made available in a glossy Zone book, presented with all the trimmings of the latest thought from Paris.[13] Clastres looks at a small nomadic society, the Guayaki Indians of South America, and writes a prose infused with lyrical identification with a people offered as a model for a sociality that has not yet arrived at the oppressions of state formation. "The Bow and the Basket" takes up their gender organization. Like many other anthropologists, Clastres insists that in this tribe, gender differences are rigidly maintained, here in an extreme form since both hunting and gathering are performed by the men, while the women tend hearth and the temporary homes established as they wander through the forest. The bow and basket emblematize for Clastres this strict separation, since members of one sex cannot touch the object associated with the other sex without disastrous consequences. Clastres's view is, however, a heterosexist fantasy about these people, belied by numerous details in his account that suggest that such crossings do in fact occur: "women do scarcely any collecting" (103), Clastres admits at one point, thus revealing that women do occasionally gather—at which point gathering is redivided by Clastres to posit the form of that activity which "properly belongs to the category of masculine activities" (103). "Men do the hunting, which is only natural" (103), Clastres writes, voicing and ventriloquizing Guayakan belief. "Natural" and "proper" assume their place within a heterosexist taxonomy. Yet the account slips again as Clastres reveals that it is the women, who supposedly never touch the male bow, who make the strings for them (104). Moreover, their "proper" activity, the preparation of food, and the fact that, because of demographic inequalities, they may take more than one husband, belies the division that Clastres sets up in which men are the "producers" and women are, as he calls them, the "consumers." These may be people living before the state, but as Clastres's misogyny writes them they are already protobourgeois.

The sole place in which Clastres registers the possibility of the violation of his schema of division (one that he thinks is a model of equality and balance but which is, as he writes it, a hierarchy always affirming the place of men over women) is in the existence within this group of twenty-odd people of two cross-dressed men who carry baskets rather than bows. Tellingly, with their presence, Clastres thinks that all the permutations possible in his mathematical schema have been realized; it never occurs to him that there might be bow-carrying women, or any arrangement for female/female sexual expression, nor (if such is the case) to remark their absence among the Guayaki.[14] These two men are the only named figures in Clastres, and although both cross-dress, they are otherwise quite different. One of them is the maladjusted Chachubutawachugi, who refuses to carry his basket as women do, and who refuses to behave as a woman. How he came to be a basket-carrier is not spelled out—bad luck in hunting, or some such event, has led him to be stigmatized and denied male prerogatives. The other basket-carrier, Krembegi, Clastres applauds as a model of social adjustment, and he offers his liberal endorsement of the tribe that has found room for him. Yet who is Krembegi? Clastres offers in the space of a paragraph several explanations: "Krembegi was in fact a sodomite" (108), we are first told. He was "an incomprehensible pederast," Clastres continues. "Krembegi was homosexual"; he was "an unconscious invert" (109). He's also naturally artistic. Each peg, of course, names not some singular form of sexual identity, but various behaviors that at historically different times have been available for sexual self-identification or that have served—as they do here—as prejudicial markers. Clastres may think he is telling us who Krembegi is or what his cross-dressing means, but the figure of the well-adjusted male basket carrier panics him into a proliferation of incoherent, utterly confused explanations.

My point, however, is not simply to dismiss Clastres's homophobic and ignorant interpretations, but to suggest that his response to Krembegi is endemic to all readings of cross-dressing. Even as Clastres celebrates how well Krembegi fits into his tribe (his "homosexuality had permitted him to find the topos he was logically consigned to by his unfitness to occupy the space of men" [110]), he also mentions his exclusion; unlike both men and women in the tribe, whose singing Clastres examines in highly invidious ways (the men turn out to be protopoststructuralists whose songs discover that language is not a means of communication but a way of enunciating an *I*, while the women turn out to sing indistinguishably one from another in songs that Clastres redescribes as howling and wailing; "one can scarcely speak of singing where the women are concerned" [111]), Krembegi is distinguished from both the men and the women. "Krembegi never sang," Clastres informs his readers in a footnote (113 n. 2).[15] "He was a *krypy-meno* (anus-make-love)" (109), Clastres tells us, giving the native word as a final "true" definition. But what of the men who slept with him? They "would make him their sexual partner," and play their "erotic games" (this form of sex couldn't possibly be serious, we are assured) in a spirit of "bawdiness" and not of "perversion" (109); they were not anus-make-loves. Before anyone seizes upon Krembegi as a model for the wonders of "Indian" acceptance of sexual diversity, of "tolerance," that "invidious descriptor one finds laced throughout this literature," as Gilbert Herdt puts it (489), it would be good to see how excluded Krembegi is, by the label he is given, by the place he occupies, and by his silence. It might almost be better to seek to identify with the maladjusted Chachubutawachugi, whose behavior at least protests the space to which he has been consigned.

Consigned by whom? It would be hard finally to disentangle the Guayaki from their sympathetic interpreter. As the essay ends, Clastres offers a last idyllic glimpse: "Such is the life of the Guayaki Indians. By day they walk together through the forest, women and men, the bow in front, the basket behind" (127–28). The hierarchy of male and female is thus quietly but unmistakably affirmed. But what is denied is that it is not only cross-dressers who have bows and baskets, a front and a behind. Such a "preposterous" admission would be too threatening to the heterosexism that marks Clastres's reading. For it suggests that, in any clothing, bodies are not singular. Clastres fastens on a male anxiety among the Guayaki—their dislike of having to share their wives with other men. But nowhere does he think that sexual relations between men are a possibility except for cross-dressed men who play the woman's part; nowhere, that is, does he acknowledge the preposterous truth that the bow and the basket are not only a figure for man in opposition to woman but also for a cross-identification that could define men's bodies or women's bodies, and the multiple possibilities for sexual relations of men with men and of women with women.

~

"They are all sodomites"; so reads the dispatch sent from Vera Cruz, July 10, 1519, in the first so-called letter of Cortés.[16] The sentence comes after several paragraphs describing "the people who inhabit this land" (30; Mexico, from the Yucatan northwards); it is the first—and only—mention of "that abominable sin" (37) in the letter, perhaps the first in any of the accounts sent back to Spain, although once made, few reports failed to repeat the charge. By 1525, Tomás Ortiz claimed that the Caribs were not merely cannibals (as Columbus first has declared), but "were sodomites more than any other race." And a year later, Gonzalo Fernández de Oviedo can repeat this formula over and again: "The Indians eat human flesh and are sodomites."[17] Balboa's forty sodomites have escalated in these blanket condemnations, but the mechanism was already at work in Peter Martyr's narrative as the accommodating Indians delivered up their fellows to the Europeans. The production of sodomites seems unstoppable; indeed, it was to halt this roller-coaster effect that Las Casas wrote. In his 1542 *Brevisima relacion de la destruccion de las Indias,* Englished as *The Spanish Colonie* in 1583, Las Casas provided not only the first text for the construction of the black legend, but singled out as most diabolical the Spaniards' accusation that the Indians "all were polluted with the abhominable sinne against nature: which is a wretched and false slaunder." "Our selves can testifie," Las Casas continues, denying the allegation, "who made diligent inquisition & search, even from the beginning." All he found were a "few" sodomites, "for whose sakes nevertheless all that world is not to be condemned. We may say as much," he goes on, "of the eating of mans flesh."[18] Las Casas may have been the friend of the Indians, but, as this defense reveals, he was no friend of sodomite or cannibal. Within the logic of his defense, moreover, were all the Indians sodomites and cannibals, their extirpation would have been justified.[19]

Las Casas's denials provide a counterpoint to the wholesale

condemnations that we will be pursuing in the pages that follow; but it is important to register at once that the attempt to "save" the Indians by denying their sexual practices also is an annihilative gesture. There is a long tradition from Las Casas on that finds its full articulation in the Enlightenment. There, as in Joseph François Lafitau's condemnation of Balboa in *Customs of the American Savage,* the fault of Europeans was to entertain "shameful suspicions" about practices that Lafitau believed were spiritual ones, revivals of ancient customs.[20] This tradition continues to our own day. Anthony Pagden, for example, footnotes the sentence declaring all the Indians of Mexico to be sodomites with this comment in his Yale edition of the Cortés letters: "There is little evidence to support this accusation," he writes (458 n. 38), summoning up some evidence we will soon be considering from Bernal Díaz; he concludes: "it seems, however, to have been severely punished in most areas." Granted, as framed in these accounts, sodomy is an accusation; but one does not rise to the defense by assurances that the natives condemned the practice as much as Europeans did—or still do.[21] Pagden's assurances, no more than the writer's condemnation, fail to explain the presence of the charge in the report. It is to that question that I turn: in seeking the sites for the production of sodomy, I pursue, once again, sodometries, multiple explanations, incongruent and "utterly confused."

One explanation for the charge that all Mexicans are sodomites lies in seeing where in that first dispatch from Vera Cruz the Spaniards think they are. The landscape is described—meadows and streams, "some so beautiful that in all Spain there can be none better" (29); there is, in short, "no difference between this land and Spain," the account proceeds to say. But if no difference, there are people in this Spanish landscape, and "in each province their customs are different" (30). The people introduce difference into a landscape of the same; but since this same is an extension of Spain, difference is also registered in Spanish terms, as can be seen in descriptions of native clothing, "highly colored yashmaks . . . thin mantles which are decorated in a Moorish fashion" (30). The discovery of Moors in this landscape is not surprising; Columbus, for example, had opened his journal by praising the Spanish for making "an end of the war with the Moors" in the 1492 conquest of Granada, and for "having driven out all the Jews" in the same year.[22] Events in the New World parallel these. But Columbus thinks that he is off the shore of China; Mandeville is his guide to these regions; he never reports sodomites in the kingdom of the Great Khan, and Columbus sees none either. His geographical projection imagines a series of analogies: Moors, Jews, and the natives of the islands. The dispatch from Mexico, however, works in terms of identities. The natives are Moors; to make what will be called New Spain identical to old Spain, they must be extirpated, as the Moors were. Accusations of sodomy, responsible for deaths in the thousands in Spain, are transported to the New World.[23] Sodomites "are" Moors.

The identification of Moors and natives might be enough (as Walter Williams has suggested) to answer the question of the logic of the accusation that all are sodomites. For it seems entirely unmotivated; no sexual practices of the inhabitants are mentioned, for instance, to support the claim—nor is it necessary to suppose that the accusation reads as merely or entirely a sexual accusation. In fact, the claim that all are sodomites appears as a kind of afterthought; the sentence begins "in addition" (37). To what, then, is the charge of sodomy added? In what context is it produced? Again, there is nothing surprising here: it is the practice of human sacrifice, the clearest indication in this letter and elsewhere that the natives need Christianity to be rescued from their abominations. One abomination presumably answers another (cannibalism, the evil that Columbus records, joins the set); several pages of the letter detail the practice of human sacrifice and the necessity of removing it. A logic guides the discussion of sacrifice, however, and it appears to be complete. So our question returns; if sodomy is congruent with these other practices, why *add* it to the charge, and in a way that draws attention to its incongruence? For unlike the witnessed practice of sacrifice, sodomy has not been seen by the Spaniards: "we have been informed, and are most certain it is true, that they are all sodomites and practice that abominable sin" (37). Here, then, is a certainty that requires no proof, an argument that needs no logic to support it. This is the final word, and it need not be argued. What does sodomy mean in this document?

It names something otherwise unnameable, something that goes beyond the evidentiary and the logical; it is a category of a violation that violates categories. It is the worst that can be said; what is presented as a kind of afterthought—"in addition"—goes beyond all thought, and thus ends the discussion. There is nothing more to be said after "they are all sodomites." But why should this be so? Have the Spaniards seen nothing to trigger this response? Is "sodomy" an entirely empty category? The answer to such a question does not necessitate an examination of sexual practices, at least not in this case. They have seen something: the bodies of men. For while they have "well-proportioned bodies," the report says, differences in local customs are registered on their bodies, and what is well-proportioned becomes grotesque:

> Some pierce their ears and put very large and ugly objects in them; others pierce their nostrils down to the lip and put in them large round stones which look like mirrors; and others will split their lower lips as far as the gums and hang there some large stones or gold ornaments so heavy that they drag the lips down, giving a most deformed appearance. (30)

The "well-proportioned" bodies of these men are "deformed"; orifices have been opened and distended in ways they should not be. The male body is violated, pierced. And these practices are continued in self-mutilations that stop just short of the ultimate violation of life. According to the account, the day begins with a visit to the temple where may be seen "some cutting their tongues, others their ears, while there are some who stab their bodies with knives" (35). The pierced male body "is" the sodomitical body, it appears. Sodomy is not merely continuous with the logic of sacrifice, however; for unlike the ultimate violation that kills, sodomy is, these "deformed" bodies suggest, a life practice, routinized, ritualized, differentiated by locale. "They are all sodomites": as the Spaniards see them, these violated bodies register a resistance to Spanish violation. For if the accusation of sodomy is meant to signal how unlike the Spaniards the Indians are, how repugnant their practices and very beings must be, how much their relations to each other and to their own bodies fail to communicate with Spanish practices, they also offer an uncanny mirror of Spanish desires, above all the desire to violate. For the Spaniards want these bodies, to trade them as possessions, to enslave them to do their work. They want the gold that distends their orifices. Here are "well-proportioned" bodies apt to serve; indeed, here are people who keep being seen as Spanish counterparts: they live in well-constructed houses, their society is striated by class/status divisions, some of the people displaying untold wealth and elegance—all this, despite the fact that they look like Moors and engage in unspeakable practices. They are, in short, people "who live in a more civilized and reasonable manner than any other people we have seen in these parts up to the present" (36). Their men "cover their shameful parts" and their women are veiled (30). Are these Moors, or Spaniards? "They are all sodomites": does this mean these are (violated) bodies we want (to violate)?

So much is suggested when the text pauses over what it regards as the ultimate horror of human sacrifice. "They take many girls and boys and even adults, and in the presence of the idols they open their chests while they are still alive and take out their hearts" (35). *Even adults.* The syntax of the sentence quietly registers what is horrific in these practices as it passes by the (mis)use of the bodies of boys and girls, to pause over the violated adult (male?) body—the body the Spaniards want, the desire projected as the desire of the natives. We can see something similar in the letter of Diego Alvarez Chanca, the physician on Columbus's second voyage.[24] There are no sodomites, as mentioned above, in the initial accounts of the Caribbean; but more and more, the Caribs, the cannibals, occupy a similar place in the narrative. Chanca describes their practices: "They castrate the boys whom they capture and employ them as servants until they are fully grown, and then when they wish to make a feast, they kill and eat them, for they say that the flesh of boys and women is not good to eat" (1:32). In this account, as in the letter from Mexico, violation of the bodies of boys and women hardly gives pause; the boys are castrated, made into women, and "the flesh of boys and women" is said to be equally unpalatable. These undigestible bodies are akin to those that later accounts will redescribe as the bodies of sodomites, the monstrous piercing of ears, lips, and nostrils there a displacement of the castration named as a cannibal practice. What is good to eat in the Caribbean is what is most monstrously sacrificed on the mainland: the adult male body as the object of desire.

Without ever naming the Caribs sodomites, accounts of the exploits of Columbus are further related to the reports from Central and South America, as when Columbus, for instance, describes the Caribs as having long hair like women; or when he describes the women with whom they mate as engaged in entirely masculine activities; indeed, the men and women in the first letter dispatched by Columbus are said to live on separate islands (1:16; compare *Journal,* 140, 147, 152). Gender norms are violated; Caribs are the male version of Amazons. Columbus will recommend their enslavement (1:92); he will also come to believe that where there are cannibals, there is gold. It is only left for Chanca to record that the Caribs, unlike the easily conquered Arawaks, are a more civilized nation despite their awful habit of eating human flesh (1:30). Caribs . . . or Spaniards? Peter Hulme has taught us how to answer that question, arguing that the figure of the cannibal projects Spanish rapacity and, even, Christian belief (the Eucharist): it figures Spanish divisions that have their counterpart in native populations.[25] Such an analysis helps to make sense of the claim that opens the account of the conquest of Spain written by Francisco López de Gómara, secretary to Cortés in his final years. The Spaniards, he says, not only rid the Mexicans of their practice of human sacrifice and of cannibalism; they also got them to forgo polygamy and sodomy, "for they were taught how filthy and unnatural a sin it is"; not, presumably, by regarding what López de Gómara also records: that Cortés, when he found his way back into favor with the governor of Cuba (whom he later betrayed), spent the night in bed with him.[26] Not by witnessing what Diego Méndez attests, making his final will: that when Columbus wanted to show his approval of his bravery, he did so by "embracing me and kissing me on the cheeks" (2:122; compare 2:130). These are not necessarily sodomitical practices, although as Alan Bray has argued, they are just the signs of normative friendship and power relations capable of being mobilized as evidence of criminal sexual behavior. Unstable in their signification, they need to be guarded from (mis)recognition, or to be recognized only elsewhere. But what guards the natives from (mis)reading the Spaniards, or the Spaniards from reading themselves in native bodies? Nothing but declarations of what *they are* ("they are all sodomites"), incapable of stabilization, always in danger of crossing the boundary between Spaniard and native.

To further trace these complicities, let us turn to another account of the conquest of Mexico, Bernal Díaz's *The Conquest of New Spain*; there, more than in any other account of the initial encounters of the Spaniards with the native inhabitants of the New World, sodomy comes to occupy a significant place in the narrative. Indeed, as if in confirmation of the judgment that all the natives of Mexico were sodomites, the first encounter reveals native sodomy. After a skirmish on the Yucatan, the Spaniards enter a town square and its temple; in it is not only the gold that will stand as unsurpassable until Peru is discovered, twenty years hence, Bernal Díaz claims, but also the idols that will as systematically be destroyed. The prayer-houses "contained many idols of baked clay, some with demons' faces, some with women's, and others equally ugly which seemed to represent Indians committing sodomy with one another."[27] This is as close as Bernal Díaz ever comes to seeing the sexual acts that he assumes to be endemic; it's noteworthy, moreover, that he barely can recognize, or feigns an inability to recognize, what is being represented, a self-protective gesture no doubt meant to ensure that what the natives do cannot be numbered among the practices of the Spaniards.

Accusations of sodomitical practices are not made after this initial discovery, nor does the charge appear for many pages. However, when it does recur, it retroactively assumes the position of the blanket accusation in the dispatch from Vera Cruz. Having many times described Cortés's behavior upon entering a village—his call for native practices to be abandoned and Christianity to be embraced—Bernal Díaz sums up the ritualistic nature of these encounters as "Cortés' customary exposition of our holy faith, and his injunctions to give up human sacrifice and robbery and the foul practice of sodomy" (120). Retroactively (and prospectively), the unspecified "evils" and "abominations" regularly listed as part of the routine can be assimilated to the unnameable crime of sodomy, here named explicitly for the first time as part of Cortés's litany. If, at first, sodomy is represented but not actualized in terms of native practice (do the statues that "seem" to depict sodomy indicate that that is what the Indians do?), sodomy comes to occupy a place in the ritual of possession and justification. Bernal Díaz wearies, as he tells us more than once, of describing the practice of human sacrifice, but he cannot stop himself from recounting it, or keep himself from recording the nausea of his entrance into the chief temple in Mexico City, or from confessing his fear that he might have been captured, had his heart plucked out, his limbs cut off to serve as food for the Aztecs; but he never describes anyone performing an act of sodomy.

Sodomy would thus seem to be an empty category, merely part of the ritual of Cortés's performance. Thus, while his charge to conquered villages provokes various responses (sometimes a statue of the Virgin is allowed to be placed where the idols stood, sometimes not; sometimes human sacrifice is abandoned, sometimes not), no response is ever made to the accusations of sodomy. Or, to put it another way, there is no indication that the practice (if it is a practice) is either acknowledged or abandoned. Rather than suggesting that sodomy is an empty category, then, this could indicate that sodomy is present in the text precisely by remaining unacknowledged, just as the first description of the representation of sodomy hovered on the verge of indecipherability. And this further suggests a complicity between the Spaniards and those whom they are condemning. Granted that sodomy comes to be the nonspecific "evil" of the natives, it's thus worth asking further what causes it to be named at the moment it is.

Sodomy is named when Cortés addresses the inhabitants of Cingapacinga; this occurs in the context of his pacification of the town of Cempoala, his making of an alliance with the "fat cacique" who rules that town. This is an alliance that will be of inestimable value in his conquest of the Aztecs, since the Cempoalans will be among those natives who fight beside the Spaniards to throw off Aztec oppression. Cingapacinga also joins Cortés; moreover, Cortés forges an alliance between the two towns. It is upon first meeting men from Cempoala that Cortés learns "that Montezuma had opponents and enemies, which greatly delighted him" (99); in Bernal Díaz, it is the men from Cempoala who look the way all men are said to look in the so-called first letter of Cortés: in Bernal Díaz, it is the men from Cempoala that have too many holes in their bodies: "The men had great holes in their lower lips, in which some carried stone disks spotted with blue, and others thin sheets of gold. They also had great holes in their ears, in which they had inserted disks of stone or gold" (98). In this text, these men are exemplary, not because they are like all Mexicans. Rather, they are declared not to be like them: their language is different, and they are unwillingly subservient to Montezuma, supplying bodies for sacrifice. For Cortés, these men with holes in their bodies are exemplary because it is with them that he can best succeed in representing himself as their liberator from Aztec oppression. If these men "are" sodomites (it is in addressing them that the term is used), sodomy would seem to name (as a supposed sexual practice) a political availability—to Cortés, the availability that the first letter masks by deploring as improper the horrific local customs; the horror now more clearly mirrors Spanish designs upon their bodies.

Hence, it requires (mis)recognition. Having used the term *sodomy* in addressing the natives of Cingapacinga, Cortés deploys it a page later, as he speaks to the Cempoalans and clarifies the terms of his proposed alliance with them, providing terms that will make proper what was improper:

> He said, however, that before we could accept the ladies and become their brothers, they would have to abandon their idols which they mistakenly believed in and worshipped, and sacrifice no more souls to them; and that when he saw those cursed things thrown down and the sacrifices at an end, our bonds of brotherhood would be very much firmer. The girls, he added, must become Christians before we could receive them, and the people must give up sodomy, for they had boys dressed as women who practised that accursed vice for profit. (121–22)

The conversion of the girls offered to the Spaniards will be a repeated condition in the text: to legitimize illegitimate sexual practices (that is, to make the Indian women acceptable mistresses), the Cempoalans must become Christian. The conditions of what is called "brotherhood" are spelled out only here. The men must give up sodomy, here specified (as nowhere else in the text) as transvestite prostitution. If sodomites "are" men with too many holes in their bodies—if sodomites "are" men who behave like women—the conditions for alliance produce "proper" men and women, "brothers" and pious women. (The conversion to Christianity is used to make it seem as if enslavement or prostitution could not enter into the question; converted, the native women are in the same position as Spanish women.) As if to clarify what giving up sodomy means, the term is specified again, as the idols in the temple at Cempoala are destroyed; the priests in charge of them are described, men with long hair, down to their waists and further, "so clotted and matted with blood that it could not be pulled apart. . . . Their ears were cut to pieces as a sacrifice, and they smelt of sulphur. But they also smelt of something worse: of decaying flesh. As they told us, and we afterwards found out for ourselves, these *papas* were the sons of chiefs, and had no wives, but indulged in the foul practice of sodomy" (124). The long hair and mutilated ears perhaps feminize the priests' bodies in ways congruent with the cross-dressers (there is no reason to assume that the term *sodomy* refers to the same people in these two descriptions), but here the stench of human sacrifice is attached to sodomy; what is sacrificed in these men without wives who "indulged in the foul practice of sodomy" is the proper masculinity (and femininity) prescribed by Cortés.

A series of substitutions mark Bernal Díaz's text: the Virgin for the idols; Christian women for native mistresses; brothers for sodomites. Brotherhood is the topic of Cortés's sermon to Montezuma:

> The favour he now begged of the great Montezuma was that he should listen to the words he now wished to speak. Then he very carefully expounded the creation of the world, how we are all brothers, the children of one mother and father called Adam and

Eve; and how such a brother as our great Emperor, grieving for the perdition of so many souls as their idols were leading to hell, where they burnt in living flame, had sent us to tell him this, so that he might put a stop to it, and so that they might give up the worship of idols and make no more human sacrifices—for all men are brothers—and commit no more robbery or sodomy. (222)

Montezuma refuses to give up his religion, but, as a token of his embrace of brotherhood, he registers his awareness that Cortés and his followers are not gods, but men, and that he too is no god: "my body is made of flesh and blood like yours" (224). Countering any anxiety this fleshly brotherhood might arouse, Bernal Díaz assures his readers that Montezuma "was quite free from sodomy" (225), though suspicions lingered that he dined on the flesh of young boys. Cannibalism, robbery, sodomy: one is always capable of being transformed into the other, but "brotherhood" in this text is meant to replace sodomy as the proper way for men to come in proximity with the bodies of other men. Not many pages later, Cortés gives Montezuma "his own young page Orteguilla" (231):

> Cortés threw his arms round the prince and embraced him, saying: "How right I am, Lord Montezuma, to love you as dearly as I love myself!" Then Montezuma asked Cortés that the page called Orteguilla, who already knew the language, might attend him, and this was of great benefit both to him and to us. For from this page, of whom he asked many questions, Montezuma learnt a great deal about Spain, and we learnt what his captains said to him. So useful was Orteguilla to the prince that he became quite fond of him. (250)

The page—messenger, ambassador, translator, go-between, a male Doña Marina—comes between Cortés and Montezuma; on his body their love is transported. This is the socially acceptable practice that replaces sodomy in the text—the Spanish equivalent for native practices—the consuming of the flesh of young boys, treating boys as women.

The position that Orteguilla occupies is not merely parallel (and thus identical) to that held by Doña Marina, Cortés's mistress and translator, it is also the position that Cortés himself has in Díaz's text. For throughout *he* is addressed *by the natives* as "Malinche," the name that is also Doña Marina's. "They called

Cortés Malinche, and I shall call him by this name henceforth in recording any conversations he had with Indians . . . The reason why he received this name was that Doña Marina was always with him, especially when he was visited by ambassadors or *Caciques*, and she always spoke to them in the Mexican language. So they gave Cortés the name of 'Marina's Captain', which was shortened to Malinche" (172). Bernal Díaz's explanation is hardly coherent—*Malinche* is a Hispanicization of her native name, and does not have the meaning claimed for it. Has Bernal Díaz mistaken native addresses to Doña Marina as directed to Cortés? Has she, by speaking for him, become him, and he her? Bernal Díaz praises Malinche's "manly valour" (153) and often commends her persuasive force. Hers . . . or his? Considering the opprobrium that surrounds La Malinche in later Mexican thought (she represents, as Octavio Paz comments, an availability to exploitation and the malignancy of the conquered turncoat),[28] as the embodiment of the feminine principle against which macho masculinity defends, it is extraordinary to find her position taken by Cortés, her name his. The only parallel to this extraordinary moment might be found in the highly self-conscious political mobilization of La Malinche by Chicana lesbian feminists as a protest against the kinds of gender opposition that the figure has hitherto served. Clearly, the slippage in Bernal Díaz does not have this purpose. Nonetheless, despite itself, it registers a movement across gender, an embrace of everything the text consciously despises.

For if the name Malinche floats between Cortés and his translator/companion/conquest, it occupies the position of Cortés's love, the page boy who moves between him and Montezuma, "always telling Montezuma things that he wanted to know" (253)—for instance, by revealing Cortés's duplicity (260); Orteguilla is the sole Spaniard present when Montezuma speaks with the caciques who are fomenting rebellion against him and his policies of accommodation (264), and it is thanks to Orteguilla that the Spaniards know it; but it is Orteguilla who serves as the trusted messenger from Montezuma to Cortés (278) when "brotherhood" begins to fail. The last we see of Orteguilla, he is weeping (280). A page later, Alvarado has massacred the Aztecs in the temple; soon,

Cortés will be weeping over the corpse of Montezuma (294). Whose tears are these?

"They are all sodomites": cross-dressers, robbers, practitioners of human sacrifice, mutilators, idol worshippers. Multiple, incoherent, overlapping, discontinuous designations. For others. For brothers.

~

Thus far, I've been writing about these colonial texts as if one could speak of them in terms of oppositions: Spaniards, on the one hand, Indians on the other. This is useful in a discussion of sodomy in the New World only insofar as sodomy comes to occupy a position that throws those oppositions into question. For unlike other supposed native practices—cannibalism or human sacrifice, most notably—sodomy crosses the dividing line. False religion can be converted into true religion, the Virgin can replace the "idol," the wafer the actual body, but when brotherhood or shared beds replace sodomy, the act has not changed, but only what it is called. If sodomy functions as the unspeakable, the excessive, it is precisely because of this fundamental categorical violation (what can't be said is the complicity between the excoriated practices of the Indians and the normative ones of the Spaniards). The page boy who is transferred from Cortés to Montezuma, like the captive women in Columbus who serve as native informants about the practices of the Caribs (2:30, 32, 38, 40), assume the positions of go-betweens; they cross the dividing line. Insofar as boys or women do this, they assume a normative position that need not raise the specter of a European sodomy (though it is just that connection that makes cannibalism intelligible to Chanca). But if an adult male were to be in this place, what then?

The remarkable relation that Alvar Núñez Cabeza de Vaca wrote can begin to answer this question.[29] In 1527, he went to Florida, second in command under Pánfilo de Narváez; the attempted conquest was an utter failure, and of the four hundred men who went, only four returned, some ten years later, and after having wandered through the American Southwest, eventually to arrive in western Mexico and among Spaniards once again.

Cabeza de Vaca's relation, addressed to the king, and written after his return to Spain, describes those ten years, often spent with no fellow Europeans, but living for a two-year stretch, as he reports, "alone among the Indians and naked like them" (67). His is not, however, an account of going native, or becoming one with the Indians—"naked like them" also implies difference; yet it is not a difference that preserves unviolated a Spanish identity. Indeed, there is no such singular thing, and the point is made succinctly by recalling that the man under whom Cabeza de Vaca served was the opponent whom Cortés defeated in Mexico. For if Cortés capitalized upon the divisions among the inhabitants of Mexico, he also faced Spanish division. Cabeza de Vaca came back to Spain with nothing—no gold, no conquests—with nothing but a "relation . . . offered Your Majesty for truth." "I beg," he concludes the prefatory letter to Charles V, "that it may be received as homage, since it is the most one could bring who returned thence naked" (26). What is the naked truth about a text written by one who lived "alone among the Indians and naked like them"?

The answer to the question, as I've begun to suggest, involves crossing the line between oppositional identity (Spaniard vs. Indian) and the possibility of a simple or absolute identification (Spaniard = Indian), and this not only because of Spanish resistance to such assimilation (although there are examples to be found)[30] but also because of Indian refusals. While it would falsely regularize Cabeza de Vaca's relation to plot it as moving from the first of these poles towards the second, in broad terms one can, keeping in mind that the narrative is not simply a straightforward one. (Cabeza de Vaca lived with the Indians sometimes in a position of prestige and power but as often as a slave; he insists that he never lost his desire to return to Spain, and his later career as a colonial administrator would seem to bear out what may nonetheless be to some degree a retrospective construction.) Thus, he begins as loyal second to his governor; but soon he is refusing commands, and eventually he is abandoned, as Narváez floats off on a barge (to his destruction), leaving Cabeza de Vaca to his uncertain fate. The Spaniards are literally divided, but what also slips away (but not entirely) is the basis for Spanish identity, at least one normative component of it:

> I yelled to him to throw me a rope so we could stay with him. He called back that if he were to do what he hoped that night, he must not further sap his men's strength. I said that since we were too feeble to carry out his orders to follow him, he must tell me how he would that I should act. He replied that it was no longer a time when one should command another; that each must do as he thought best to save himself; that that was what he was doing now. So saying, he pulled away in his barge. (53)

Part of Cabeza de Vaca's identity disappears at this moment, as the chain of command, and the expectations of hierarchical order dissolve. But, at the same moment, Narváez constitutes Cabeza de Vaca as his equal (in this unequal situation—Narváez has the stronger men on his barge, and he has the greater chance of survival); he is left on his own, in command of a situation that one cannot command. Yet the ideal of individual mastery, so central to Spanish identity, is not abandoned. Indeed, it is part of Cabeza de Vaca's equipment for survival and he never gives it up; Cabeza de Vaca's relation is laced with advice on how properly to win the territories through which he wanders, naked, often starving, and, for several periods, serving as a slave to various Indian tribes, who, at various moments, seemingly capriciously, kill Spaniards for their sport.

Yet, their behavior also is reunderstood. Initially, after the landing on Galveston Island that marks the end of their voyage on makeshift barges and the beginning of the long trek overland, captured by Indians, those among the Spaniards who had been to New Spain before predict "that the Indians would sacrifice us to their idols," and the ragged crew spend the night waiting for "the hour they should make us victims" (58). That is not what happens. Instead, they are compelled to become medicine men. "They insisted we should do this . . . and be of some use to them. We scoffed at their cures and at the idea we knew how to heal. But they withheld food from us until we complied" (64). As Cabeza de Vaca finally reports, "in the 2,000 leagues we sojourned by land

and sea . . . we found no sacrifices and no idolatry" (133). Nor any native cannibalism. But on Galveston Island, the Spaniards ate each other. "The Indians were so shocked at this cannibalism that, if they had seen it sometime earlier, they surely would have killed every one of us" (60). Does Cabeza de Vaca know this because that's what Spaniards would do faced with Indian cannibalism or because these Indians genuinely would find such an act unthinkable and bestial? These Indians often go for long stretches with scarcely any food; and according to Cabeza de Vaca, in their extremity they do not do what the Spaniards do. Of course, what the Spaniards do here is what they claim elsewhere Indians always do. At this very moment of slipping into the stereotypical Indian identity of cannibal, Cabeza de Vaca also refuses to condemn Spanish practice as an Indian slippage. This is no instance of Spaniards becoming Indians, since all Indians are not the same in this text; but it is also not an instance of Spaniards not being Spaniards either, although Spaniard and cannibal are usually antithetical and supposedly inviolable categories.

What anyone is, what one knows, always is in question in this text. Cabeza de Vaca begins ignorant of Indian languages; by the end of his journey, he can speak six and is aware of countless others and of "a thousand dialectical differences" (120). In the very paragraphs in which he first records becoming a shaman (a practice at which he becomes increasingly, if intermittently, proficient, and which accrues to him great powers, even the ability to raise someone supposed dead [88]), he also mentions that he has "tried" the native practice of sucking and cauterizing wounds, "with good results" (64), he adds. So he becomes a shaman, adding to the native practice of sucking, burning, and blowing, only the recital of the Pater Noster and Ave Maria. In what does Cabeza de Vaca believe—the native practice into which he enters, or the prayers that he recites? There is no simple answer to this question, nor later when, preaching to the Indians, he tells them that the god they pray to is the same as the one he calls Dios (132); who has converted whom? A partial answer to such questions lies in realizing the position that Cabeza de Vaca has been compelled to take up.

The shaman is a go-between. It is precisely as an outsider that he is supposed to have extraordinary powers; it is because Cabeza de Vaca is not like the Indians, not one of them, that he is made to play the part. Moreover, it is not simply a religious or medical role; as Cabeza de Vaca travels from village to village, he is the site of exchanges, sometimes, it seems to him, forced, sometimes voluntary. He moves from group to group; those with whom he travels expect or extort gifts from those villages at which they arrive; depleted villagers then follow him on to the next place, where the pattern is repeated, this time to the benefit of those who lost in the prior round of exchanges. Each time, the visited village hands over their most valuable goods to Cabeza de Vaca; and each time he, in turn, hands them over to the group with whom he is traveling, who, in turn, feed and reward him. Cabeza de Vaca's "cures" also are economic. The Spaniard who began his journey with the usual trinkets and things of no value to give in exchange for expected food and hoped-for treasure instead is inserted in a circuit of native exchanges that serve to make shifting and fragile alliances among peoples often at war and on the brink of starvation. Cabeza de Vaca's nomadic life becomes part of a native nomadism, but not identical to it. The natives, as much as he, have an investment in his not becoming one of them; for it is thanks to his separateness that he also can serve them.

Falling ill, Cabeza de Vaca's shamanistic abilities fade (his body shows that he is not as separate as he seemed to be); he is enslaved, and escapes, turning to the life of a wandering merchant, bartering valued inland products for coastal ones (66–67), recognizing and capitalizing upon genuine native needs and economies. "Wherever I went, the Indians treated me honorably and gave me food, because they liked my commodities" (67). Once again, he serves as a go-between for tribes unable to trade with each other because of their "incessant hostilities" (66). Working for them, he never abandons his goal—"an eventual road out" (67); but even for them, well-known as he becomes, he remains definitionally not one of them; a neutral. No one else can do this in Cabeza de Vaca's text—except women: "women can deal as neutrals anywhere, even during war" (112). They appear in this text as go-betweens, messengers, traders (96, 101, 105), although more often—in the ethnographical descriptions, as opposed to the narratives—in highly determinate gender-inscribed positions as mothers, wives, and performers of "female" labor. We need to ponder the place of native women in Cabeza de Vaca's text, and the relation between his place and theirs.

Women are not all the same in this text; besides the discrepancies between the appearance of women in the narrative as opposed to the several ethnographic sections, the ethnographies mark local differences—though these, we may come to see, are dialectical variants upon a single conception of women. What's remarkable (not that Cabeza de Vaca ever remarks this) are the complex trajectories of identification across gender that take place. Recording the life of the Malhado, for instance, he says that the women "toil incessantly" (61), but also are able to move freely from parental home to the home of their husband and his family: "The woman, however, is free to fraternize with the parents and relatives of her husband" (62). Cabeza de Vaca also toils incessantly, of course, and he too moves freely where others cannot. The Malhado are described as a society in which the "people love their offspring more than any in the world and treat them very mildly" (61); the woman's role seems to guarantee this peace between generations who otherwise are separated by marriage. Nothing like this is the case among the Mariamnes, however. There, daughters are fed to dogs rather than allowed to be married to enemies—or to kin: "they said that marrying relatives would be a disgusting thing; it was far better to kill them than give them to either kin or foe" (78). But males fare no better: "Couples kill their own male children and buy those of strangers" (79). Wives are likewise bought, and marriages last for only a short time. The difference between these groups lies in the precariousness of Mariamne life; they live surrounded by enemies and cannot afford to make alliances or marriages, nor do they have the luxury to invest in the family. Nor does Cabeza de Vaca ever enter into any such regularized relation. (Indeed, it is not clear whether he was married when he sailed to Florida, although late in his life, in disgrace and sent back, captive, to Spain, it was his wife's money that bailed him out.)

Or take the case of the Yguaces, among whom famine prevails (Cabeza de Vaca's case too for long stretches of his narrative), and who also show little love for children. "The men bear no burdens. Anything of weight is borne by women and old men, the people least esteemed" (79). These women workers, like the Malhado, are root diggers. Enslaved, this is Cabeza de Vaca's position too: "My life had become unbearable. In addition to much other work, I had to grub roots in the water or from underground in the canebreaks" (66). The valuable go-between can also, in an instant, be the unvalued one, like the old men or women, who work for the "real" men. The women who can go anywhere can also be the cause of war (96). These go-betweens go between men—that is the underlying pattern beneath these local variations. But if this defines the positions of women in this text, is it also the position of Cabeza de Vaca? Where is he in relation to men? Indeed, what are the men doing while the women work?

One of Cabeza de Vaca's more detailed ethnographies of the plains tribes gives this picture: the men are smoking peyote, drinking a special brew; and when the drink is ready, the women must stand motionless; when the tea is brewing, it must be kept covered, for if a woman passes by while it is being made or being drunk, it will be spoiled. "Should a woman make a motion, they dishonor her, beat her with sticks, and in great vexation throw out the liquor that is prepared" and vomit what has already been consumed (99). These Indians, the Aguanes, elsewhere receive high marks from Cabeza de Vaca, who praises them for the acuteness of their relation to their senses, keener than those of "any in the world. . . . I have wanted to say this much, not merely to indulge the curiosity of humans about each other, but to impart a knowledge of usages and artifices which would be of value to those who might sometimes in the future find themselves among these people" (97). And, included in this knowledge is an account of their warfare, and how they can be defeated by Spanish infantry. Cabeza de Vaca has found himself "among these people" (but where? enjoying male leisure or female labor? on which side of the sharp divide sketched in the fear of female pollution and male separateness?); in that euphemistic phrase, which does not quite locate him, although at the moment of writing it serves to separate him from those he has been among, he can also project other Spaniards who will find themselves—as Spanish conquistadores—among these people too.

If this, like other moments of admiring description, quickly becomes a fantasy of mastery, an attempted solidification projected into a future when he will regain his full Spanish conquistador identity, it is not quite borne out when Cabeza de Vaca finally does meet up again with Spanish conquerors. Rather, he excoriates them for their slave-trading and for conquests that devastated the native Mexican populations and rendered the landscape bare and defiled. Attempting to stop his "fellow" Spaniards from such depredations, and to ensure Indian cooperation for kinder treatment (kinder conquests are what Cabeza de Vaca advocates, telling the king that "to bring all these peoples to Christianity and subjection to Your Imperial Majesty, they must be won by kindness, the only certain way" [123]), he assures the Indians that he is one of the Spaniards, and thus can guarantee their behavior. The Indians are not convinced when his fellow Spaniards insist that Cabeza de Vaca is one of them: "They replied that the Christians lied. We had come from the sunrise, they from the sunset; we healed the sick, they killed the sound; we came naked and barefoot, they clothed, horsed, and lanced; we coveted nothing but gave whatever we were given, while they robbed whomever they found and bestowed nothing on anyone" (128). "We" are Cabeza de Vaca and his three fellow "Christians"; "they" are "the Christians." The Indians speaking do not see a single Spanish identity. But they do not see Cabeza de Vaca as one of them either. And as he records their words, he speaks as them—as if "the Christians" were not a category that included him, even as he declares that he is one with them. "To the last I could not convince the Indians that we were of the same people as the Christian slavers" (128). But can he convince himself? When he arrives at the governor's residence, his response to the governor's hospitality suggests not: "At Compostella the Governor received us graciously and outfitted us from his wardrobe. I could not stand to wear any clothes for some time, or to sleep anywhere but on the bare floor" (134). If Cabeza de Vaca never ceases to believe that he is a Spaniard, has he, in the very nakedness of his body, become an Indian? Or something else, a go-between that cannot inhabit either body fully?

But what body has he come to have? Here we can return to some observations left suspended above—about the gendered identity of the go-between position. For if the go-between is definitionally the woman (or, at least, not the native adult male), the naked body is a male prerogative. In clinging to his undressed state, Cabeza de Vaca also registers on his body, in his bodily response to the offer of Spanish civilization, his identity with the native male body, the attempt to secure his body against the gender transformation that marks his position as go-between. The desire to remain naked, which could be read as some zero degree of nature or even as a sign that despite himself Cabeza de Vaca has come to identify fully with those among whom he lived, naked like them, is itself a differential sign of gendered identity, as he records it; it is only the adult male body that is uncovered. "The inhabitants of all these parts [in Galveston and its vicinity] go naked, except that the women cover some part of their persons with a wool that grows on trees, and damsels dress in deerskin" (63). Is this naked adult man, acting as shaman and merchant, go-between and neutral, root digger and burden carrier, any determinate gender? Is the very movement across genders a sign that Cabeza de Vaca has come to occupy the position that other texts would mark as that of the sodomite? The word does not appear in the text. But the practice is named in its familiar roundabout way. The Yguaces, who do not love their children, have in their midst some "accustomed to sin against nature" (79).

As this discussion of Cabeza de Vaca's unstable identity has aimed to suggest, what it calls into question again and again is the "nature" upon which it rests, its naked truth. For Cabeza de Vaca's fractured and divided identity is striated by oppositions that it never fully inhabits. The axes of identification and difference are not separated by the normative Spanish/Indian opposition; nor is the absoluteness of gender difference, which Cabeza de Vaca seems to endorse as he writes his ethnographies, borne on his naked and burdened body.

Just after the description of the plains Indians, with their men and women tensely opposed, Cabeza de Vaca records once again the existence of the "diabolical practice," and this time in sufficient detail so that one could suspect that the identity of the "sodomite" haunts the identity that Cabeza de Vaca inhabits; the practice involves "a man living with a eunuch. Eunuchs go partly dressed, like women, and perform women's duties, but use the bow and carry very heavy loads. We saw many thus mutilated. They are more muscular and taller than other men and can lift tremendous weight" (100). The so-called "eunuch" refuses the stabilization of gender boundaries; feminine in dress and work, masculine in musculature and size, bearer of the bow and the basket. "Mutilated," in this description, would seem to set these male bodies apart; yet, at several points in the text, it is a feature of the normative naked male body. The Capoques and Han on Galveston Island, for instance, "bore through one of their nipples, some both, and insert a joint of cane two and a half palms long by two fingers thick"; they "also bore their lower lip and wear a piece of cane in it half a finger in diameter" (61). The Yguaces, also "have a nipple and a lip bored" (79). Is Cabeza de Vaca's body secure against such representations? "I have already said that we went naked through all this country. . . . The sun and air raised great, painful sores on our chests and shoulders, and our heavy loads caused the cords to cut our arms. . . . Blood flowed from us in many places where the thorns and shrubs tore our flesh" (92).

Cabeza de Vaca's sole consolation at this moment is to think of the bleeding and lacerated body of Christ. But he might have thought too of the story he had told just before, of Indians who say they have been visited by *Mala Cosa.* "He had a beard. . . . A blazing brand would suddenly shine at the door as he rushed in and seized whom he chose, deeply gashing him in the side" (90), violating the entrails, slashing arms, but then healing the wounds. Whose body is this? Bearded and armed, it appears to be a Spaniard's. Wounding and healing, it is that of Cabeza de Vaca as shaman, cutting and closing the wound. "They said that frequently . . . he appeared in their midst, sometimes in the dress of a woman, at other times in that of a man." Cabeza de Vaca scoffs at this superstition, assures them that the Bad Thing is the devil—and, presumably, that the Indians are talking about a diabolical practice. The Indians display their wounded bodies to vouch for the truth of what they tell (in which a Spaniard Bad Thing is responsible for wounding and healing them, producing their scarred bodies; in which the Spaniard is in the position of the cross-dressed man, the man who goes between the categories of gender). The wounded body is the point of identification between Cabeza de Vaca and them—and between adult males and the mutilated bodies of the "eunuchs."

"Eunuch," in the most recent translation, has decided something about these men that other translators are more reticent about—and also more hysterical. A 1907 translation has Cabeza de Vaca observing the horrible practice of "a man living with another"—a more neutral identification in which the "eunuch" has not put in an appearance that differentiates one man from another and has decided that that difference is registered as a physical one. A qualifying clause follows, one that attempts to do what "eunuch" does: "one of those who are emasculate and impotent. These go habited like women."[31] Nonetheless those called "emasculate" are not quite identical to those called "eunuchs"; indeed, whether these men have been castrated is further thrown into doubt in a 1922 translation. This reports the practice of "a man married to another" and goes on to describe these: "Such are impotent and womanish beings, who dress like women. . . . Among these Indians we saw many of them."[32] Are "womanish beings" castrated men? The 1922 translation is close to the first Englishing of the text in the 1613 *Purchas His Pilgrimes*, which raises similar questions:

> In the time that I continued among them, I saw a most brutish and beastly custome, to wit, a man who was married to another, and

> these be certaine effeminate and impotent men, who goe cloathed and attired like women, and performe the office of a woman; they carry no Bowes, but beare very great and waightie burdens: and among them we saw many such effeminate persons, as I have said, and they are of greater lims and taller then the other men.[33]

The translations boggle at the gendered being of what the most recent translator calls the "eunuch"; is what is seen two biologically identical men differentiated by what they wear or do, or does genital mutilation explain and differentiate them? Are "effeminate" men "emasculate" men? The earliest translation is least committed to a physical explanation, but even as it stacks its cards in producing the effeminate man who cannot carry the male bow, it also never ceases calling the effeminate man a man. If it, like the 1922 translation, heterosexualizes the relationship between men as a marriage—and if the "office of a woman" reads as a sexual arrangement as much as it indicates a sphere of female labor—it has not quite produced a body that can be assimilated to a female body along the route of castration assumed in the most recent translation as the "explanation" of male/male sexual behavior.

These questions of translation are not resolvable ones,[34] for no accurate translation will simply deliver what Cabeza de Vaca saw—what the naked truth was—of these male/female plains Indians, although one may venture the guess that the arrangements described are related to modes of life least served by the production of children or the exogamous practices of marriage, not that such explanations will ever serve as a full account of the "cause" of the practice of men living with and sleeping with each other, as even a sixteenth-century Spaniard or Englishman well might know, if never admit. Cabeza de Vaca never identifies himself with these dressed (therefore female, therefore cross-dressed) bodies—his naked body guards against a full identification, though his go-between status and his wounds keep nudging his body into "female" and "emasculate" positions (so that even naked he is not fully a man among the Indians, and naked among the Spaniards, he is not fully a Spaniard). Such is the naked truth of this endlessly nonidentical text, anything but "impotent" even as—precisely because—it destabilizes the powerful differential markers of national, racial, and sex/gender identity that colonial texts seek to deliver.

~

As an afterword to this consideration of Cabeza de Vaca, the relation written by Diego de Landa might be considered.[35] On the face of it, this might seem an odd juxtaposition. Landa was a Franciscan, head of the order in the Yucatan, where he ruthlessly tortured over four thousand natives accused of backsliding into idolatry (official reports admitted the death of 158 of these)[36] and commanded an auto-da-fé in which, along with the humiliation of the people, virtually all of the holy books of the Mayans were burned ("We found a great number of books . . . , and since they contained nothing but superstitions and falsehoods of the devil we burned them all, which they took most grievously, and which gave them great pain" [82]). Called back to Spain after these events of 1562, Landa was exonerated, and after the death of the Bishop of Yucatan in 1571, he returned in his place. During these years in Spain, Landa wrote his relation, and it is, as Inga Clendinnen puts it, an "odd" text. As she notes, it barely mentions the auto-da-fé or his own role in instituting it ("the friars held an Inquisition," the text laconically reads [30]), omits all mention of torture or of the reasons for it (after the auto-da-fé, Landa extracted confessions of human sacrifice and even of crucifixions, yet none of this "information" appears in the relation); when it mentions a native informant, it omits telling that Landa has his body exhumed and burned. Clendinnen reads these omissions as signs of a guilty text which has "repressed" (125) all the evidence Landa had produced as a way to maintain his authority. This allows Landa to recreate Yucatan before the Inquisition, an account that Clendinnen calls nostalgic, "tranquil" (118), and "tender" (119). It is here, of course, that the comparison with Cabeza de Vaca proves relevant. Since Landa has virtually effaced his brutal part in the destruction of Mayan civilization, what his text offers is an ethnography (the most detailed extant) that preserves an otherwise inaccessible past. More than that, there are indications throughout it of Landa's engagement with the Mayans (he has tasted their food, been made privy to highly esoteric information) and with the Yucatan (the stony landscape, in his descriptions, blossoms with flora and fauna summoned up in warm and appreciative terms). In short, if we didn't know what Landa did, his text would, like Cabeza de Vaca's, suggest someone who had crossed over, gone beyond his Spanish identity to assume some in-between status.

Clendinnen chooses to read the repressed and guilty text in that way, and to celebrate it. (She also believes that the confessions Landa extracted only exaggerated the extent of the continuation of native practices of human sacrifice, and she thinks it likely that crucifixions also were held, not in mockery of Christianity but as part of the way in which the Mayans assimilated the imposed religion—certainly one of the most interesting of her arguments is that one form of Mayan resistance to the Spaniards lay in such accommodations of Spanish beliefs and practices to Mayan ones, a crossing in the opposite direction from the one I have been pursuing here.) For Clendinnen the text "confesses" the falsity of what was done in 1562 and reveals a truth despite itself—the truth of Landa's engagement in what he attempted violently to efface, and then lovingly recreated. (For her, the behavior is that of a disappointed father discovering that his supposedly docile children have been harboring revenge [113], an oedipal scenario.) Thus, although her account tells us what Landa's does not, it also takes his relation as if what it omits has nothing to do with what it produces. Landa's "great *Relacion* . . . steeped in pride and nostalgia" (69) "suggests that Landa, like so many other great travellers, saw the small lost world of Yucatan the more vividly for being distanced from it, and sought to record its clear bright shapes before they were dimmed by age and failing memory" (118). Thus Clendinnen herself effaces the fact that the loss and distance upon which the relation rests were Landa's violent doing. Calling the man and his text "great" will not settle the unsettling complicity between its valuable knowledge and its violent base.

By bringing the torture and burning and the book into relation with each other, we can resist the notion that some easy or easily acceptable crossing is represented by Landa. Moreover, the very extremity of his case can also reflect upon the precariousness of the go-between status of Cabeza de Vaca, a middle without a secure foundation, a crossing secured only contradictorily. The even less supportable contradictions in Landa point to the sustaining ones in Cabeza de Vaca, and suggest how close to crisis his text is too. In the case of Cabeza de Vaca, as I have argued, the crisis lies in the proximity of his identity to that of the (cross-)dressed plains Indians. Rather than reading Landa's as simply a text of omission/repression, can we locate the points of crossing that might bring together the violent act of repudiation and the written restoral of the destroyed civilization? I think we can—not, I hasten to add, in order to compose these responses and to stabilize them, but to suggest the locus from which these opposing and mutually canceling desires arise.

Persistent idol worship, human sacrifice, mock crucifixions: these are the accusations leveled by Landa in 1562. His relation mentions the first two, but only as part of a Mayan past—a past that Landa hopes to have made past by his Inquisition. Yet, they are also made present in his writing, anything but effaced. Why preserve them? Perhaps because the Mayans had their own ceremonies of baptism, in which they believed "they acquired a predisposition to good conduct and habits" (43); because "the Yucataneans naturally knew when they had done wrong, . . . believed that death, disease and torments would come on them because of evil-doing and sin, and thus had the custom of confessing to their priests" (45); because they held their temples and idols "in as great veneration as we have in our pilgrimages to Jerusalem and Rome" (46); indeed, because "as regards the images, they knew perfectly that they were made by human hands, perishable, and not divine; but they honored them because of what they represented" (47). Landa's text is one in which his identity appears to have been effaced—there is scarcely an autobiographical "I" to be found in it; but is there not a perilous identification between Mayan idolatry and Christianity, the locus of Landa's identity, the justifying site of his Inquisition, but also of his conversion activity? Does not conversion rest upon the supposition of an identification? Is that not what is supposedly achieved, as in this instance: "They desire many children, and she who lacks them invokes their idols with gifts and prayers; and today they pray to God for them" (55). Indeed, don't ethnographies—especially those like Landa's deemed especially valuable—depend upon identification too, the bedrock belief of anthropology being of course that beneath all local differences lies the human or, as the discipline calls itself, hardly uncontentiously, the logos of man?

Once, in his relation, Landa pauses to pray, as he ponders the horrors of Mayan religion, above all, bloodletting, scarification, self-mutilation, profound acts of self-mortification ("fasts and continence" [91]), and human sacrifice. "From all such miseries may the merciful Lord see fit to free us forever," Landa writes, continuing to define his deity as "He who saw fit to sacrifice himself to the Father, on the cross for all men" (91). Then the prayer follows, begging for the strength to go on combating these practices, enjoining his fellow Franciscans to be at least as strenuous in their zeal as the Mayan priests were in theirs: "How much more burdensome were their fasts than yours, and how long and many; how much longer were their vigils and their prayers than those you give, how much more serious and careful they were of the affairs of their office than you are of yours; with how much more zeal than you they understood how to teach their pestiferous doctrines" (93). "Give me grace to leave the house of my sensuality and the kingdom of my vices and sins," Landa prays (92); "live in cleanness," with "the cleanness of an angel rather than of a man," Landa enjoins his coreligionists. Live the exemplary sacrifice of the Son—or of the Mayan priests and their victims. If there is, as Clendinnen suggests, an oedipal dimension in Landa's violent repudiation of his Mayan children, it goes back to his faith, to his identification with Father and Son, riven and identified by sacrifice—and that identification also joins him to the inhabitants of the Yucatan, to their human sacrifices and their mock crucifixions, and to the Yucatan itself, flowering in the hard stones.

And to their "cleanness." Remarking, as he does in a number of instances, the separation of male and female spheres in Mayan life and religion (only the blood of men is required in the mutilations and sacrifices), Landa pauses over the fact that young men lived with each other in the years between childhood and marriage. "And since I have heard it said that in other parts of the Indies they were guilty of unnatural offenses in these houses, I have not learned of their doing this in this country, nor do I believe they did so" (52).[37] What is this belief based upon? That, as Clendinnen writes, "with the Indians of Yucatan [Landa] had a special relationship," that "it is possible that his friendship with the old men who were his informants were among the most emotionally rewarding of his life" (123); and not just with old men—one of the informants was Gaspar Antonio Chi, "the Indian brought up from childhood by the friars (and if we are to believe one biographer, by Landa himself)" (119). Special relationships, friendships, surrogate father and son; are these euphemized versions of the unspeakable crime?

It is spoken one other time in Landa's relation, just after one of several passages on the remarkable calendrical and mathematical knowledge of the Mayans (they had a "calendar, by which they regulated their festivals, their counting and contracts as business, as we do ours" [68]—another moment of identification), as he enjoins his fellow believers in the struggle already won, he claims, by missionaries to Asia and Africa: "All of this God already had permitted for us, as we stand, were it not that his Church cannot pass, neither that which is said concerning her: *Nisi Dominus reliquisset semen, sicut Sodoma fuissemus*" (69). "Except the Lord of Sabaoth had left us a seed, we had been as Sodom" (Rom. 9:29, citing Isa. 1:9). The priests are the chosen seed, sown against the sterility of Sodom. But the Mayans are not sodomites; indeed, their bloodlettings ensured the sowing of seed.

> At other times they practised a filthy and grievous sacrifice [that is, worse than the cutting of ears or the perforations of cheeks and lips]. . . . Each made a pierced hole through the member, across from side to side, and then passed through as great a quantity of cord as they could stand; and thus all together fastened and strung together, they anointed the statue of the demon with the collected blood. The one able to endure the most was considered most valiant, and their sons of tender age began to accustom themselves to this suffering; it is frightful to see how much they were dedicated to this practice. (47–48)

Thus were Mayan men literally bound to each other, by ropes joining penis to penis, blood poured out in sacrificial insemination. Such was the literalization, at once filthy and yet clean (they are not sodomites), so did they chastise their unruly members, thus did they practice, boys together living apart. In the final paragraphs of his relation, Landa takes up some common misrepresentations of the Mayans: were they circumsized? Not at all—penis-incised. Had they ever heard of the crucifixion before the Spanish arrived, were crosses a native belief? Not at all, Mayan crosses appeared only after the first Spaniards came, "some small party" that "quickly disappeared, with no memory left" (113). Remembering the Mayans, Landa has no memory left for his attempt to efface them, no memory left for what his text nonetheless continually records, his identification with them, violently repudiated and as violently recreated in his relation.

CHAPTER 7

Bradford's 'Ancient Members' & 'A Case of Buggery . . . Amongst Them'

LANDA'S ACCOUNT OF the Yucatan, his ability to represent the Mayans textually, depends, I have argued, on violent acts of suppression—not only the Inquisition that he ordered but also the denials and forgetting that make his text possible. Denying that the Mayans were guilty of practices of sodomy allowed Landa to identify with them. (This is a *saving* denial—for Landa—it allows him to write of those he destroyed; it did not save the Mayans.) I move from Landa now to William Bradford's *Of Plymouth Plantation* to pursue further these paths of negation and their relation to representations of sodomy. From many perspectives Bradford's text could seem out of place in this discussion, and indeed the introduction of an Anglo-American text in the context of Spanish-American texts poses great problems, and not merely those of national, chronological, and geographical difference. Such issues could be explored, but to do so might deflect the focus of this inquiry too far afield; it might also serve the purposes of the enforcement of disciplinary and nationalist differences which are no part of my design. I choose to place Bradford after Landa because his text allows us to see further—and perhaps in an extreme way—the productive relations between the negation of sodomy and the incoherent refashioning of European identity in the New World. What makes Bradford's text of particular interest is that for him the sodomite is not an Indian, but an inhabitant of Plymouth. In Bradford's text the accusation of sodomy, no longer deflected, realizes what has also been the case in the Spanish texts I have been looking at, the nonidentity of the European, the divisions within a supposed (proto)national identity that facilitate the various phenomena of crossing and cross-identification that are also stigmatized under the name of sodomy.

What is at issue in Bradford, and some of the ways in which his text can be considered next to Landa's, are suggested by Wayne Franklin's account in *Discoverers, Explorers, Settlers: The Diligent Writers of Early America.*[1] Franklin is interested, as his title suggests, in acts of textualization. He sees acutely that Bradford's work was (like Landa's) composed in retrospect, and is not simply the year-by-year chronicle that it appears to be. (Indeed a comparison of *Plymouth Plantation* to that part of *Mourt's Relation* written by Bradford would show how much Bradford suppresses and compresses in his later account of events.) Against those who read Bradford as enunciating an ideal,[2] Franklin finds instead the pathos of its lack as Bradford's true contribution to the making of America. The combination of forward-moving chronicle and backward-glancing composition that produces Bradford's text, Franklin argues, offers a "counterpoint between the ideal and the real" (150) written along the axes of inclusion and exclusion; in attempting to represent the community of Pilgrims as insulated and unified in its goals and beliefs, Bradford's story is continually undone by all those forces represented as outside that exclusive sphere. By the end, Franklin writes, Bradford "is forced to see how blurred are the lines of inclusion and exclusion, how hard it is to attribute inner tensions solely to figures who presumably are outside the colony" (151). Franklin thus points to divisions in Bradford's text and to its multidirectionality.

As the representative moment for his reading, Franklin chooses the late chapter in *Plymouth Plantation* in which Bradford lamentingly records the decision to move to Nauset and the abandonment of the "ancient mother" (370) church at Plymouth. The moment, as Franklin finely notes, is one in which demarcations are blurred: "Having defined itself by a series of 'removals' . . . the church has found that the ritual of departure, invented at first for the sake of preserving the ideal, now has become in America a primary means for its dissolution" (166). Franklin writes about the Nauset removal and cognate moments in Bradford with great sympathy and identification. The pained realization of failure, for Franklin, opens the vista of "competing views" (180) rather than the exclusivity to which Bradford clung. From Bradford's pathos, however, Franklin fetches an even more ideal notion than that of the exclusive community, the community made of its differences, irreconcilable and progressive. "Opposition itself is what organizes Bradford's prose" (180), Franklin writes; "opposition itself" translates into an "abundance of centers in New World experience . . . rather than any old scheme of cultural domination" (181). The end of Bradford's text serves an emblematic function for Franklin; the final page of *Plymouth Plantation* records Edward Winslow's departure for England, never to return ("which has been much to the weakening of this government" [385]), and below it, the years 1647 and 1648 inscribed with no entries beneath them. From such "blankness" Franklin derives Bradford's "positive insight" (177) that history is always the history of loss, and that from it the historian can fetch "the only abiding terrain of wonder, the human spirit" (178) that survives loss, if only in writing it. For Franklin, finally, there are no blanks in Bradford's text.

The proof of this is what Franklin terms the "rogue's gallery" of grasping newcomers and strangers, "along with worse figures like Weston, Morton, Allerton, Lyford, and Thomas Granger" (172) that are represented in Bradford and who point to a future unimaginable from the narrow perspective of Plymouth. In celebrating the diversity that can be read in Bradford (despite his designs), Franklin tacitly endorses the exclusions upon which his list rests; there are no women named here, no Indians either, and Franklin fails to note their omission even as he celebrates the pluralism of Bradford's text. Moreover, the final figure on the list, the "bugger," Thomas Granger, is treated as if blandly equivalent to the other men named. Yet Bradford devotes a merciless paragraph to

Granger, recording his death, over which he presided. However much he is "in" Bradford's text, that difference cannot be ignored. If Granger should be read, as Franklin suggests, in conjunction with those on his list of rogues in Bradford, he needs also to be considered with the "blanks" in Bradford's text, in relation to those who do not make it onto the list. My purpose in the pages that follow is not to suggest some monolithic identification between sodomites, women, and Indians in Bradford. Each is accorded a different representational status, as I will suggest; yet there are also convergences and crossings that need to be taken into account. A consideration of these can go further than Franklin's "multiplicity" and "opposition" do to suggest how divided Bradford's text is. From these convergences we can take stock of the fierce negations in Bradford's text—and what they produce—too easily glossed over in Franklin's idealizing reading. Thus, rather than reading Bradford from the vantage point of the Nauset removal, the pages that follow are conducted from the site provided by the execution of Thomas Granger.

Franklin's reading of Bradford occurs in a chapter that derives its title, "Like an Ancient Mother," from the lament over the Nauset removal. From it, Franklin's notion of ideal and real is fetched, and the possibility that however bodily separate its members are, the church remains one, an ideal that can be said to continue to animate those dispersed bodies. Reading the passage, it's not hard to see how that analysis could be made:

> And thus was this poor church left, like an ancient mother grown old and forsaken of her children, though not in their affections yet in regard of their bodily presence and personal helpfulness; her ancient members being most of them worn away by death, and those of later time being like children translated into other families, and she like a widow left only to trust in God. Thus, she that had made many rich became herself poor. (370–71)

For Franklin, this passage offers a "benchmark from which Bradford's most important historical measurements are run in the book. The ancient mother church is still a point of uncorrupted ideals" (168). If the origin has been lost, the future has not, and the dispersed community will expand beyond its original design. The ideal will be located elsewhere, but it will not be lost in the realized multiplicities that follow.

Such a reading responds to the pathos of the passage but not to antagonisms that can also be read in it, and not merely, I would argue, in some "counterpoint" of "real" and "ideal." Rather, these oppositions are more entangled: the "ideal" is an ideological production. One can see this if one asks (as Franklin does not) why the church is represented as a woman, and what that gendering has to do with the relations between men that the passage also imagines and depends upon. Such questions are related to the "rogue's gallery" of "outsiders" that has no space for women in it, but also and fundamentally to the all-male community that animates Bradford, the "ancient members" that are Bradford's signal point of attraction and identification.

In the passage, the "ancient members" (I will have more to say about the locution), the first settlers, are pitted against those that came after, not only the newcomers, but also their own children.[3] A fierce antagonism between generations operates in Bradford as one of the dividing lines *within* the community. "Translated" names obliquely the regular practice of putting out children to be raised by other families, a division within the patriarchy that virtually operates to redraw class lines (it was not only the children of poor families who became servants in others' houses) and that ensures the division of labor (children are a commodity in this system) and the increase of wealth finally lamented.[4] Having crossed class lines, the children of the founding fathers are also allied with the so-called strangers (many of whom remained apart from the community), or the newcomers, or those who arrived on their "particulars" and who did not become incorporated within the "general" body. Despite all these removals, of children and ancient members, the widowed mother-church is represented as yet married—to God. Thus, an ideal of the family and of the enclosed community is preserved—as an ideological construct at some distance from and yet as the sustaining rhetoric for what actually happened at Plymouth. As Bradford records, the early attempt to form extended households—so that unmarried men, or men who arrived without their families, were incorporated into families—eventually had to be abandoned. That initial arrangement "farmed out" all single men—in the name of the family. Promoting this ideal, Bradford's prose gains resonance from biblical citation and paraphrase. What palpably holds the passage together is an ideal of union despite which and out of which these abandonments are recorded—an ideal of union *between men* represented through the ideal union of the mother-church with God.

Hence, Bradford's lament in the "ancient mother" passage, structured as it is by the breaking of the mother/child bond, by divisions of age and class, by its yearnings for the community of "ancient members," cannot be read without considering questions of sexuality and gender. The "ancient mother" in this passage—the woman—is represented as abandoned, and to serve as an ideal from which one departs never to return. The pathos (from Franklin's perspective) of this historical plot (the triumph of capitalism) is, after all, based in a paradigm of marriage and procreation in which the men venture out and leave their wives and mothers behind. That movement is virtually enacted in the passage when the "ancient mother" is transmuted into the "ancient members"; the pathos quickly becomes one of a division between older and younger men, the Pilgrims and other men, a pathos generated by the yearning for the ancient members.

One of the differences between the settlement in Plymouth and the earlier exploits of conquistadores lies precisely in the fact that these founding fathers came with their families and servants. Yet, while Bradford records tensions between the old comers and the newcomers, between the general and the particular, family life is hardly his concern except in terms of questions of property; women appear remarkably infrequently in his account.[5] When they do appear it is in moments like this one, recording the death of the first governor of Plymouth, John Carver, "whose death was much lamented and caused great heaviness amongst them, as there was cause. He was buried in the best manner they could, with some volleys shot by all that bore arms. And his wife, being a weak woman, died within five or six weeks after him" (95). Carver dies as a strong man—although ill, he puts in a hard day of work in the fields and in the blazing sun, suddenly to be felled; his death requires a quasi-military ceremony and causes a lamentation which, however generally it is presented, seems retrospectively to involve only the men in the community. The neutral "they" and "them" so characteristic of Bradford's prose become "all that bore arms" (the trusted men, those inside the community). Carver is an isolated individual, with his own first name, and he is lamented by a community of men who have their arms and their ceremonies. His wife's death is an afterthought, a response to his, and a sign of her "weakness." She has no part in the production of the manly ideal and the community of men around Carver—no place in Bradford or in Franklin. Unthinkingly, for them history is only the story of what men do; the purple passage about the mother-church is a late admission of a principal exclusion in Bradford's text—an exclusion, as I've been suggesting, that sustains the production of the ideal all-male community.

Elizabeth Carver or the ancient mother-church are put into Bradford's text only to be put out of them; if these passages adhere to the pattern that Franklin finds—of exclusions that are inclusions—they do so in a way that radically calls into question the "multiplicity" he celebrates. Real women are translated in that late passage into a trope of ideal femininity, a phantasmatic female that secures male/male arrangements and an all-male history. Written under the sign of an ancient mother, these male arrangements are secured beneath a spirituality that is nominally female and which serves a normative protoheterosexuality that barely obscures the fact that Bradford's attention is always on other men, whether the rogues or his divided fellow members—on other white men, that is, since Bradford's text excludes Indians as much as it can.

Unlike most other accounts of the settlement of North America, Bradford's text has no space for even a minimal ethnography; Indians figure only in the spheres of trade and war, treaties and betrayals; in this Bradford's text represents a kind of limit case in New World writing. Revisionist historians like Francis Jennings and Neal Salisbury have begun to write the other side of the story that Bradford fails to tell, and have seized upon his suppressions and misrepresentations to make comprehensible from the Indian side the story of relations that Bradford offers.[6] Such revisionary history is not (or need not be) merely in "counterpoint" or contributory to the great American multiplicity that Franklin reads.[7] The armed band shooting off their guns at Carver's death might be for Jennings or Salisbury a trope for the murderous impulses behind English settlement. Another late moment in Bradford—another purple passage, but not among those listed as memorable at the end of Samuel Eliot Morison's edition of his text—records that genocidal impulse, the burning of the Pequot Indians at Mystic:

> All was quickly on a flame, and thereby more were burnt to death than was otherwise slain; It burnt their bowstrings and made them unserviceable; those that scaped the fire were slain with the sword, some hewed to pieces, others run through with their rapiers, so as they were quickly dispatched and very few escaped. It was conceived they thus destroyed about 400 at this time. It was a fearful sight to see them thus frying in the fire and the streams of blood quenching the same, and horrible was the stink and scent thereof; but the victory seemed a sweet sacrifice, and they gave the praise thereof to God, who had wrought so wonderfully for them, thus to enclose their enemies in their hands and give them so speedy a victory over so proud and insulting an enemy. (331)

A page later, Bradford slips, recording the beheading of Sassacus, the Pequot sachem, done he says first "to satisfy the English" and then, immediately after, "or rather the Narragansetts" (332), at this point the English allies and here visibly scapegoated for English atrocities. But also, in this slippage from English to Indian, an admission of identification; after the ritual holocaust (like the passage about the ancient mother, resonant in its biblical allusion), the enemies who were "enclosed[d] . . . in their hands" are literally in Bradford's hand; momentarily, the English are their savage counterparts.

My point here, in moving from Anglo women to Indian men, is not to suggest that they are identical in Bradford's text, except in the single regard in which I have been considering them: as those who must be effaced in order for history to move forward as the exclusive preserve of white men. While real white women barely put in an appearance in Bradford's text, they are "saved" by him in the figuration of the mother-church (and this, in turn, saves male/male relations from sexual stigmatization); Indians, on the other hand, appear more often, especially in the opening and closing chapters of the book—as helpers or hindrances, providing food or beaver pelts to the Puritans, who are always represented as innocent peacemakers; although there is occasional sympathy for Indians (when they are dying thanks to plagues believed sent by God, for instance), they are never "saved" by any idealizing trope; they remain, for Bradford, "savages." Despite differences in the representational status of Anglo women and Indian men, it is worth pointing to the ways in which they are joined (a connection not noticed by Jennings or Salisbury, although it is central to Ann Kibbey's discussion of the Pequot War)[8] to take a full measure of Bradford's genocidal text. In Bradford's description of the bloody massacre at Fort Mystic (one that featured the slaughter of women and children, as Kibbey notes), an impulse buried in his initial description of the New World as "vast and unpeopled" (26) begins to be realized—the impulse to *make* it unpeopled;[9] there, as throughout, others—the rogues, never the Puritans—are blamed for what is done to them, other Englishmen like Weston or the supposed gun-running Morton of Merrymount, or the Indians themselves as savage betrayers of Puritan peace and civility. The slip of the pen of English to Narragansett quickly covers over what the text never more openly admits, its own savagery, "removals" and blanks that cannot be accommodated to Franklin's benign reading of them.

These lethal energies against women and Indians can be found even in so ideal a moment as the "ancient mother" passage, deflected onto the bodies of other white men, in that case, the next generation. That this is related to the divided constitution of Plymouth is suggested by the "providential" story Bradford tells about the crossing on the *Mayflower,* when a "lusty" young man refuses to help those who are sick and helpless: "It pleased God before they came half seas over, to smite this young man with a grievous disease, of which he died in a desperate manner, and so was himself the first that was thrown overboard. Thus his curses light on his own head, and it was an astonishment to all his fellows for they noted it to be the just hand of God upon him" (66). Two pages later, Bradford records that only one passenger died in the crossing, "William Butten, a youth, servant to Samuel Fuller, when they drew near the coast" (68), and the death "before they came half seas over" of the "lusty" young man has been expunged. The nameless young man is not the named youth—the designation of his master further assures that. Similarly, the "Civil Body Politic" (84) compacted on the *Mayflower* in the face of mutiny was signed only by those who represented the "better part" (84), the "ancient members." They have their dutiful servants, others' children, single men, housed under their roofs; nameless dissolute young men have no place in this compact except insofar as they are willing servants of their masters. One consequence of these arrangements (fearful to be named, Bradford would write) is just that division of the society between hierarchically disposed male bodies that, Alan Bray has convincingly argued, facilitated male/male sexual behavior, and the bodies of "lusty" and rebellious young men on whom the sin of sodomy could be attached.[10] No wonder then that age and generational tensions mark Bradford's text.

It is thus worth pausing over the nature of the all-male ideal that Bradford espouses, before we consider further the ways in which such dissolute young men are attached to those whom Bradford would expunge. *Plymouth Plantation* opens by situating the notion of "removal" (to Amsterdam, to Leyden, to Plymouth) as a strategy for narrowing the perimeters around the community, for ensuring the separateness of "the better part" (4). Theirs is the history of a true church whose removals made it possible for "the truth" to "spring and spread" (3). What necessitates removal to America is the fear of the "dissolution" and "scattering" (24–25) of the chosen seed, the "sowing" of the seeds of error, a worry manifest in what is said to be happening to the dispirited and wayward youth in Leyden. Bradford's terms—seed, fruit, sowing, scattering, and dissolution—are fetched from the Bible; they are also insistently sexual. So read, they can help us understand both the energies that animate Bradford as he regards the "ancient members" (in this context, it's hard not to hear the sexual meaning of the term), but also the lethal energies unleashed on Thomas

Granger. One might well wonder why a sixteen- or seventeen-year-old boy caught having sex with a mare should figure as the last on Franklin's list of who are the "worst" in Bradford (this does not misrepresent Bradford in the least) and what he might share with Weston (the backer that failed Bradford), the "atheist" Morton (whose crime seems to have been his attempt to form a more egalitarian community), or Allerton, Bradford's partner who cut his own deals, or the backsliding minister Lyford. One answer lies in seeing that there are networks of connection between these allowable figures (the excluded who can be included) and those who do not even figure in this list, women and Indians. By pursuing these connections, we can come closer to understanding the function of sodomy in Bradford and its relation to the ideal of community that animates his text.

Consider the case of Lyford, the minister offended by Puritan exclusivity, the rule of the so-called "better part"; "the smallest number in the Colony . . . appropriate the ministry to themselves" (177), Lyford is discovered to have written in an intercepted letter, and his wife is called upon to give the clinching evidence against her husband. "She feared to fall into the Indian's hands and to be defiled by them as he had defiled other women" (185). The good wife here (a woman entirely complicitous or represented as being so) is admitted into the community in order to voice Lyford's identification as an Indian, to represent the Indian as a fornicator bent on the capture and rape of white women. Lyford's willingness to extend the community of believers beyond the limits of tolerability is signaled by the case mounted against him, of his use of his ministry as a way to the bed of other women, usually serving women, but, in the most fully detailed instance, the future wife of one of his parishioners: "Lyford had overcome her and defiled her body before marriage"; even worse it seems, "though he had satisfied his lust on her, yet he endeavoured to hinder conception" (187). Lyford's religious "crimes" are translated into sexual ones, fornication and adultery, but in "hinder[ing] conception," his crime could also fall under the label of sodomy (in the broad sense of the term, as any form of sexual activity without procreation as its ostensible aim).[11] The last charge, which seals the case against him for Bradford—it is the worst that can be said about Lyford—is also palpably excessive.

Yet it is how Lyford can come to be on a list that ends in Thomas Granger. Such associations can be found throughout the text. Take Ashley, for instance, a worrisome partner for Allerton, Bradford opines, since he had a history of living "among the Indians as a savage" and going naked (242); when his financial abuses were found out, he also was discovered guilty of "uncleanness with Indian women" (258). If the "rogues" are associated with Indians and women (condensed into the figure of the promiscuous Indian woman), this also links them to sodomy. Thus, Morton's threat to the Puritans' "lives and goods" is represented as even more fearsome than that of "the savages themselves" (230). If the proof of his profligacy is the allegation that his followers (lower-class men whom Morton rescued from being sold into slavery) take "Indian women for their consorts" (227),[12] Morton's "School of Atheism" implies even worse deeds. Just as Lyford's "bad" religion translates into sodomitical sex, "atheism," as Bray points out, is a charge regularly made against sodomites. In Protestant England, Catholics or Catholic sympathizers were so charged; in Puritan New England, the Anglican Morton is redubbed an atheist. Beyond the explicitly named debauchery of Indian consorting (a "savage" debauchery that could itself fall under the broad label of sodomy), "worse practices" are hinted, "the beastly practices of the mad Bacchanalians," the "fairies, or furies" whirling about their "idle or idol maypole" (227), as Bradford puts it in prose whose doublings and allusions—in its refusals to name more directly—circle about the unnameable crime, and about the maypole erected in defiance of the ancient members. Such locutions only imitate what Richard Slotkin has read in the multiply named pleasures of Merrymount—Marrymount, where whites and Indians joined; Marymount, where high church and "pagan" rituals mixed; and Maremount, evoking, as Slotkin concludes, "the image of sodomy, or buggery, a crime that troubled New England not a little (by Bradford's account)."[13] And which found its only detailed representation in Thomas Granger, "discovered by one that accidentally saw his lewd practice towards the mare" (355).

Granger is thus the worst of these unclean members, the site towards which these representations move. Tensions of age, race, class, and gender fasten on his body to unleash homophobic energies that serve the all-white male ideal in Bradford. Why the threat should be crystallized there—how it is that Granger is even admitted into Bradford's text—can be further understood if we look at another of the purple passages in Bradford, a very late (probably the last) retrospective addition to Bradford's manuscript. On one side of the page, a letter jointly penned by John Robinson, the leader of the church in Leyden who never joined his congregation in Plymouth, and by William Brewster, whose death is lamented by Bradford in the chapter immediately following the one devoted to sodomy. "We are knit together as a body" (34), the letter declares; on the facing page, Bradford replies:

Bradford's 'Ancient Members'

> O sacred bond, whilst inviolably preserved! How sweet and precious were the fruits that flowed from the same! But when this fidelity decayed, then their ruin approached. O that these ancient members had not died or been dissipated (if it had been the will of God) or else that this holy care and constant faithfulness had still lived, and remained with those that survived, and were in times afterwards added unto them. But (alas) that subtle serpent hath slyly wound himself under fair pretences of necessity and the like, to untwist these sacred bonds and tied, and as it were insensibly by degrees to dissolve, or in a great measure to weaken, the same. I have been happy, in my first times, to see, and with much comfort to enjoy, the blessed fruits of this sweet communion, but it is now a part of my misery in old age, to find and feel the decay and want thereof (in a great measure) and with grief and sorrow of heart to lament and bewail the same. And for others' warning and admonition, and my own humiliation, do I here note the same. (34–35)

The intensity of male bonds in this passage is unmistakable. Women have no place here, not even figuratively (once the "ancient mother" becomes the "ancient members," she disappears). The "blessed fruits of . . . sweet communion" may look like a procreative metaphor, but these are sweets and fruits that flow between men, ideally between the "ancient members," who, in this fantasy either never would die or would be replaced by newcomers identical to the old. This is that fantasy of the seed and of the truth that opens Bradford's book, a fantasy about the spirit that has not been expended in a waste of shame. If this sacred bond looks like marriage, it is worth recalling that Bradford's first act as governor of Plymouth, duly recorded just beneath the description of the death of Carver and his wife, was to reinstitute marriage as a secular relation, taking it out of the hands of the church; the bond that ties men together is propagated in fruits that are not the children of heterosexual procreation but an overflow from member to member, a preservation of the chosen seed, here sadly dissolved and disseminated. Rather than spending their seed upon each other, those who have betrayed Bradford's vision have sowed seeds into the void. The death of the "ancient members" marks the end of the fantasy of the preservation of the "better part."

What part that is is suggested by another of Robinson's letters, the one read out to the Pilgrims before their passage across the Atlantic; here are its opening lines:

> Loving and Christian Friends, I do heartily and in the Lord salute you all as being they with whom I am present in my best affection, and most earnest longings after you. Though I be constrained for a while to be bodily absent from you. I say constrained, God knowing how willingly and much rather than otherwise, I would have borne my part with you in this first brunt, were I not by strong necessity held back for the present. Make account of me in the meanwhile as of a man divided in myself with great pain, and as (natural bonds set aside) having my better part with you. (55)

The "better part" is a presence made in absence, an affection carried by a letter that attempts to overstep the limits represented by "natural bonds," the ties to women. ("We are well weaned from the delicate milk of our mother country" [34], Brewster and Robinson write, in a phrase that foretells the "ancient mother" trope.) This is what Franklin idealistically termed the eternal spirit, but it is more exactly the materiality of the letter; Robinson is not divided between body and spirit but between part and part. One part is the "natural" bond of home and kin; his "better part" is on the page, but it was realized too in the "Civil Body Politic" compacted on the *Mayflower* and signed by the "better part" (84). This vision of "loving and Christian friends" bound together is further conveyed in another letter—from Charles Gott, founding the first Congregationalist church in New England. "Every member (being men) are to have a free voice," he writes (248); among the separatists, every old member, being a man, has a voice so long as he is among the better part. "I may say, as the eunuch said," Gott begins another declaration; as the eunuch, he locates himself, dismembering the members and severing the "natural" bond to women in order to make "free" male members—free to have relations with each other that are nominally desexualized and are resexualized, nominally, in the very words on the page, in their loving exchanges, member to member.

The sexuality that flows at such moments in the representation of the ideal male community suggests how close sodomy is to this discourse and why, when sodomy "broke forth," as Bradford puts it (351)—when it became visible—it was violently repudiated. The fundamental nonrecognition in Bradford's text, I would argue, is the proximity of the ties that bind these men together and the possibility of literally enacting them. Let me be clear here: I am not suggesting that Bradford is secretly homosexual, or latently so. Nor am I framing this as the accusation voiced by a late-seventeenth-century Englishman who wrote that "there be some of the Brethren that do love to embrace their likeness, (to wit, a Beast,) choosing rather to have familiarity with a Beast or a handsom Boy, than use their own wives."[14] Rather, Bradford's text is (to follow Eve Kosofsky Sedgwick's use of the term in *Between Men*) eminently homosocial, and it preserves its fantasy of all-male relations precisely by drawing the line—lethally—between its sexual energies and those it calls sodomitical. (It is this that makes a text like Bradford's foundational for the national imaginary upon which the U.S. Supreme Court depended in *Bowers v. Hardwick.*) The burst of energy in Bradford's evocation of the "sacred bond," like that in so many other of his purple passages, comes against the other more usual impulse in his prose: the desire not to say, the desire to efface which is variously aimed at women, Indians, and sodomites. "I omit," "I have been too long," "etc." are the frequent marks in a text in which the writer rarely inhabits an "I" (more often a "they"; and "William Bradford" appears in this text as another—the Governor—or as the signatory of letters included in the text). Bradford writes in a plural "general" voice. "Etc." is the mark inserted in the letters he so frequently cites, with the aim of letting others speak—but only so far. Announcements of omission or overstepping the limits of what he would tell appear as he dilates on his "rogues," and he stops himself to keep his prose from becoming dissolute (this happens twice in his pages on Morton). "To cut things short" (167), this, despite its prolixity, is the desire of Bradford's text. This desired cut is exactly the place of meeting between the holy eunuch and the condemned sodomite.

Always extending himself, Bradford would, if he could, not tell anything. The case of Thomas Granger, and his unspeakable sin, is, Bradford writes, "horrible . . . to mention" but must be told since "the truth of the history requires it" (355). The truth of the history, as I am reading it, is the entanglement of the "ancient members" with and the desire to separate from the figure of the sodomite who represents at once the negation of the ideal and its literalization. Even the mention of Granger, Bradford claims, goes only so far: "I forebear particulars" (355–56). His acts are not described, just the satisfaction of their punishment. "I forebear particulars": it could be Bradford's refrain—"particulars" are also how he names all those who are not part of the "general," all the dissolute members that Bradford would cut off. Granger's execution is recorded in the middle of Bradford's 1642 chapter, devoted to the "breaking out of sundry notorious sins," drunkenness, incontinence, uncleanness, and "that which is worse, even sodomy and buggery (things fearful to name)" (351). His "buggery," as I've been suggesting, is the dense site of a series of crossings and displacements in Bradford. It's to those now that I turn.

First, the relation of sodomy and buggery needs to be discussed. Legally, sodomy and bestiality were synonymous, both "fearful to name," both warranting death. However, in New England, a distinction was made between male/male sexual misconduct and having sex with an animal.[15] As Robert Oaks remarks, "Puritans were less resistant to punish buggery with death than they were sodomy" (70). (Bradford's list of crimes thus arrives at buggery last, as the worst.) This inconsistency has been variously explained—usually by asking which activity was more likely to have been practiced in the period and thus more in need of policing, and by pointing to the fears of monstrous offspring that such matings were thought to produce.[16] Rather than asking the question about which sexual activities were more common in New England, it seems to me more useful to ask what the body of a man caught sleeping with an animal could serve that a man sleeping with another could not, why one body would be destroyed, while the other could be preserved. Here the notion of monstrous births seems worth pursuing; in imagining that possibility, "buggery" is given the potential to realize—literally—the debasement of procreative sexual behavior against which sodomy in general was measured. By killing someone for an act that was believed capable of bearing fruit, the tacit relation between prohibited and metaphorically idealized male/male relations could remain undisturbed. Thus, the body of the "bugger" could serve as the site for the assaultive energies against "sodomy," and at the same time preserve ideal male/male relations untouched by the crime—could, by displacing male/male sodomy onto male/animal buggery, fail to bring sodomy into relation with the overflow of spirit and seed Bradford favored.

The punishment of an interspecies crime rather than one between men insists upon the "unnaturalness" of sodomy, and thus its lack of relation to bonds between men. Granger, undistinguished in his punishment from that meted out upon the animals, is, in effect, not granted membership in the human race. His punishment is the one specified in Leviticus, but it can't help but recall Balboa's mode of dealing with the Panamanian "sodomites," allowing his dogs to rend their bodies. And it suggests that in equating Granger with his animal partners, Bradford's racist energies fasten on his body too. Bradford, after all, believes that Indians are "wild beasts," "savage and brutish men" (26). In his bestiality, Granger momentarily—and finally—steps into that blank in Bradford's text reserved for the bodies of Indians.

But Granger's act is with a female of the species, a mare, and the crossing of species serves to mark a gender crossing as well as a racial one. To see that, we need to recall that Granger's story surfaces only midway in Bradford's chapter. Bradford opens his chapter by lamenting the appearance of sodomy "here," but by the end of a paragraph "here" becomes "in this land" (351), and the lament seems, a page later, to have been occasioned by a "letter from the Governor in the Bay . . . touching matters of the forementioned nature" (352). "Here" becomes "there," and it appears that Governor Bellingham's case of "uncleanness" (353) is motivating Bradford, not Granger's case at all. Retrospectively, they will be connected (explicitly so, as we will see momentarily). The case in Massachusetts Bay involved what would, in modern terms, be thought of as rape—two female children were said to have been violated numerous times over the course of a couple of years, and by several different men. Appeals were sent to Plymouth and elsewhere (there was no statute that covered the case) and opinions were solicited; "sodomy" seemed a capacious enough category under which the case might fall, and Bradford polled various divines (the opinions of three are recorded in his text). "Besides the occasion before mentioned in these writings concerning the abuse of those two children," Bradford finally admits, "they had about the same time a case of buggery fell out amongst them, which occasioned these questions, to which these answers have been made" (355). Granger's case and the Bay case are considered together. Much as Bradford has attempted to displace Granger's case, and to act as if the outbreak of sodomy really hasn't happened at Plymouth, he finally admits otherwise. But displacement is still taking place: Granger's buggery is being thought of in relation to a crime against women.

In their opinions, the learned divines keep measuring the Massachusetts case against their own. They are divided by many issues, particularly, as Bradford summarizes the documents, whether death is warranted for crimes of bestiality and sodomy "if there be not penetration" (354). In that case, there should have been no question what punishment was apt for the rape of the two girls; that's not how the Plymouth minister John Rayner understood the issue, however: "because there was not the like reason and degree of sinning against family and posterity in this sin as in some other capital sins of uncleanness" (Morison, 405). Sodomy and buggery, when penetration can be proved, are capital sins; rape is "uncleanness," a lesser charge. The "logic" here is the same that led Bradford to regard Lyford's unprocreative adultery as more horrific than a "natural" adulterous act. Raping girls is less criminal than *any* sexual act between men or between a man and an animal. Thus the men charged in the Bay case were whipped severely, and one of them had his ears mutilated. They did not receive Granger's punishment. Crossing species—sleeping with a female horse—Granger's case is nominally sodomitical but also, and more significantly, a violation of the procreative act between sexes. However awful the Bay case was, at least it recognized that the female body was a site of procreation—such is Rayner's opinion: I need hardly point out how this hideous misogyny countenances rape and yet "saves" women for their "proper" procreative role. The Bay case therefore was not a case of sodomy. Granger's was and deserved death. But it deserved that punishment precisely because it represented the worst male/female sexual behavior.

Thomas Granger thus is a transfer point for energies directed against Indians and women; his crossing of species is also a racial and gender crossing. His death along with his barnyard companions would seem to mark an absolute point of termination (the polluted animals, following the dictates of Leviticus, were not even allowed to serve as food—this could be related to Chanca's discussion of the economies of cannibalism, the question of which bodies are too degraded to be eaten). But, as Bradford puts it, Granger's case "fell out amongst them" and it remains to be said that his case *is* theirs. However much Granger displaces the anxieties about male/male sodomy, he also is a locus for them. This explains why the learned divines were so troubled about questions of penetration. To understand this, we need to notice yet another retrospective recontextualization of Granger in Bradford's text. For, after describing Granger's death, Bradford backtracks to a summary of his examination. When Granger is questioned, his story is linked to one told by someone else "that had made sodomitical attempts upon another"; both said they learned such wickedness "in old England. . . . This youth last spoken of said he was taught it by another that had heard of such things from some in England when he was there, and they kept cattle together" (356). As usual, Bradford forbears particulars; here he seems to be conflating a March 1642 sodomy trial with Granger's September 1642 case. The earlier case had decided that the two men involved, Edward Michell and Edward Preston, had been engaged in "lewd & sodomitical practices tending to sodomy."[17] Public whippings were their punishment, to be witnessed by their townsmen, and by John Keene, a boy they had attempted, who was not found guilty, but not exactly innocent either ("in some thing he was faulty"). Michell had also attempted to "abuse" Lydia Hatch, and she in turn was said to have shared a bed with her brother. She too was whipped, the brother banished from the community. These are all acts "tending to sodomy," acts in which penetration was not proved; none of these "sodomitical practices" (whether male/male or male/female—and incest seems to be included here) led to the death penalty. "Normal" sodomy, practices "tending to sodomy," were part of the usual fabric of sociosexual life.

The men, Bradford reports, confessed that they learned their crime when "they kept cattle together" (Bradford thus conflates their sodomy with Granger's buggery, misrepresenting the differences in their fates). Once, as Bradford tells the story, that was what all the Puritans did. "They were not acquainted with trades nor traffic," Bradford writes of those English who originally removed to Amsterdam, "but had only been used to a plain country life and the innocent trade of husbandry" (11). They all started as Thomas Grangers. For Granger was, after all, a quite ordinary English boy, indeed one of those farmed-out children upon whom Bradford's ideal community rests, "servant to an honest man of Duxbury, being about 16 or 17 years of age. (His father and mother lived at the same time at Scituate)" (355). Granger's case testifies to the unspeakable *continuity* between Bradford's ideal and the unmentionable horror of sodomy.

No wonder, then, for all its deflections and despite the condensations upon Granger's body as the site of all that must be repudiated, the question that Bradford keeps asking in his 1642 chapter—in both its opening and its closing pages—is, how could this happen here? The initial answer is supernatural: Satan, most incensed by so righteous a community, plagues them with the worst of sins (351–52). But this is immediately replaced with a natural explanation—like waters that have been dammed up and which will have out, so too with wickedness despite the severity of laws and their enforcement (352). The natural becomes social, and it is yet another social explanation that Bradford himself favors—the very enforcement acts to reveal what elsewhere would be hidden. There is not more sodomy among them, it is simply more visible thanks to the intensity of scrutiny. Bradford all but admits that the righteous community produces sodomy.

Alan Bray has remarked how Bradford displays the characteristic Elizabethan belief that sodomy is something which anyone is capable of doing, an eruption in "our corrupt natures, which are so hardly bridled, subdued and mortified" (351). Incipiently, Bradford (and Bray following him) reads sodomy as the repressed, as a component inherent in human sexuality. Dammed up, it will out.[18] Yet, Bradford's view is insistently social and it seems worthwhile taking that seriously; not, obviously, to endorse his analysis, but because it suggests the social conditions through which sodomy comes to be that which is discovered as *the* repressed, conditions in which repression is invented. "They are here more discovered and seen and made public by due search, inquisition and due punishment; for the churches look narrowly to their members" (352). The final locution connects of course to the object of Bradford's most rapturous desire, the ancient members to which he is always looking. Not surprisingly, then, it has its locus in the love letter from John Robinson that serves as the founding document of Plymouth. Robinson preaches the necessity of "watchfulness" (56): "Let every man repress in himself and the whole body in each person" (57). Repression here is a means of production; sexuality is not inherently within, it is produced as that which is within, the unseen that corresponds to what is seen. The gaze of members upon members produces what must be repressed—by inquisition and punishment when made visible, but "ideally" never made visible at all: this invisibility preserves the "ancient members" from sodomitical penetration; this invisibility ensures the life of sodomites as well.

Thomas Granger is killed as a sodomite but the chapter does not end with his death: it is part of the mechanism for the production of sexuality. Hence, the end of the chapter swarms with a multitude of bodies, those of the strangers, the profiteers, the servants, represented as those who have diluted the community of first comers. They are said to be the *origin* of sodomy, the outsiders who have insidiously undermined the true members of the body politic. This is the import too of the letter from Massachusetts Bay which asks for advice about three things, not only their case of "uncleanness," but also what is to be done about "the Islanders at Aquidneck" (the "heretics," including Roger Williams and Anne Hutchinson),[19] and about the beaver trade. These are only apparent nonsequiturs. So-called "heretics" and Indians occupy the same discursive space in colonial writing, as more than one historian has noticed.[20] What has further to be remarked is the insistent sexualization of the connection. The heretics are represented as "sowing the seeds of Familism and Anabaptistry" (353) and spreading "infection"; the Massachusetts Bay colony fears that "the Indians will abuse us" in trade (353). In other texts, this sexual language implicates the bodies of women; in Bradford, the language is that of the sodomitical body with its bad seed, infection, and abuse.

Bradford's answer to the multiple query from Boston is epitomized in his decisively singular reply about the "heretics": "We have no conversing with them, nor desire to have, further than necessity or humanity may require" (354). "Necessity" makes clear, in its understated way, that the community cannot be sealed off; it explains why there is room for the "rogues" in Bradford. Morton may be sent off, but Allerton brings him back: the lapsing Lyford is given more than one chance. And Allerton, of course, the figure who dominates page after page of Bradford's text, is the only one who is never directly accused of sexual crimes. The reason is not far to seek. He was one of the "ancient members," a signer of the *Mayflower* Compact; moreover, he was married to William Brewster's daughter. With Allerton, Bradford repeated a relation he celebrates in the eulogy of Brewster that fills the chapter after the one devoted to sodomy. Allerton was Bradford's right-hand man, as Brewster had been when he served the chief secretary of Elizabeth I: "[Secretary Davison] esteemed him rather as a son than a servant, and for his wisdom and godliness, in private he would converse with him more like a friend and familiar than a master" (360). Such are the proper connections between "ancient members," and the fallen Allerton never falls so far as to be connected with stigmatized forms of male/male familiarity. But humane treatment has its limits, and Thomas Granger is beyond the pale.

Who was Thomas Granger? The court records tell what Bradford omits: "late servant to Love Brewster" (Shurtleff, 2:440). Love Brewster was one of two sons—the other was named Wrestling—that came over on the *Mayflower* with their father, William Brewster. Love and Wrestling: the names are too allegorically perfect to describe the tensions between generations, or the sacrifice of Granger made in the name of the love between men. "Your loving friend, William Bradford" (355), so the Plymouth Governor signs his letter to his fellow leader of the rival colony, who signs himself "Your loving friend, Richard Bellingham" (353).

Is there penetration here? Penetration is supposedly requisite for the death penalty in cases of sodomy, but not in Granger's case. Hence the "sad spectacle" that Granger's death offered this community of loving friends eyeing each other: "For first the mare and then the cow and the rest of the lesser cattle were killed before his face, according to the law, Leviticus xx.15; and then he himself was executed. The cattle were all cast into a great and large pit that was digged of purpose for them, and no use made of any part of them" (356). The large pit: the holes in Bradford's prose. The spectacle: they watch those brought before Granger's face, those animals that he had been seen to penetrate. Because in "that carnal knowledge of man or lying with man as with woman," Rayner writes, "it was a sin to be punished with death (Leviticus xx.13) in the man who was lyen withall, as well as in him that lieth with him. . . . His sin is not mitigated where there is not penetration." Because bestiality and sodomy are fully analogous, and "if a woman did stand before or approach to a beast for that end, to lie down thereto (whether penetration was or not) it was capital." Because in these cases—when men lie with men *as* with woman, when a woman *looks* to an animal as she might to a man—it is "equivalent to penetration" (Morison, 404). Strange equivalence that must deny these equivalences, but no stranger than the gaze of the ancient members upon each other, or upon the bugger, Thomas Granger. "One wicked person may infect many," Bradford intones, and all must take care "what servants they bring into their families" (356). There is no stopping this wickedness, however, for its origin is not where Bradford puts it, outside the community, outside the pale of humanity. There always is penetration.

CHAPTER 8

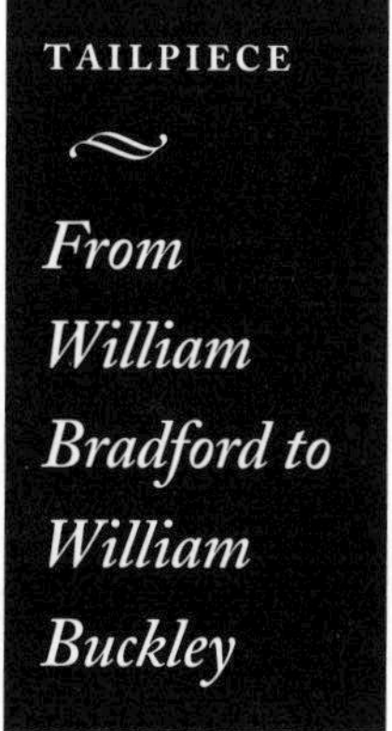

TAILPIECE

From William Bradford to William Buckley

In the summer of 1990, the *National Review* printed a letter from Marvin Liebman, longtime participant in the conservative movement, to his equally longtime friend (or should I say, longtime companion?) William Buckley.[1] "We've known each other for almost 35 years now," Liebman noted; "I am almost 67 years old. For more than half my lifetime I have been engaged in, and indeed helped to organize and maintain, the conservative and anti-Communist cause" (17), he wrote, making his friendship with Buckley—"you are my best friend," the letter opens by declaring (16)—coincident with his political engagement. Liebman's public declaration of this coincidence was not, however, the aim of his letter; it was rather to announce his homosexuality. The letter was a public coming-out by a man haunted by what he characterizes as the increasing homophobia of his political allies. Liebman explained why being gay and being conservative were compatible: that he had not chosen to be gay: "It is how I was born; how God decreed that I should be" (17); that "the conservative view, based as it is on the inherent rights of the individual over the state, is the logical political home of gay men and women" (18). To this letter, Buckley replied, oozing pity at his friend's pain, but pointing as did the justices in *Bowers v. Hardwick* to "the Judeo-Christian tradition" and to the contradictory demand that Liebman's letter voiced, that a tradition "which is aligned with, no less, one way of life, [should] become indifferent to another way of life." Even granting that God made Liebman the way he is, Buckley went on, that could not shake "convictions rooted . . . in theological and moral truths," in what "we deem to be normal, and healthy" (18). At best, Buckley promised that the *National Review* would not engage in "thoughtless gay-bashing," though he qualified this promise by licensing the *Review* to indulge in "humor" (18): "I qualify this [promise] only by acknowledging that humor (if wholesomely motivated) is as irresistible to us, as it is to you."

Liebman's coming-out letter is a performance of the closet, with repeated hints that what he is declaring publicly in his letter will not surprise Buckley in the least. Buckley's sanctimonious reply is equally such a performance, trading in what "is as irresistible to us, as it is to you." Licensed by theological truths, by his own wholesomeness, Buckley can announce, in terms more open than anything Liebman says to his friend: "My affection and respect for you are indelibly recorded here and there, in many ways, in many places" (18), and can end his letter by declaring, "you remain, always, my dear friend, and my brother in combat." Drawing on the irresistible path that brought them together in the "cause I joined, along with you, 35 years ago," as Liebman puts it, Buckley trades on their affection, their brotherhood, their comradeship. Calling his dear friend "unnatural" (18), immoral, and unhealthy, he can, exercising Christian "toleration and compassion," also call him brother. Calling him *that* he need never notice how such terms of so-called compassion cover his irresistible bond to his friend, how irresistibly he can count on Liebman to take his humor as *thoughtful* gay-bashing, backed as it is by the church: "Ten years ago," Liebman notes, "you served as my godfather when I entered the Catholic Church" (17). Recloseted, reconverted, Liebman is instructed in Buckley's quasi-paternal message to recognize how he may remain the friend and comrade, what he must do to retain his love. And also, to maintain that precious individuality that joins him to the cause by subsuming it within the brotherly cause. It is at this point—as individuality is subsumed within brotherhood—that Buckley's language touches on the arguments of the liberal justices, the dissenting voices in *Bowers v. Hardwick*; that is, it is at this point that the conservative denial of homosexuality and the liberal affirmation of individuality meet in their insistence on the maintenance of the closet.

But whose closet is it? What does this exchange between Buckley and Liebman testify to, if not a continuation, however different the terms and the historical situation may be, of the calculated nonrecognitions that structure the terms of brotherhood in the sermon Cortés delivered to the man he was bent on defeating, or the letters penned by William Bradford to his fellow governor in the rival colony, united only in their persecution of sodomites and heretics? Or even in the familiar letters that constitute Elizabethan high literariness? What do these letters, written "here and there, in many ways, in many places," do, if not to vehiculate the (non)relation of an abjected sexuality and an exalted love between men, guarding against the recognition that *there always is penetration*? Liebman worries in his letter that "without the anti-Communist and anti-tax movements as sustaining elements" (18) that the assaults that he notices in TV evangelism and in the attempts to squash the National Endowment for the Arts may burgeon into a campaign against gays as the uniting bond of the Christian brotherhood. Buckley assures him otherwise, even as he suggests just how that campaign will continue.[2] What neither of them knew as they wrote in July 1990 was that a month later, a new campaign would be launched, and that it would be aimed at someone all too conveniently named Saddam.

REFERENCE MATTER

NOTES

CHAPTER I

1. *Rolling Stone,* November 15, 1990. I am grateful to Karin Cope for clipping this ad for me.

2. Michel Foucault, *The History of Sexuality,* vol. I, *An Introduction,* trans. Robert Hurley (New York: Pantheon, 1978), 101. Further citations appear parenthetically in the text.

3. 25 Hen. VIII. c. 6. The law was first passed in 1533; it was renewed in 1536, 1539, and 1541. It was repealed and then reenacted under Edward VI; the 1548 version of the law (2 & 3 Edw. VI. c. 29) is less stringent in its punishment than Henry's act, since, unlike the original statute, it allows the property of the person condemned to death under the statute to be inherited by his heirs. Mary repealed the law upon ascending the throne in 1553; in 1563, Elizabeth I reinstated it with the original Henrician terms (5 Eliz. c. 17), claiming that "Sithens wch Repeale so hadde and made dyvers evyll disposed psons have been the more bolde to committ the said most horrible and detestable Vice of Buggerie." The death penalty for sodomy remained on the books until 1861, when it was abolished in the Offenses Against the Person Act (24 & 25 Vict. c. 100). For a history of English sodomy laws, see H. Montgomery Hyde, *The Other Love* (London: Heinemann, 1970), 29–57; Jeffrey Weeks, *Coming Out* (London: Quartet, 1977), 11–22; and Ed Cohen, "Legislating the Norm: From Sodomy to Gross Indecency," in Ronald R. Butters, John M. Clum, and Michael Moon, eds., *Displacing Homophobia* (Durham, N.C.: Duke University Press, 1989), 169–205. For a detailed description of the passage of these laws, see Bruce R. Smith, *Homosexual Desire in Shakespeare's England* (Chicago: University of Chicago Press, 1991), 41–53.

4. I owe this characterization of Puttenham to Barbara Herrnstein Smith.

5. George Puttenham, *The Arte of English Poesie,* the Edward Arber

edition with an introduction by Baxter Hathaway (1906; reprint, Kent, Ohio: Kent State University Press, 1970), 182. Further citations appear parenthetically in the text.

6. The image is reproduced in Richard Goldstein, "Season of the Kitsch: Watching and Shopping the War," *Village Voice,* March 15, 1991, 30. The complicities between *Saddam* and *Sodom* might well underlie a phenomenon noted by several commentators, President Bush's inability to pronounce properly Saddam Hussein's name. Calvin Trillin speculates on that question in a piece that appeared in the Raleigh, North Carolina, *News and Observer* (and I assume in many other newspapers that carry his column) on March 11, 1991, "Reading Bush's lips for the key to victory." Trillin observes that the day that the war was declared won, Bush suddenly found he could say the name correctly. While Trillin believes that this manipulation was purposeful (some derogatory slur involved in the mispronunciation), it never occurs to him that (not) saying *sodomy* was involved; despite all Trillin's attempts to uncover a strategy, sodomy remains unthinkable for him, and thus his analysis remains within the complicities that the strategy depends upon, what Eve Kosofsky Sedgwick has termed "the privilege of unknowing" in an essay that bears that title in *Genders* 1 (1988): 102–24.

For an incisive discussion of relationships between the war against Iraq, Bush's mispronunciations, misogyny, homophobia, and demonization, see Michael Bronski, "The Rape of Kuwait," *Gay Community News*, January 28–February 3, 1991, 9, 11. I'm grateful to Heather Findlay for sending me the clipping.

7. The questions raised here and the suppositions guiding my discussion are everywhere informed by Eve Kosofsky Sedgwick's *Epistemology of the Closet* (Berkeley and Los Angeles: University of California Press, 1990), especially 44–48. My discussion of *Bowers v. Hardwick* also follows Sedgwick's remarks on 6–7, 86.

8. "Survey on the Constitutional Right to Privacy in the Context of Homosexual Activity," *University of Miami Law Review* 40 (1986): 521–657. Further citations appear parenthetically in the text.

9. The fullest historical critique is offered by Anne B. Goldstein, "History, Homosexuality, and Political Values: Searching for the Hidden Determinants of *Bowers v. Hardwick,*" *Yale Law Journal* 97 (1988): 1073–1103, especially 1081–89.

10. Goldstein makes the point eloquently on p. 1086 of "History, Homosexuality, and Political Values." For a review of nineteenth-century judicial decisions in which fellatio explicitly was ruled not to be included under sodomy statutes, see Lawrence R. Murphy, "Defining the Crime Against Nature: Sodomy in the United States Appeals Courts, 1810–1940," *Journal of Homosexuality* 19 (1990): 49–66.

11. *Padula v. Webster,* 822 F.2d 97 (D.C. Cir. 1987), is one such case. For a comment on the chilling effect that similar recent decisions may have on attempts to argue for gay rights within Fourteenth Amendment guarantees of Equal Protection, see the Harvard Law Review volume *Sexual*

Orientation and the Law (Cambridge: Harvard University Press, 1990), 168–70.

12. Justice Harry Blackmun points this out in his dissenting opinion; see 106 S. Ct. 2849 and n. 1 for the failure of the previous Georgia sodomy law to be upheld in a case involving lesbians. Justice John Paul Stevens also stresses the point in his dissenting opinion; see 106 S. Ct. 2857.

13. See Sedgwick, *Epistemology of the Closet,* 40–44, 83–90.

14. See "The Constitutional Status of Sexual Orientation: Homosexuality as a Suspect Classification," *Harvard Law Review* 98 (1985): 1285–1309, especially 1288–92.

15. See Robert L. Caserio, "Supreme Court Discourse vs. Homosexual Fiction," in *Displacing Homophobia,* 262–64.

16. See Janet E. Halley, "The Politics of the Closet: Towards Equal Protection for Gay, Lesbian, and Bisexual Identity," *UCLA Law Review* 36 (1989): 915–76, which has guided my discussion throughout. Halley develops her argument further in "Misreading Sodomy: A Critique of the Classification of 'Homosexuality' in Federal Equal Protection Law," in Julia Epstein and Kristina Straub, eds., *Body Guards* (New York: Routledge, 1991), 351–77.

17. For the texts of the statutes, see the appendix to "The Right of Privacy and Other Constitutional Challenges to Sodomy Statutes," *Toledo Law Review* 15 (1984): 868–75. This piece seems to have been influential for the minority opinion in *Bowers v. Hardwick.* It is, of course, the case that citation of early English statutes in current law does not exhaust the question of the archaic quality of these formulations; descriptions of sodomy as the crime against nature or as an "unnatural" act have medieval origins, as James A. Brundage notes in his appendix 3, "Survivals of Medieval Sex Law in the United States and the Western World," in *Law, Sex, and Christian Society in Medieval Europe* (Chicago: University of Chicago Press, 1987), 612.

18. For further consideration of this decision, see Halley, "Politics of the Closet," 954–55. In the confusions of definition that I pursue, I follow Halley's discussion on 949–56. For details about state laws, see Halley, 919 n. 14, and *Sexual Orientation and the Law,* 9–10. On the presumptions about knowledge, see Sedgwick, *Epistemology of the Closet,* 45 and chapter 4 *passim.*

19. I owe this point to Lee Edelman, "Capital Offenses: Sodomy in the Seat of American Government" (Paper delivered at the 105th Annual Meeting of the Modern Languages Association, Washington, D.C., December 1989); to be reprinted in Edelman's forthcoming *Homographesis: Essays in Gay Literary and Cultural Theory.*

20. See Sylvia Law, "Homosexuality and the Social Meaning of Gender," *Wisconsin Law Review* (1988): 187–235. Further citations appear parenthetically in the text.

21. See Norman Vieira, "*Hardwick* and the Right of Privacy," *University*

of Chicago Law Review 55 (1988): 1181–91. Further citations appear parenthetically in the text.

22. For some telling statistics for 1880, see Jonathan Katz, *Gay American History* (New York: Thomas Y. Crowell, 1976), 36, which shows that of the 63 people in jail at that time on sodomy convictions, 32 were classified as "colored," while of the 31 whites, 11 were foreign-born.

23. See Blackmun 2845, Stevens 2857, and Andrew Koppelman, "The Miscegenation Analogy: Sodomy Law as Sex Discrimination," *Yale Law Journal* 98 (1988): 145–64.

24. See Jonathan Ned Katz, *Gay/Lesbian Almanac* (New York: Harper & Row, 1983), 31–65, and, following Katz, John D'Emilio and Estelle B. Freedman, *Intimate Matters: A History of Sexuality in America* (New York: Harper & Row, 1988), 15–38. For a brilliant inquiry into the (non)relations of gays and the family, see Michael Warner, "Fear of a Queer Planet," *Social Text* 29 (1991): 3–17, especially 9–11.

25. Alan Bray, *Homosexuality in Renaissance England* (London: Gay Men's Press, 1982); "Homosexuality and the Signs of Male Friendship in Elizabethan England," *History Workshop Journal* 19 (1990): 1–19.

26. The fullest discussion of lesbianism in the Renaissance that I know appears in the introduction to Judith C. Brown, *Immodest Acts* (New York: Oxford University Press, 1986). Valerie Traub, in her unpublished essay "The (In)Significance of 'Lesbian' Desire in Early Modern England," advances the discussion considerably by looking beyond legal discourse to other discursive sites (such as gynecology) in which same-sex desire can be imagined, and by paying attention to national differences in the understanding of sexual regimes.

27. Ian Maclean, *The Renaissance Notion of Woman* (Cambridge: Cambridge University Press, 1980).

28. Most of the work in English history, following Mary McIntosh's "The Homosexual Role" (1968), reprinted with a postscript in Kenneth Plummer, ed., *The Making of the Modern Homosexual* (London: Hutchinson, 1981), has concentrated on the late seventeenth century and on—the emergence of the "molly" as a recognizable form of an alternative sexual identity, the earliest manifestation of a protogay identity; such work, often committed to a transhistorical definition of homosexuality, has been variously resistant to Bray and to Foucault; for some representative examples, one might consult the essays gathered in Kent Gerard and Gert Hekma, eds., *The Pursuit of Sodomy: Male Homosexuality in Renaissance and Enlightenment Europe* (New York: Harrington Park, 1989), or in Robert Purks MacCubbin, ed., *'Tis Nature's Fault: Unauthorized Sexuality During the Enlightenment* (Cambridge: Cambridge University Press, 1985, 1987). To gauge the differences between the persecution of sodomites in Spain, by the Inquisition, in those places where sodomy fell under its purview, and by civil codes, to see how variously sodomites were prosecuted *even in the same city,* one can consult the arguments and evidence presented in Mary Elizabeth Perry, *Gender and Disorder in Early Modern Seville* (Princeton:

Princeton University Press, 1990), and in William Monter, *Frontiers of Heresy* (Cambridge: Cambridge University Press, 1990). For Italy, one can look to Guido Ruggiero, *The Boundaries of Eros* (New York: Oxford University Press, 1985), for data, if not much in the way of analysis, about sodomy in Renaissance Venice.

29. Joseph Pequigney, *Such Is My Love: A Study of Shakespeare's Sonnets* (Chicago: University of Chicago Press, 1985), 64–80.

30. Joel Fineman, *Shakespeare's Perjured Eye* (Berkeley and Los Angeles: University of California Press, 1986). Fineman's argument that Shakespeare "invents" heterosexuality in the sonnets is structured for much of the book in terms of invidious distinction between a narcissistic homosexuality and a misogynistic heterosexuality that is claimed at least to recognize alterity. Here and there, from the middle of the book on, Fineman relaxes his absolute opposition between hetero- and homosexuality.

31. This is also the case in Thomas Laqueur's *Making Sex* (Cambridge: Harvard University Press, 1990), much as the evidence he presents about classical and Renaissance biology might have led to quite other conclusions since, unlike later constructions of biological sex, these do not suppose male and female as opposite, that is, do not root procreation in some vision of a biological necessity registered in "opposite sexes" and their need to join. The biology that Laqueur details seems to me one that follows from the indistinction of hetero- and homosexuality. Laqueur's difficulties in reconciling this biology with all the social injunctions to marry and procreate can, I think, be handled through a recognition that the demands of alliance are not rooted in sexual desire.

32. Eve Kosofsky Sedgwick, *Between Men: English Literature and Male Homosocial Desire* (New York: Columbia University Press, 1985).

33. See Judith Butler, *Gender Trouble: Feminism and the Subversion of Identity* (New York: Routledge, 1990).

34. See Denise Riley, *Am I That Name?* (Minneapolis: University of Minnesota Press, 1989). Gregory W. Bredbeck attempts to raise such questions about the identity of the sodomite in chapter 4 of his *Sodomy and Interpretation* (Ithaca: Cornell University Press, 1991).

35. One would not have even the suspicion that that is the case from perusing *Representations* 33 (1991), a volume devoted to the special topic of "The New World."

36. This work is extended brilliantly in Michael Warner's "New English Sodom," *American Literature* 64 (1992): 19–47, the initial essay in a project that aims at uncovering the relationships between liberalism and sexuality in the United States. Other related essays by Warner include "*Walden*'s Erotic Economy," in Hortense J. Spillers, ed., *Comparative American Identities* (New York: Routledge, 1991), 157–74, and "Thoreau's Bottom," *Raritan* 11 (1992): 53–79.

37. There is, of course, a large corpus of critical literature that has exposed much in the prevailing discourses; exemplary here is Cindy Patton, *Inventing AIDS* (New York: Routledge, 1990).

CHAPTER 2

1. See especially Louis A. Montrose, "Of Gentlemen and Shepherds: The Politics of Elizabethan Pastoral Form," *ELH* 50 (1983): 415–59, especially 433–59.

2. "The substitution of Puttenham for Sidney as the authoritative English commentator on the poetry of his contemporaries could be taken as one striking occurrence in the brief history of the new historicism," Crewe writes in *Hidden Designs* (New York: Methuen, 1986), 71. (Further citations appear parenthetically in the text.) Crewe complicates the familiar story in a number of ways: by showing that Puttenham already has written what critics have "discovered" in him—that poetry is political—but also by suggesting that there is a yet "undiscovered" and perhaps undiscoverable story to be told, one in which Sidney no longer secures some idealist position but one too in which Puttenham as a cover for Spenser or for Spenserian ambitions points to a malign power of poetry that threatens rather than simply supports constituted power.

3. See " 'Those Terrible Aproches': Sexuality, Social Mobility, and Resisting the Courtliness of Puttenham's *The Arte of English Poesie*," *ELR* 20 (1990): 179–208, especially 190–91, 196–98.

4. George Puttenham, *The Arte of English Poesie*, the Edward Arber edition with an introduction by Baxter Hathaway (1906; reprint, Kent, Ohio: Kent State University Press, 1970), 146–48. Further citations are to this edition and appear parenthetically in the text.

5. " 'The Lady Was a Little Perverse': The 'Gender' of Persuasion in Puttenham's *Arte of English Poesie*," in Joseph A. Boone and Michael Cadden, eds., *Engendering Men* (New York: Routledge, 1990), 53–65.

6. Fundamentally implicated in Lezra's account are the assumptions that govern Patricia Parker's *Literary Fat Ladies* (London: Methuen, 1987), with its determinately reductive plot of gender difference.

7. For further thoughts along these lines, see pp. 242–47 of my "Speculations: *Macbeth* and Source," in Jean Howard and Marion O'Connor, eds., *Shakespeare Reproduced* (New York: Methuen, 1987), 242–64.

8. See especially " 'Shaping Fantasies': Figurations of Gender and Power in Elizabethan Culture," *Representations* 2 (1983): 61–94, especially 77–79. Further citations appear parenthetically in the text.

9. See "Shakespeare's Comic Heroines, Elizabeth I, and the Political Uses of Androgyny," in Mary Beth Rose, ed., *Women in the Middle Ages and the Renaissance* (Syracuse, N.Y.: Syracuse University Press, 1986), and, in greater detail, *Puzzling Shakespeare* (Berkeley and Los Angeles: University of California Press, 1988), 55–105, from which I will be citing parenthetically in the text. For similar arguments, see Gabriele Bernhard Jackson, "Topical Ideology: Witches, Amazons, and Shakespeare's Joan of Arc," in Kirby Farrell, Elizabeth H. Hageman, and Arthur Kinney, eds., *Women in the Renaissance* (Amherst: University of Massachusetts Press, 1990), 88–117, especially 107–8. The essay originally appeared in *ELR* in 1988.

10. On the problem of female rule, see Constance Jordan, "Woman's Rule in Sixteenth-Century British Political Thought," *Renaissance Quarterly* 40 (1987): 421–51, and her discussion in *Renaissance Feminism* (Ithaca: Cornell University Press, 1990), 116–33.

11. Montrose's fondness for this formulation is suggested when he repeats it verbatim in "The Work of Gender in the Discourse of Discovery," *Representations* 33 (1991): 27.

12. Contrasting Elizabethan England with non-Western cultures that find a place for "dazzling multiform" women, Marcus suggests that there was no such place for Elizabeth's image "that would have allowed it to be separated from the merely deviant" (61). Elsewhere, she describes Greenblatt's work on male/female biological identity as dealing with "deviant male sexuality" (68). That by "deviant" Marcus means homosexual is suggested when she endorses Lisa Jardine's work on "deviance and homoerotic display" (239 n. 88).

13. For a Lacanian reading of this passage, see Christopher Pye, *The Regal Phantasm* (London: Routledge, 1990), 36–37.

14. For a sampling of texts that seem to depend on the slippages from *vir* to *virago* to *virtus,* see Winfried Schleiner, "*Divina virago*: Queen Elizabeth as Amazon," *Studies in Philology* 75 (1978): 163–80, especially the verse cited on 168. I am grateful to Elizabeth Hines for pointing out to me the play on the signifier here, one that destabilizes sex and its location.

15. For some representative samples, see Allison Heisch, "Queen Elizabeth I: Parliamentary Rhetoric and the Exercise of Power," *Signs* 1 (1975): 31–55; for example: "I have as good a corage awnsuerable to my place as evere my fathere hade" (35), a statement echoed at Tilbury.

16. "As a young woman, Elizabeth had liked to place herself directly in front of the giant Holbein portrait of Henry VIII at Whitehall, challenging those present to measure her own bearing and authority against the majestic 'splendour' of her father," Marcus writes, going on to link the Tilbury appearance with Henry's militarism (*Puzzling Shakespeare,* 55). For further discussion of the Holbein portrait and its relation to a later representation of the queen, see Catherine Belsey, "Richard Levin and Indifferent Reading," *NLH* 21 (1990): 449–56. Harrington's remark that Elizabeth "left no doubtings whose daughter she was" is cited in Stephen Greenblatt, *Renaissance Self-Fashioning* (Chicago: University of Chicago Press, 1980), 169.

17. See Marcus, *Puzzling Shakespeare,* 97.

18. Philippa Berry, *Of Chastity and Power: Elizabethan Literature and the Unmarried Queen* (London: Routledge, 1989). Arguing against received accounts of the "cult of Elizabeth" (those of Frances Yates, Roy Strong, Leonard Tennenhouse), Berry writes, "at the heart of this cult were numerous depictions of a woman *with other women*" (65), a fact generally ignored. John Lyly is the writer that Berry sees most often insisting on this all-female world as a sexual one; see, for example, 123–24; she also writes acutely about Spenser's "Aprill" eclogue on 79–82.

19. This is the telling argument of Eve Kosofsky Sedgwick's *Epistemology of the Closet* (Berkeley and Los Angeles: University of California Press, 1990).

20. Constance Jordan, "Representing Political Androgyny: More on the Sieve Portrait of Queen Elizabeth I," in Anne M. Haselkorn and Betty S. Travitsky, eds., *The Renaissance Englishwoman in Print* (Amherst: University of Massachusetts Press, 1990), 157–76. Further citations appear parenthetically in the text. Jordan's analysis bears comparison with the one I offer in *Endlesse Worke: Spenser and the Structures of Discourse* (Baltimore: Johns Hopkins University Press, 1981), 153–57.

21. Pye, *Regal Phantasm,* 34–36.

22. On this point, see Pam Wright, "A Change in Direction: The Ramifications of a Female Household, 1558–1603," in David Starkey, ed., *The English Court* (London, Longman, 1987), 147–72.

23. Citations from Hall's *Chronicles* and state papers from David Starkey, "Intimacy and Innovation: The Rise of the Privy Chamber, 1485–1547," in David Starkey, ed., *The English Court,* 80. A fuller narrative is offered by Starkey in *The Reign of Henry VIII* (London: Franklin Watts, 1986), 70–81. Further details about the control of signature and finances are presented in Starkey's "Court and Government," in Christopher Coleman and David Starkey, eds., *Revolution Reassessed* (Oxford: Clarendon, 1986), 29–58.

24. Quoted in Eric Ives, *Anne Boleyn* (Oxford: Basil Blackwell, 1986), 130.

25. Henry Savage, ed., *The Love Letters of Henry VIII* (London: Allan Wingate, n.d.), 40. In a note, Savage remarks that "lieu" usually means "room" but that "there can be little doubt as to Henry's meaning"—little doubt, that is, that the meaning that I am suggesting is there. A facsimile of the letter (Savage, *Love Letters,* 104) makes it unclear why Ives brackets the phrase "wisheth you [were here] instead of your brother" in his translation (*Anne Boleyn,* 103).

26. Or so Retha M. Warnicke argues in *The Rise and Fall of Anne Boleyn* (Cambridge: Cambridge University Press, 1989); she believes that George Boleyn and Mark Smeaton were lovers; see 216–19.

27. See Alan Bray, "Homosexuality and the Signs of Male Friendship in Elizabethan England," *History Workshop Journal* 29 (1990): 1–19.

28. See Jean Kaulek, ed., *Correspondance Politique de Mm. de Castillon et de Marillac Ambassadeurs de France en Angleterre (1537–1542)* (Paris: Félix Alcan, 1885), 364, a dispatch of November 22, 1541, from Marillac. I was drawn to this account by Lacey Baldwin Smith, *Henry VIII: The Mask of Royalty* (London: Jonathan Cape, 1971), 173.

29. "Although Flamock's indiscreet 'rappe' appears to challenge the hierarchy which placed him at the heels of his king as they entered the park, the standard-bearer enlists his 'rappe' in an effort to reinforce that hierarchy. By pairing the King's blast for the keeper with his own for the keeper's man, he decorously claims that even his potentially subversive 'rappe' actually occurred at the command not of his belly but of his King" (Rosemary Kegl, "'Those Terrible Aproches,'" *ELR* 20 [1990]: 188).

30. Puttenham's "etc." covers more than Flamock's fart, as another version of the story that quotes his reply in full suggests: "Within this hour / She pist full sower / And let a fart," cited in Smith, *Henry VIII,* 66.

31. Louis Adrian Montrose, "Of Gentlemen and Shepherds: The Politics of Elizabethan Pastoral Form," *ELH* 50 (1983): 438. The final phrase cites Puttenham, "Poets them selves cunning Princepleasers" (32).

32. Jonathan Crewe, *Trials of Authorship* (Berkeley and Los Angeles: University of California Press, 1990), 49.

33. Jonathan Crewe, *Hidden Designs,* 126; see also chapter 5 *passim.*

34. On the trope of the fatality of homosexual desire, see, among others, Jeff Nunakawa, "*In Memoriam* and the Extinction of the Homosexual," *ELH* 58 (1991): 427–38. I am grateful to Tim Dean for alerting me to the drift of Crewe's argument. Crewe follows a suggestion first made by S. P. Zitner in "Truth and Mourning in a Sonnet by Surrey," *ELH* 50 (1983): 509–29. Noticing the sexual implications in Surrey's description of putting his will into Clere's hands in "Norfolk sprang thee, Lambeth holds thee dead," Zitner declares "no problem" and endorses the "regularity" of Surrey's marriage against "going further with the possible implications of 'will'" (516). To his credit, Crewe goes further. Zitner's fantasy of the exclusivity of hetero- and homosexual relations is simply that, and it is worth recalling that after Surrey's marriage in 1532, he traveled with Richmond to the Continent, spending time in the court of Francis I; Surrey began living with his wife in 1533, the year that Richmond married Surrey's sister—which hardly distanced himself from him. In this context, it is worth recalling that from 1543 on, Surrey served as Henry VIII's cupbearer—his Ganymede; he was one of the minions Henry gathered around him in the 1540s. The fact that Henry rewrote—in his own hand—the writ accusing Surrey of treason suggests how extraordinarily close they were; Henry loathed writing. On the latter point, see Starkey, *Henry VIII,* 158, and Lacey Baldwin Smith, *Henry VIII,* 256–57, for details.

35. Sir Thomas Wyatt, *The Complete Poems,* ed. R. A. Rebholz (1978; reprint, London: Penguin, 1988). Further citations appear parenthetically in the text. Besides the notes mentioned below, see the comments on 369, where a poem is presented as being alternatively about Wyatt's political life or his "private life," or notes on 401–2, where Rebholz again denies the legitimacy of Tottel's title and so doing desexualizes the poem.

36. For a fine discussion of the poem and the subjectivity effects it produces, see Stephen Merriam Foley, *Sir Thomas Wyatt* (Boston: Twayne, 1990), 39–42. Foley sees as mutually implicated the languages of love and friendship, of amorous and political courtship, and ends his account of the poem with a description of Wyatt's behavior at the death of Cromwell.

37. The essay first appeared in 1977 and has been reprinted in Joan Kelly, *Women, History and Theory* (Chicago: University of Chicago Press, 1984), 19–50, from which I cite. Further citations appear parenthetically in the text.

38. Barbara Correll, "Malleable Material, Models of Power: Woman in

Erasmus's 'Marriage Group' and *Civility in Boys*," *ELH* 57 (1990): 241–62. Further citations appear parenthetically in the text.

39. Stephen Greenblatt, *Renaissance Self-Fashioning*, chapter 3, reviewed by Marguerite Waller, "Academic Tootsie: The Denial of Difference and the Difference It Makes," *Diacritics* 17 (1987): 2–20. Waller's essay appears in a somewhat expanded form in Sheila Fisher and Janet E. Halley, eds., *Seeking the Woman in Late Medieval and Renaissance Writings* (Knoxville: University of Tennessee Press, 1990).

40. "Dyvers thy death doo dyverslye bemone," #29 in Surrey, *Poems*, ed. Emrys Jones (Oxford: Clarendon Press, 1964). Extraordinarily, Crewe endorses an editorial note on the conclusion of this poem which reverses the ending of the Pyramus and Thisby story (*Trials*, 76), presumably in the interest of rescuing Surrey from being displaced by the "feminine" Wyatt. Further citations of Surrey are to this edition.

41. See Surrey, #22–24; of the first, "Gyrtt in my giltlesse gowne," Jones comments that "the woman speaks for herself" (118), a remark that may be truer than he supposes since, as he notes, the poem is assigned to Surrey only in the second edition of Tottel, and even there not all of the poem, as it is found in manuscripts, is printed. On #23, "O happy dames, that may embrace," Jones describes the poem as "written for the Countess of Surrey," following the note in Frederick Morgan Padelford's edition of *The Poems of Henry Howard Earl of Surrey* (Seattle: University of Washington Press, 1928), who not only sees it as "for the Countess" but also as "perhaps . . . for Mary Shelton" (215). For a brilliant consideration of these poems and the problem of Surrey writing as a woman, see Anthony Scott, "The Fatality of Surrey's Desire," forthcoming. On Wyatt, see, for example, Rebholz, 420 (on #115).

42. See, for example, S. P. Zitner, "Truth and Mourning." "Her hand is a scrawl," Zitner comments, and of marginalia that seem to be her writing, he goes on, "her bits of doggerel unimpressive" (513). Zitner imports both terms from the discussion by Richard Harrier in *The Canon of Sir Thomas Wyatt's Poetry* (Cambridge: Harvard University Press, 1975), 23–24. For a reproduction of Mary Shelton's italic signature in the Devonshire manuscript, see A. K. Foxwell, ed., *The Poems of Sir Thomas Wiat*, 2 vols. (London: University of London Press, 1913), facing 1:251.

43. For similar remarks, see Puttenham, 180, 184, 256.

CHAPTER 3

1. All citations from *The Poetical Works of Edmund Spenser*, ed. J. C. Smith and E. De Selincourt (London: Oxford University Press, 1912); line numbers provided for verse, page numbers for prose.

2. "A shepherd, Corydon, burned with love for handsome Alexis"; citations of Virgil and translations are informed by C. Day Lewis, *The Eclogues and Georgics of Virgil* (Garden City, N.Y.: Doubleday, 1964).

3. See Paul Veyne, "Homosexuality in Ancient Rome," in Philippe Ariès and André Bejin, eds., *Western Sexuality* (Oxford: Basil Blackwell, 1985),

26. For a brilliant historical survey, see the title essay in David M. Halperin, *One Hundred Years of Homosexuality* (London: Routledge, 1990).

4. Citations from Shakespeare are from *The Complete Pelican Shakespeare,* ed. Alfred Harbage (New York: Viking Press, 1969).

5. William Harrison Woodward, trans., *Desiderius Erasmus Concerning the Aim and Method of Education* (New York: Teachers College, Columbia University, 1964), 174. Further citations appear parenthetically in the text. In an unpublished essay, "Erasmus's 'Tigress': The Languages of Friendship, Pleasure, and the Renaissance Letter," F. Tyler Stevens has shown that elsewhere Erasmus responds more positively to male/male relations, particularly in his letters of friendship. There is a homophobic tradition of reading Erasmus's psychology noted by Barbara Correll in "Malleable Material, Models of Power: Women in Erasmus's 'Marriage Group' and *Civility in Boys,*" *ELH* 57 (1990): 260 n. 11.

6. Harry Berger, Jr., "The Mirror State of Colin Clout: A New Reading of Spenser's *Januarye* Eclogue," *Helios* n.s. 10 (1983): 151, 154. Further citations appear parenthetically in the text.

7. Alan Bray, *Homosexuality in Renaissance England* (London: Gay Men's Press, 1982), 59, 65. Further citations appear parenthetically in the text. Nothing in the critique of Bray that follows is meant to devalue Bray's book; the problem of literary evidence troubles many distinguished historians, and Bray remains the best guide to the question of homosexuality in Renaissance England.

8. My critique here follows Eve Kosofsky Sedgwick, *Between Men: English Literature and Male Homosocial Desire* (New York: Columbia University Press, 1985), 83–90. Further citations appear parenthetically in the text.

9. See my "Sodomy and Society: The Case of Christopher Marlowe," *Southwest Review* 69 (1984): 371–78.

10. Michel Foucault, *The History of Sexuality,* vol. 1, *An Introduction,* trans. Robert Hurley (New York: Pantheon, 1978), part 4.

11. For the role of "open secrets" to secure the secret subjectivity of the modern subject, see D. A. Miller, "Secret Subjects, Open Secrets," in *The Novel and the Police* (Berkeley and Los Angeles: University of California Press, 1988), 192–220.

12. See Michel Foucault, *The Use of Pleasure,* trans. Robert Hurley (New York: Vintage Books, 1986), 187–225. In Virgil's second eclogue, much depends, in the final lines of the poem (69–73), upon whether Corydon continues to address himself or is being addressed—something that remains undecidable and thus keeps open the question of the perspective taken on his "dementia" (69).

13. For further discussion of these issues, see my "Consuming Texts: Spenser and the Poet's Economy," in *Voice Terminal Echo: Postmodernism and English Renaissance Texts* (New York: Methuen, 1986).

14. I have in mind the Lacanian framework, in which the refusal ever to embody Rosalind as a "real" woman would testify to the structure of desire

shaped by an Other that is, by definition, inaccessible. This leads, within the Lacanian schema, to the postulate that there is no woman per se; and this leads, within an argument like Sedgwick's, to a realization of the homosocial structure between men that covers over the place of woman. Thus, Berger's ethical complaint—that Colin is in love with a projected idea of woman—can be supported by the recognition of psychic and social structures that make the place of woman insupportable. Yet this structure obtains not only in the case of Rosalind, but underwrites the divided place of Colin Clout—and that place also writes itself into the real, although never in the same way for each gender.

15. The translation, by Rudolf Gottfried, is from *Spenser's Prose Works*, vol. 9 of the Variorum Edition, ed. Edwin Greenlaw et al. (Baltimore: Johns Hopkins Press, 1949), 258.

16. Gottfried, 258, translating these lines: "Utinam meus hic *Edmundus* adesset, / Qui nova scripsisset, nec Amores conticuisset / Ipse suos, et saepe animo, verbisque benignis / Fausta precaretur" (*Poetical Works*, 638).

17. The first phrase, from Shakespeare's sonnet 116, is invoked by Arthur Marotti in "'Love is not love': Elizabethan Sonnet Sequences and the Social Order," *ELH* 49 (1982): 396–428, and is the guiding thesis as well in his *John Donne: Coterie Poet* (Madison: University of Wisconsin Press, 1986). The translation of pastoral *otium* into *negotium* is the theme in a number of essays by Louis Adrian Montrose, several of which deal with Spenser: "'The perfecte paterne of a Poete': The Poetics of Courtship in *The Shepheardes Calender*," *Texas Studies in Literature and Language* 21 (1979): 34–67; "'Eliza, Queene of shepheardes,' and the Pastoral of Power," *ELR* 10 (1980): 153–82; and "Of Gentlemen and Shepherds: The Politics of Elizabethan Pastoral Form," *ELH* 50 (1983): 415–59. My argument here attempts to modify the point made repeatedly in this work, that love must be translated into something "real"—ambition—or that pastoral functions as a cover for a place in the world and negotiates the desire for it.

18. Cited in Virginia Stern, *Gabriel Harvey: His Life, Marginalia and Library* (Oxford: Clarendon Press, 1979), 237; for information on Spenser's secretaryship to Bishop Young, see 48–49. For the significance of secretaryships for class and subject formation in this period, see my *Writing Matter: From the Hands of the English Renaissance* (Stanford: Stanford University Press, 1990), chapter 5. For a study that situates Spenser in these secretarial contexts, see Richard Rambuss, *Spenser's Secret Career* (Cambridge: Cambridge University Press, 1992). Harvey's parasitic relationship to texts, living in his marginal annotations, I take also to describe a modus vivendi, an argument I make in part thanks to unpublished work by Jennifer Summit.

19. Gottfried, 256, translating these lines: "Spiritus ad summos, scio, te generosus Honores / Exstimulat, maiusque docet spirare Poetam, / Quam levis est Amor" (*Poetical Works*, 637).

20. "Per tuam Venerem altera Rosalindula est: eamque non alter, sed idem ille, (tua, ut ante, bona cum gratia) copiosè amat Hobbinolus. O mea

Domina Immerito, mea bellissima Collina Clouta, multo plus plurimum salve, atque vale" (*Poetical Works,* 632); my translation depends on the one offered in Frederic Ives Carpenter, *A Reference Guide to Edmund Spenser* (Chicago: University of Chicago Press, 1923), 58.

21. Roger Ascham, *The Schoolmaster* (1570), ed. Lawrence V. Ryan (Ithaca: Cornell University Press, 1967), 80. The secret of the shared bed is more usually declared in patronage and servant/master relations where, as Alan Bray argues in "Homosexuality and the Signs of Male Friendship in Elizabethan England," *History Workshop Journal* 29 (1990): 1–19, shared beds (or tables) suggest intimate power and influence. Thus, Archbishop Laud recorded in his diary on August 21, 1625, a dream of sleeping with Buckingham. When these relations were politically suspect, such intimacies could fall under the shadow of sodomy. In "Pederasty in Elizabethan London" (Paper delivered at the International Scientific Conference on Gay and Lesbian Studies, Free University, Amsterdam, December 15–18, 1987), Robert M. Wren starts with the *Januarye* eclogue and extends Bray's arguments to the theaters and schools—pointing as well to shared beds in such plays as Middleton's *Michaelmas Term,* Chapman's *Sir Giles Goosecap,* and Shakespeare's *Henry V* and *Othello*—suggesting, too, that medical manuals may have encouraged masturbation in a widespread and culturally countenanced pederasty.

22. I cite the texts of the 1609 edition of Shakespeare's sonnets from Stephen Booth, ed., *Shakespeare's Sonnets* (New Haven: Yale University Press, 1977).

23. Jacques Lacan, *Ecrits I* (Paris: Seuil, 1966), 92: "Faits qui s'inscrivent dans un ordre d'identification homéomorphique qu'envelopperait la question du sens de la beauté comme formative et comme érogène." In *Ecrits: A Selection,* trans. Alan Sheridan (New York: Norton, 1977), the passage reads: "Such facts are inscribed in an order of homeomorphic identification that would itself fall within the larger question of the meaning of beauty as both formative and erogenic" (3).

24. See Jacques Derrida, *The Post Card from Socrates to Freud and Beyond,* trans. Alan Bass (Chicago: University of Chicago Press, 1987).

25. Virgil B. Heltzel and Hoyt H. Hudson, eds. and trans., *Nobilis; or, A View of the Life and Death of a Sidney* (San Marino, Calif.: Huntington Library, 1940), 19; their translation reads: "For the courts are, as it were, common inns of kingdoms, in which live a great many of the base along with the upright. By no discipline can it be avoided that day by day a foison of delights and desires newly abound, and variously transform men into women, women into men, men into beasts, the scrupulous and devout into sodomites and gallants" (78).

Work on this section would not have been possible without the important collaborative work of a seminar at Johns Hopkins on writing by Renaissance women that met in the spring of 1990: in particular, Charles Barker's work on the Countess of Pembroke has been of enormous help, as has Jennifer Summit's on Nashe and Harvey and their relation to Spenser.

26. Edmund Spenser, *The Minor Poems, Volume 1,* vol. 7 of the Variorum Edition, ed. C. G. Osgood and H. G. Lotspeich (Baltimore: Johns Hopkins Press, 1943), 7:487. The editors also wonder who Stella is in *Astrophel,* but do not address the question; I defer it too.

27. Most recently in Michael Brennan's *Literary Patronage in the English Renaissance* (London: Routledge, 1988), which summarily assigns the poem to Spenser, 62.

28. Margaret P. Hannay, *Philip's Phoenix* (New York: Oxford University Press, 1990), 65.

29. Thomas Perrin Harrison, Jr., *The Pastoral Elegy: An Anthology* (Austin: University of Texas, 1934), 285.

30. Peter Sacks, *The English Elegy* (Baltimore: Johns Hopkins University Press, 1985), 338 n. 17.

31. Richard C. McCoy, *The Rites of Knighthood* (Berkeley and Los Angeles: University of California Press, 1989), 187 n. 50; McCoy cites the Variorum for the usual attribution; the reference to Josephine Roberts is to her bibliographical essay in *ELR* 14 (1984): 426–39, reprinted and updated in Kirby Farrell, Elizabeth H. Hageman, and Arthur F. Kinney, eds., *Women in the Renaissance* (Amherst: University of Massachusetts Press, 1988).

32. Frances Berkeley Young, *Mary Sidney Countess of Pembroke* (London: David Nutt, 1912), 134.

33. Gary F. Waller, "Introduction" to *The Triumph of Death and Other Unpublished and Uncollected Poems by Mary Sidney* (Salzburg: Institut für Sprache und Literatur, 1977), 56. Waller further supports Friedrich's views in his *Mary Sidney, Countess of Pembroke: A Critical Study of Her Writings and Literary Milieu* (Salzburg: Institüt für Anglistik und Amerikanistik, 1979), 92–93.

34. Things are changing, however; I have been told by an editor that Oxford University Press is negotiating with Margaret Hannay for an edition of Mary Sidney.

35. See George Chauncey, "From Sexual Inversion to Homosexuality: Medicine and the Changing Conceptualization of Female Deviance," *Salmagundi* 58/59 (1982/83): 114–46, and Carroll Smith-Rosenberg, "The New Woman as Androgyne: Social Disorder and Gender Crisis, 1870–1936," in *Disorderly Conduct* (New York: Oxford University Press, 1985). On the relationship between the female vote and questions of the feminine, see Denise Riley, *Am I That Name?* (Minneapolis: University of Minnesota Press, 1989).

36. William Oram, introduction to *Astrophel* and *The Doleful Lay of Clorinda,* in *The Yale Edition of the Shorter Poems of Edmund Spenser,* ed. Oram et al. (New Haven: Yale University Press, 1989), 565. Further citations appear parenthetically in the text.

37. See G. W. Pigman III, *Grief and English Renaissance Elegy* (Cambridge: Cambridge University Press, 1985), 152 n. 23; Pigman finds the

consolation offered by Clorinda to be part of his "rigorist" tradition of questioning grief; no surprise, then, that the rigorous view must have been written by a man.

38. Alternatively, Elaine Beilen has no hesitation in treating the *Lay* as the countess's, since, in her reading, it offers utterly conventional Christian, and therefore female, consolation; see her *Redeeming Eve* (Princeton: Princeton University Press, 1987), 137–39.

39. Sacks defends against what I am suggesting here when he insists that "the familiar motif of piercing and breeding" (52) must be heterosexually generative; the familiar breeds the family in a "displaced sexual energy" which is a literary heterosexuality that can carry the speaker "beyond the weaker introversions of melancholy" (52). "Introversions" is but a syllable away from the "inversions" that this reading seeks not to acknowledge, and almost does, despite itself. This "familiar motif" is also defamiliarized in the letters prefatory to the *Arcadia,* which I cite below.

40. Nashe makes these charges in *Have with You to Saffron-Walden* in *Works of Thomas Nashe,* ed. R. B. McKerrow (London: Adelphi, 1910), III.35, 92, 111–12, 123. Nashe also charges Harvey with sexual sycophancy—the letters produced in his commendation before *Pierces Superrogation* were, Nashe claims, written by "his minions and sweet-harts" (108).

41. George Whetstone, *Sir Phillip Sidney: his honourable life, his valiant death* (London, 1586), B2v; the claim that Whetstone is an accurate reporter in all other respects is made by A. J. Colaianne and W. L. Godshalk in their introduction to *Elegies for Sir Philip Sidney* (Delmar, N.Y.: Scholars' Facsimiles, 1980).

42. For Lodowick Bryskett's authorship and Milton's borrowings from the poem, see Bryskett's *A Discourse of Civill Life,* ed. Thomas E. Wright (Northridge, Calif.: San Fernando Valley State College, 1970), xviii nn. 1 and 5. Bryskett's dialogue, largely a translation of Guazzo, features a speaker called Edmund Spenser; by the end, the author of the dialogue is represented as "being betrayed by M. *Spenser*" (205) into writing what Spenser should have written; as the dialogue opens, Spenser claims he has already written what the dialogue says he should have, in *The Faerie Queene,* which, he also claims, he has yet to write (22–23). These dizzying claims, which hardly exhaust Spenser's contribution to the book, are recognizably Spenserian.

43. Sir Philip Sidney, *The Countess of Pembroke's Arcadia,* ed. Maurice Evans (Harmondsworth: Penguin, 1977), 57, 59; cited from the prefatory letters signed by Sidney and H. S. (Hugh Sanford, secretary to the countess).

44. The letter is printed by Hannay (63–64), who argues (like others before her, including Waller) for its status as evidence of the countess's authorship of the *Lay.*

45. Sir Philip Sidney, *A Defence of Poetry,* ed. J. A. Van Dorsten (Oxford: Oxford University Press, 1966), 22. This description of the psalms bears, of course, on the countess's hand in that Sidney text.

CHAPTER 4

I wish to express my gratitude to Eve Kosofsky Sedgwick, Jonathan Crewe, and David Riggs for comments on an earlier draft of this chapter. This chapter continues an earlier essay of mind, "Sodomy and Society: The Case of Christopher Marlowe," *Southwest Review* 69 (1985): 371–78, an analysis of accusations against Marlowe circulated by Richard Baines. A slightly revised version of this essay appears in David Scott Kastan and Peter Stallybrass, eds., *Staging the Renaissance* (New York: Routledge, 1991), 75–82.

1. All citations from *The Complete Plays of Christopher Marlowe,* ed. Irving Ribner (Indianapolis: Odyssey, 1963).

2. Sara Munson Deats, "Marlowe's Fearful Symmetry in *Edward II,*" in Kenneth Friedenreich, Roma Gill, and Constance B. Kuriyama, eds., *"A Poet and a filthy Play-maker": New Essays on Christopher Marlowe* (New York: AMS Press, 1988), 260 n. 13.

3. All page references to the edition of Edward Arber in the *English Reprints* 3 (Birmingham, 1868).

4. As Jonathan V. Crewe argues persuasively in "The Theatre of the Idols: Marlowe, Rankins, and Theatrical Images," *Theatre Journal* 36 (1984): 321–33, the discourses of Marlovian theater and antitheatricality are mutually (de)constitutive. Priority is less the issue than an ongoing and internalized debate.

5. Cited in Ed Cohen, "Legislating the Norm: From Sodomy to Gross Indecency," in Ronald R. Butters, John M. Clum, and Michael Moon, eds., *Displacing Homophobia* (Durham, N.C.: Duke University Press, 1989), 176, and in Alan Bray, *Homosexuality in Renaissance England* (London: Gay Men's Press, 1982), 75, accompanied with a full discussion of foreign projection as a favored English way of misrecognizing native behavior.

6. Stephen Orgel, "Nobody's Perfect: Or, Why Did the English Stage Take Boys for Women?" in Butters et al., *Displacing Homophobia,* 7–29, and Laura Levine, "Men in Women's Clothing: Anti-theatricality and Effeminization from 1579 to 1642," *Criticism* 28 (1986): 121–43. Further citations appear parenthetically in the text.

7. See especially the opening pages of Valerie Traub's "Desire and the Difference It Makes," in Valerie Wayne, ed., *The Matter of Difference* (Ithaca: Cornell University Press, 1991), 81–114. I am grateful to Professor Traub for making her essay available to me before its publication.

8. Jean E. Howard, "Crossdressing, the Theatre, and Gender Struggle in Early Modern England," *Shakespeare Quarterly* 39 (1988): 418–40. Further citations appear parenthetically in the text. Howard lists and briefly describes the work on cross-dressing that precedes hers (419 n. 3); I will be looking at some of these items in the pages that follow. To her list could be added Katherine E. Kelly, "The Queen's Two Bodies: Shakespeare's Boy Actress in Breeches," *Theatre Journal* 42 (1990): 81–93, which largely es-

pouses the liberal constructivist line of Catherine Belsey; Kelly's contribution to this subject lies in her argument that the revelation of the boy beneath the woman's part is something that the plays work to undo, charting a path from male immaturity to female maturity. However much the argument means to show that gender is a construction, Kelly has very determinate and invidious notions of the differences between boys and women. Belsey, on the other hand, however much she seeks to loosen gender definitions, insists on maintaining heterosexuality in "Disrupting Sexual Difference: Meaning and Gender in the Comedies," in John Drakakis, ed., *Alternative Shakespeares* (London: Methuen, 1985), 166–90; her concern, she says in her closing sentence, is "relations between men and women" (190), and in teasing out "romantic" implications, she denies that possibility to homoerotic ones (see, for example, 185).

9. This is an argument that is implicitly called into question by Karen Newman's discussion of Ben Jonson's *Epicoene,* in which women are located in the market as prototypical consumers; see *Fashioning Femininity* (Chicago: University of Chicago Press, 1991), 129–43.

10. Phyllis Rackin is more on the mark when she refers to the homophobia of the play in "Androgyny, Mimesis, and the Marriage of the Boy Heroine on the English Renaissance Stage," *PMLA* 102 (1987): 31, 35. Nowhere, however, does Rackin take up any question of a positive representation of male/male sexuality in her essay. Rather, for her the boy-girl is, when viewed approvingly (in Lyly or Shakespeare), a divine androgyne, the product of the poet's imagining of a golden world in which femininity does not constrain as it does in the real world. The androgyne for Rackin is a thoroughly heterosexual figure, indeed, a marriage of male and female that is said to liberate women. Shakespeare's "ambivalent" creatures thus offer in their mediation of opposites "a kind of marriage" (37), so much so that Rosalind/Ganymede is said in the epilogue to *As You Like It* to intimate that the play's relation with its audience is "a kind of sexual transaction or marriage" (36). Clearly, for Rackin, "sexual transaction" and "marriage" are synonymous.

11. As Traub writes: "To whom is same-sex love between women funny? . . . Howard . . . assumes (without contextualizing this assumption in an essay replete with historical reference) that love between women was readily available as both a source of humor and humiliation for members of Shakespeare's audience" (82–83). In fact, judging by *A Midsummer Night's Dream,* female friendship was capable of being seen erotically—as Helen's extraordinary speech about Hermia's betrayal (3.2.195–220), with its invocation of a shared double cherry, suggests. Howard links the "humiliation" of Olivia with Titania's punishment, and the connection is suggestive along these lines; she is given an ass so her husband can have her boy, and her punishment echoes Oberon's desire, an exchange in which he acquires the boy lover he wants (with all the proprieties and prerogatives of male/male relationship), while he bequeaths to Titania the sodomitical residue of Bottom's ass.

12. See Kathleen McLuskie, "The Act, the Role, and the Actor: Boy Actresses on the Elizabethan Stage," *New Theatre Quarterly* 3 (1987): 20–30, and *Renaissance Dramatists* (Atlantic Highlands, N.J.: Humanities Press International, 1989), 100–122.

13. Orgel characterizes all the tracts as pathological.

14. Levine's approach is implicitly Freudian and builds upon the definitions of homosexuality as inversion current in the late nineteenth century; for the ways in which psychoanalysis has shaped definitions of homosexuality, see Traub, "Desire and the Difference It Makes."

15. On this point, see Alan Bray, *Homosexuality in Renaissance England,* 130–31 n. 77.

16. These presumptions are powerfully scrutinized in Eve Kosofsky Sedgwick's *Epistemology of the Closet* (Berkeley and Los Angeles: University of California Press, 1990), where such knowingness about the difference between hetero- and homosexual identity is deconstructed; and by Judith Butler's *Gender Trouble* (New York: Routledge, 1990), in which the impossibility of the performativity of gender is demonstrated. Gregory W. Bredbeck attempts to address these questions in chapter 3 of *Sodomy and Interpretation* (Ithaca: Cornell University Press, 1991). Positing sodomy as the "end" of sex—as beyond heterosexuality—he courts the danger of suggesting that homosexuality is *not* sex, and thus of reaffirming a heterosexual definition of sex that he means to question by construing sodomy as the end of sex.

17. Elaine Showalter, "Critical Cross-Dressing: Male Feminists and the Woman of the Year," *Raritan* 3 (1983): 130–49; Craig Owens, "Outlaws: Gay Men in Feminism," in Alice Jardine and Paul Smith, eds., *Men in Feminism* (New York: Methuen, 1987), 219–32.

18. Showalter's more recent work has more productively taken up a point in her essay—when she notices on p. 135 that late nineteenth-century culture mobilizes against the new woman and the newly emergent homosexual—that should have served to keep her earlier thoughts on track; that she also has come to sponsor male feminism and gay critics is attested by the introduction to Joseph Boone and Michael Cadden, *Engendering Men* (New York: Routledge, 1990).

19. Lisa Jardine, "'Girl Talk' (For Boys on the Left), or Marginalising Feminist Critical Praxis," *Oxford Literary Review* 8 (1986), 213–14. Jardine also takes Toril Moi to task for making her final point in *Sexual/Textual Politics* by way of Derrida, and thus producing "Derrida in a frock" (217 n. 16).

20. New York: Columbia University Press, 1989 (1983). Further citations appear parenthetically in the text.

21. Anthony Munday, *A Second and Third Blast of Retrait from Plaies and Theaters* (1580), facsimile, ed. Arthur Freeman (New York: Garland, 1973), 89.

22. Phillip Stubbes, *The Anatomie of Abuses* (1583), facsimile, ed. Arthur Freeman (New York: Garland, 1973), N8r–v.

23. Alan Bray, "Homosexuality and the Signs of Male Friendship in Elizabethan England," *History Workshop Journal* 29 (1990): 1–19. Further citations appear parenthetically in the text.

24. Michel Foucault, *The History of Sexuality,* vol. 1, *An Introduction,* trans. Robert Hurley (New York: Pantheon, 1978), 101.

25. Effeminization is, for Stubbes, the route to damnation. Thus, through the music and bawdy songs of minstrels, Stubbes claims that young men are "as it weare transnatured into a woman, or worse, and inclyned to all kind of whordome and abhomination" (O5r). This "worse," like the one about sodomites, can be related to the punishment Stubbes holds out for those "both men, wemen & children" who indulge in dancing; "they maye be thought nothing inferiour to *Cynoedus,* the prostitut ribauld" (M7r), and "if they repent not, & amend, it shal be easier for that land of *Sodoma* and *Gomorra* at the day of iudgement then for them" (M8r). Sodom and Gomorrah for Stubbes are the seat of pride, the cardinal vice with which the tract begins (G6r), and, elsewhere in the tract, the sins of those cities are specified as "whordom adulterie and fornication" (H2r). What Levine—or the U.S. Supreme Court—calls sodomy is not what Stubbes means by the term. It names the worst within the heterosexist construction of sex that also aligns homosexuality with transvestitism.

26. It seems fair to assume that there is some self-identification on Marlowe's part with such men. David Riggs has suggested to me that Marlowe might even have been writing with King James in mind; the scenario with Gaveston, after all, bears more than a slight resemblance to James's difficulties with favorites in Scotland, notably with his cousin, Esmé Stuart, who was banished from the realm.

27. See Sara Munson Deats, "*Edward II*: A Study in Androgyny," *Ball State University Forum* 22 (1980): 30–41.

28. Stephen Greenblatt, "Marlowe and the Will to Absolute Play," in *Renaissance Self-Fashioning: From More to Shakespeare* (Chicago: University of Chicago Press, 1980), 193–221.

29. See, for example, Claude J. Summers, "Sex, Politics, and Self-Realization in *Edward II,*" in "*A Poet and a filthy Play-maker,*" 221–40; although I think Summers errs in his emphasis on self-realization, he is quite good at detailing the class transgression in the play, noting, importantly, that Marlowe gives Gaveston lower class origins than his sources warrant, thereby emphasizing the overturning of constituted hierarchies; see 225–26.

Summers depends upon the arguments offered by James Voss in "*Edward II*: Marlowe's Historical Tragedy," *English Studies* 63 (1982): 517–30, and I have recast Voss's argument about the play representing a political conflict between traditional and personal rule into Foucauldian terms. Importantly, Voss argues that Edward can be called a weak king only from the perspective of traditions that maintain blood, and that the play dismantles that traditional point of view, thereby participating in an irreversible historic change.

Purvis E. Boyette, in "Wanton Humour and Wanton Poets: Homosexuality in Marlowe's *Edward II*," *Tulane Studies in English* 22 (1977): 33–50, notes well the willful iconoclasm of king and playwright, but rescues a spirituality in the relationship between Edward and Gaveston, arguing, like Summers, for "wholeness."

30. William Empson, "Two Proper Crimes," *The Nation* 163 (1946): 444–45. The other proper crime is atheism. Empson makes Marlowe a martyr for his causes, which perhaps overdramatizes things. He also, interestingly, slips, assigning the elder Mortimer's lines about famous kings and their minions to Edward. It is part of the fundamental strategy of the play that the defense of the relationship be offered by the opponent, and is akin to the inherent antitheatricality that Crewe reads in *Tamburlaine.*

31. Here I disagree with Jardine's claim in *Still Harping on Daughters,* 22–24.

32. To the critics cited in Simon Shepherd, *Marlowe and the Politics of Elizabethan Theatre* (New York: St. Martin's, 1986) might be added Jackson Cope, "Marlowe's *Dido* and the Titillating Children," *ELR* 4 (1974): 315–25. Cope sees that the opening scene responds to antitheatrical arguments about boys and to the fact that boys were impressed, giving further grounds for suppositions of abuse, but he nonetheless regards the opening scene as farce.

33. Shepherd, *Marlowe and the Politics of Elizabethan Theatre,* 201. Further citations appear parenthetically in the text.

34. "The Death of the Modern: Gender and Desire in Marlowe's 'Hero and Leander,'" *SAQ* 88 (1989): 757–87.

35. For the special pertinence of Ganymede to humanism, see Leonard Barkan, *Transuming Passion* (Stanford: Stanford University Press, 1991), 48–59, 67–74.

36. All citations from the March of America Facsimile Series, Number 6 (Ann Arbor: University Microfilms, 1966).

37. This is an interpretation explicitly rejected in William Ringler's *Stephen Gosson* (Princeton: Princeton University Press, 1942), 19, on the grounds that Gosson always was a moralist, never the "immoral" poet described; to believe this is to take Gosson at his word when he claims moral purpose for his plays (none of them are extant). What is valuable in Ringler is his insistence that Gosson (and many other antitheatrical writers) was not a Puritan (he became an Anglican divine), that class interest is a more coherent principle of explanation for the opposition to the theater; Ringler also provides information about John Rainoldes, among other things Gosson's teacher at Oxford, that suggests that he was not the extremist that Jardine takes him to have been; see especially 9–15.

38. John Rainoldes, *Th'Overthrow of Stage-Playes* (1599), facsimile, ed. Arthur Freeman (New York: Garland, 1974), 11.

39. *A Treatyse of the Newe India,* in the March of America Facsimile Series, Number 3 (Ann Arbor: University Microfilms, 1966), aa4r.

40. Jonas Barish, *The Anti-Theatrical Prejudice* (Berkeley and Los Angeles: University of California Press, 1981), 88.

41. The final chapter of Bray's *Homosexuality in the Renaissance* discusses the molly houses; Bray's documentation is furthered by the work of Randolph Trumbach; see "London's Sodomites: Homosexual Behavior and Western Culture in the Eighteenth Century," *Journal of Social History* 11 (1977): 1–33; "Sodomitical Subcultures, Sodomitical Roles, and the Gender Revolution of the Eighteenth Century," in R. P. MacCubbin, ed., *'Tis Nature's Fault* (Cambridge: Cambridge University Press, 1985), 109–21; "Sodomitical Assaults, Gender Role, and Sexual Development in Eighteenth-Century London," in Kent Gerard and Gert Hekma, eds., *The Pursuit of Sodomy* (New York: Harrington, 1989); "The Birth of the Queen: Sodomy and the Emergence of Gender Equality in Modern Culture, 1660–1750," in Martin Bauml Duberman, Martha Vicinus, and George Chauncey, Jr., eds., *Hidden from History: Reclaiming the Gay and Lesbian Past* (New York: Meridian, 1990), 129–40; and "Sodomy Transformed: Aristocratic Libertinage, Public Reputation and the Gender Revolution of the Eighteenth Century," in Michael S. Kimmel, ed., *Love Letters Between a Certain Late Nobleman and the Famous Mr. Wilson* (New York: Haworth, 1990). Trumbach's work valuably demonstrates that the cross-dressed "homosexual" is a phenomenon with few English antecedents before the Restoration, and that it is a newly visible form that replaces the older images of the sodomite whose sexual tastes did not run to cross-dressing, who slept with both boys and women. Trumbach's thesis that the emergence of the cross-dressed molly bespeaks a new regime of gender equality strikes me as questionable. What does seem arguable is that it marks the moment in which two genders are conceived of as oppositional and when only one form of sexuality is imagined to operate no matter what genders are involved. For a parallel argument, founded in the discourses of biology, see Thomas Laqueur, *Making Sex* (Cambridge: Harvard University Press, 1990).

42. See Joseph A. Porter, *Shakespeare's Mercutio* (Chapel Hill: University of North Carolina Press, 1988), where Mercutio is read as a figure for Marlowe, and his relationship with Romeo in counterpoint to Romeo's relationship with Juliet. Porter's view of Shakespeare is to be contrasted with the liberal humanist celebration offered by Bruce R. Smith in *Homosexual Desire in Shakespeare's England* (Chicago: University of Chicago Press, 1991), who seems to think that he is praising Shakespeare for a "more inclusive vision" than Marlowe because he reconciles "homosexual desire with established structures of ideology and power" (221). Smith ends his book exulting in Shakespeare's "more liberally imagined world for one of the many modes of human sexual desire" (270) without noting that this liberalism is one with an ideology and power structure bent on the elimination of that mode of desire.

43. See Karen Newman, "Portia's Ring: Unruly Women and Structures of Exchange in *The Merchant of Venice*," *Shakespeare Quarterly* 38 (1987): 19–

33. Newman's analysis begins, properly enough, by seeing the homosocial relation of Antonio and Bassanio as located within the paradigm of the traffic of women; what she does not consider is what happens to that relationship when Portia triumphs in the play. As I see it, the narrative of the sonnets is replayed in the play. My reading of the play finds some support in Seymour Kleinberg's "*The Merchant of Venice:* The Homosexual as Anti-Semite in Nascent Capitalism," *Journal of Homosexuality* 8 (1983): 113–26.

44. Stephen Greenblatt, *Shakespearean Negotiations* (Berkeley and Los Angeles: University of California Press, 1988), 93.

45. Beth Pittenger, "Dispatch Quickly: The Mechanical Reproduction of Pages," *Shakespeare Quarterly* 42 (1991): 389–408.

46. See Linda Charnes, "'So Unsecret to Ourselves': Notorious Identity and the Material Subject in Shakespeare's *Troilus and Cressida,*" *Shakespeare Quarterly* 40 (1989): 413–40.

CHAPTER 5

1. For the purposes at hand, the most notable exception would be Heather Findlay's "Renaissance Pederasty and Pedagogy: The 'Case' of Shakespeare's Falstaff," *Yale Journal of Criticism* 3 (1989): 229–38. Findlay is hardly entranced with Hal because she takes him as the locus of a homophobia inflicted upon the more or less sodomitical Falstaff. I agree with this point, and part of my effort here is to locate the critical complicities involved in the unknowing reproduction of this structure. Nonetheless, much as I admire Findlay's essay, and much as this chapter follows certain very similar trajectories (including considerations of class formation and its relation to the protobourgeois domestication of women), I aim here to mark ways in which the play fails to deliver the Hal that criticism reproduces and that Findlay assumes to be in place. So doing, I hope to move sodomy from the archaic and marginal position that it occupies in Findlay's essay, and to allow it the space of a recognition that would trouble received readings of the play of various critical stripes.

2. Phyllis Rackin, *Stages of History* (Ithaca: Cornell University Press, 1990), 29, 70, 79. The first time, the phrase "mirror of all Christian kings" is not in quotation marks, the second time it is, the third time its source is given: each repetition of the phrase gives it further authority even as Rackin's argument seeks in some measure to demystify what her reiteration affirms. Why this should be so, I will suggest in the course of my argument.

3. 2.Chor.6; all citations to this play are from *King Henry V,* ed. J. H. Walter (London: Methuen, 1954).

4. In fact, the mirror proclaimed in *Henry V* (2.Chor.6) is taken up by Christopher Pye, *The Regal Phantasm* (London: Routledge, 1990), 124–41, in his consideration of the spectacle of punishment that follows hard upon it in act 2, scene 2, and the complicities that structure sovereignty and its betrayal. It is to a version of that argument that my chapter also is devoted.

5. A. R. Humphreys, ed., *The First Part of King Henry IV* (London:

Methuen, 1960), xlviii. All citations from this play are from this edition, and citations of Part II from Humphreys' edition of *The Second Part of King Henry IV* (London: Methuen, 1966). For a critique of the ideological effects of such criticism, see Graham Holderness, *Shakespeare's History* (New York: St. Martin's, 1985).

6. David Bevington, ed., *Henry IV, Part I* (Oxford: Oxford University Press, 1987), 62, 64, 66.

7. *Shakespearean Negotiations* (Berkeley and Los Angeles: University of California Press, 1988), 41. Further citations from this chapter, "Invisible Bullets," appear parenthetically in the text. The essay has been published twice before, in somewhat different versions—in *Glyph 8* (1981) and in Jonathan Dollimore and Alan Sinfield, eds., *Political Shakespeare* (Ithaca: Cornell University Press, 1985)—and is, of course, one of the most widely cited pieces by Greenblatt and the essay that embodies the definition of New Historicism currently in circulation.

8. I follow Jean Laplanche and Jean-Baptiste Pontalis, in *The Language of Psycho-Analysis*, trans. Donald Nicholson-Smith (New York: Norton, 1973), 137, in defining *phantasmatic* as an unconscious structuring scenario or action. The patriarchal phantasmatic voiced by Theseus is traced by Louis Adrian Montrose in "'Shaping Fantasies': Figurations of Gender and Power in Elizabethan Culture," *Representations* 2 (1983): 70–71. Although Montrose connects the lines that Theseus speaks in 1.1.47–51 to the fight over the Indian boy, he is silent about the sexual connection that the child represents; for that point, one can turn to Jonathan Crewe, *Hidden Designs* (New York: Methuen, 1986), 148–51, for a somewhat pathologizing view of Oberon's desire for the boy as, in Crewe's terms, his "pathic." Nonetheless, Crewe sees that the boy is written much as the young man is in the sonnets, and that as changeling he is the very locus for a series of crossings in the play.

9. For further considerations of this point, see my "Rebel Letters: Postal Effects from *Richard II* to *Henry IV*," *Renaissance Drama* n.s. 19 (1988): 16–17. For a remarkable essay about what remains unassimilable to any normative patriarchal reading of *2 Henry IV*, see Jonathan Crewe, "Reforming Prince Hal: The Sovereign Inheritor in *2 Henry IV*," *Renaissance Drama* n.s. 21 (1990): 225–42.

10. Hal's imagery answers his initial accusation that Falstaff is "fat-witted with drinking old sack" (1.2.2); this image of Falstaff corresponds to the portrait of the sodomite as what Alan Bray in recent unpublished work calls the "consumptive," a self-devouring appetitiveness that could as easily take the form of gluttony as of thievery. Bray presented arguments about this conception of the sodomite in a lecture at the Johns Hopkins University on October 24, 1991, entitled "'Love Among the Muses': Sexuality, Masculinity, and Identity in the Early Modern Period." The connection between "vapours" and flatulence is made over and again in *Bartholomew Fair.*

11. On this point, see my discussion of the lines in "Shakespearean

Inscriptions: The Voicing of Power," in Geoffrey Hartman and Patricia Parker, eds., *Shakespeare and the Question of Theory* (London: Methuen, 1985), 119–20, as well as the consideration of *Henry V* in *James I and the Politics of Literature* (Baltimore: Johns Hopkins University Press, 1983), 161–63. Rackin makes somewhat similar points in her description of Henry V as an absence around which both tetralogies move.

12. Greenblatt does follow Empson, although he attributes one of two quotations supposedly from him that I cannot find in Empson (see *Shakespearean Negotiations,* 42 and 42 n. 40).

13. William Empson, *Some Versions of Pastoral* (London: Chatto & Windus, 1935), 108. Further citations appear parenthetically in the text. In *Shakespeare's Heroical Histories* (Cambridge: Harvard University Press, 1971), David Riggs has noted that the final fourteen lines of Hal's soliloquy at the end of *1 Henry IV,* act 1, scene 2, "fall naturally into the meditative frame of an unrhymed Shakespearean sonnet" (156), a formal observation that furthers Empson's thematic and semantic point.

14. See Jean Laplanche, *Life and Death in Psychoanalysis,* trans. Jeffrey Mehlman (Baltimore: Johns Hopkins University Press, 1976), chapters 1 and 5 *passim.*

15. *King Richard II,* ed. Peter Ure (London: Methuen, 1956), 5.3.10.

16. These are not unlike the terms of patriarchy described by Luce Irigaray in *This Sex Which Is Not One,* trans. Catherine Porter (Ithaca: Cornell University Press, 1985), 192–93. Where my critique parts company with Irigaray is in her supposition that such male/male relations (for example, the pederasty that lurks in father/son relations) mask homosexuality *tout court* as the secret of homosociality (this is the argument that her nonce word "hom[m]osexuality" conveys), since it leaves no room for the recognition that the policing of homosexuality is complicit with the policing of women, and that there is a world of difference between homosexuality and homophobia. This is of course the point argued against Irigaray by Craig Owens in "Outlaws: Gay Men in Feminism," in Alice Jardine and Paul Smith, eds., *Men in Feminism* (New York: Methuen, 1987), 223–24, which takes its cue from the exemplary discussions of Eve Kosofsky Sedgwick such as the one in the introduction to *Between Men* (New York: Columbia University Press, 1985), 19–20.

17. Barbara Correll, "Malleable Material, Models of Power: Women in Erasmus's 'Marriage Group' and *Civility in Boys,*" *ELH* 57 (1990): 241–62, especially 241–43.

18. For an analysis of the play along these lines, see Pye as well as Krystian Czerniecki, "The Jest Disgested: Perspectives on History in *Henry V,*" in Jonathan Culler, ed., *On Puns* (Oxford: Basil Blackwell, 1988), 62–82.

19. In Joseph A. Boone and Michael Cadden, eds., *Engendering Men* (New York: Routledge, 1990), 190–206.

20. This is most transparently to be seen in that nervous critical formation called male feminism and exemplified among Shakespeareans by the

work of Peter Erickson, who opens his *Patriarchal Structures in Shakespeare's Drama* (Berkeley and Los Angeles: University of California Press, 1985), 6–7, with assurances that the male bonding he considers could not usefully be called homosexuality (sexualizing male/male relations is regarded as an oversimplification), but since it's not, Erickson contends, capable of an idealized platonizing either, he reads male/male relations as a political formation bent on the subordination of women. This is, like Irigaray, invidiously to homosexualize heterosexuality, to lay the ills of heterosexuality elsewhere, a move parallel to the one Warner details in "Homo-Narcissism," and worth comparing too to Heather Findlay's reading of the elision of lesbianism in deconstructive equations of heterogeneity with heterosexuality; see "Is There a Lesbian in This Text? Derrida, Wittig, and the Politics of the Three Women," in Elizabeth Weed, ed., *Coming to Terms* (New York: Routledge, 1989), 59–69.

Erickson holds out the possibility for "good" male bonding (respectful of women) only to heterosexuals. In this he follows his mentor, C. L. Barber, whose work is often outrageously homophobic; Barber is, of course, the acknowledged "father" of Shakespearean feminists like Coppélia Kahn. For a critique of this work along similar lines, see Joseph A. Porter, *Shakespeare's Mercutio* (Chapel Hill: University of North Carolina Press, 1988).

21. This is assumed in *Homosexuality in Renaissance England* (London: Gay Men's Press, 1982) and argued in relation to the ideal of friendship and the practices it involved (shared bed and boards) in "Homosexuality and the Signs of Male Friendship in Elizabethan England," *History Workshop Journal* 29 (1990): 1–19.

22. Fantasmatic since the mechanisms of repression are, as Foucault argued, productive, but fantasmatic too because the private is continually policed and regulated to this day, and the sanctioned forms of sexuality that are secured are the ones that ensure the perpetuation of procreative sex within a compulsory heterosexuality. The Supreme Court decision in *Bowers v. Hardwick* makes this all too clear.

23. In Part II, Lady Percy convinces her father-in-law once again to betray his fellow rebels; this she does for the sake of an ideality constructed around the dead Hotspur, and her behavior and historical agency seem congruent with Prince John's behavior at Gaultree where, by breaking his word to the rebels, he scores a victory for the king.

24. *Hic Mulier: Or, The Man-Woman* (London, 1620), Sig. C1r.

25. Peter Erickson cashes in this inheritance in his reading of Coriolanus and Aufidius in *Patriarchal Structures*, 5. As far as Erickson is concerned, this is what homosexuality amounts to in Shakespeare. It appears, too, to be the case in the avowedly gay-affirmative treatment of *Henry V* in Alan Sinfield's forthcoming *Fault Lines*.

26. This is much less true for women given their position under patriarchy and their definitional status acquired through marriage. But it is not entirely untrue, as Valerie Traub begins to suggest in "Desire and the

Difference It Makes," and in an unpublished essay, "The (In)Significance of 'Lesbian' Desire in Early Modern England."

27. In a presentation at the 1990 MLA Convention on the lesbian phallus and the impossibility of heterosexuality—a reading of Freud's essay on narcissism immensely pertinent to the discussion here and to Warner's discussion in "Homo-Narcissism"; a longer version of this essay will appear as "The Lesbian Phallus," *differences,* May 1992.

28. Michael Moon and Eve Kosofsky Sedgwick's "Divinity: A Dossier / A Performance Piece / A Little-Understood Emotion," *Discourse* 13 (1990–91): 12–39, is a sustained meditation on these questions. For the relationships between body size and social organization in the transition to capitalist social organization—towards the modernity incipient in Shakespeare's plays—see Stephen Mennell, "On the Civilizing of Appetite," *Theory, Culture & Society* 4 (1987): 373–403, especially his discussion on p. 397 of the ways in which an older aristocratic corpulence becomes the body of the poor as the new regimes of civilization preach restraint. Falstaff's body is, in these terms, legible under both the old and new regimes.

29. The critic I have in mind here is of course Patricia Parker, who in *Literary Fat Ladies* (London: Methuen, 1987) declares Falstaff an "obvious Shakespearean 'fat lady'" (20) on the basis of his girth and tongue.

30. This is Valerie Traub's argument in "Prince Hal's Falstaff: Positioning Psychoanalysis and the Female Reproductive Body," *Shakespeare Quarterly* 40 (1989): 456–74. "The homoerotics of the Henriad deserve fuller treatment," Traub notes, only immediately to figure that sexuality as Hal's masculinity played in relation to Falstaff's femininity (465). The locus classicus for the association of Falstaff's fat body with the woman's body—indeed with the maternal pregnant body—is W. H. Auden's "The Prince's Dog" in *The Dyer's Hand* (New York: Random House, 1948), 182–208. Auden does note, on pp. 190–92, ways in which Falstaff's relationship with the prince echoes against the sonnets, but he also insists on the fat knight's narcissism, infantilism, and feminization, in short, writes the love relationship within the psychoanalytic devaluation of homosexuality. He also depicts Falstaff as a hopeless alcoholic, implying a connection between homosexuality and addiction which Eve Kosofsky Sedgwick treats in her unpublished essay, "Epidemics of the Will," and in *Epistemology of the Closet* (Berkeley and Los Angeles: University of California Press, 1990), 171–78.

31. I owe this connection to Jonathan Brody Kramnick.

CHAPTER 6

1. See Jonathan Katz, *Gay American History* (New York: Thomas Y. Crowell, 1976), 281–334; Walter L. Williams, *The Spirit and the Flesh* (Boston: Beacon, 1986), 131–51. In *Memory of Fire: Genesis* (New York: Pantheon, 1985), 58–59, Eduardo Galeano offers a stunning evocation of the Balboan moment, to which I will be turning. It also receives brief mention, as one instance in the sexualization of Amerindians, in Peter

Mason, *Deconstructing America* (London: Routledge, 1990), 56. The fullest anthology of colonial texts on sodomy is found in Francesco Guerra, *The Pre-Columbian Mind* (London: Seminar, 1971); Guerra is entirely uncritical of the material that he offers, homophobically believing that the accounts simply offer the truth about "aberrant" native practices.

2. I will be citing *The Decades of the Newe Worlde or West India* from the March of America Facsimile Series, Number 4 (Ann Arbor: University Microfilms, 1966). Richard Eden translates the 1533 edition of Pietro Martire d'Anghiera's *De rebus oceanicis et orbe novo decades tres.*

For an empassioned rebuttal of the black legend, see Roberto Fernández Retamar, "Against the Black Legend," in *Caliban and Other Essays,* trans. Edward Baker (Minneapolis: University of Minnesota Press, 1989), 56–73.

3. The image is analyzed, in ways fully complicitous with the structures of understanding that I will be critiquing here, in Bernadette Bucher, *Icon and Conquest: A Structural Analysis of the Illustrations of de Bry's Great Voyages,* trans. Basia Miller Gulati (Chicago: University of Chicago Press, 1981), 153–54. Bucher conflates effeminacy, hermaphroditism, and sodomy under the label "sexual ambiguity." The crossings that I will be arguing for keep differentials in play.

4. It is worth adding that "preposterous" is Eden's contribution to the description; in Peter Martyr, Balboa finds the royal house "nefanda infectam Venere" (infected with abominable Venus); I cite from the facsimile of the 1530 edition of *De Orbe Novo* in Petrus Martyr de Angliera, *Opera,* ed. Erich Woldan (Graz: Akademische Druck- u. Verlagsanstalt, 1966), 106 (fol. xxxvi verso in the original). For a discussion of preposterousness as a trope for what he calls the "(be)hindsight" with which Freudian *Nachträglichkeit* arrives at a primal scene of sex *a tergo,* see Lee Edelman, "Seeing Things, Representation, the Scene of Surveillance, and the Spectacle of Gay Male Sex," in Diana Fuss, ed., *Inside/Out: Lesbian Theories, Gay Theories* (New York: Routledge, 1991), 93–116.

5. For example, in Fernández de Oviedo, the enormously influential first vernacular account of the New World (*Natural Historia de las Indias* [1526]), not least because Bartolomé de Las Casas undertook to debunk it; see Guerra, 55: "they are hated extremely by the women"; 56: "this abominable sin against nature, very much practised among the Indians in this island [Santo Domingo], hateful to women." Of course, it hardly needs to be said, these claims are not to be taken as the truth about what native women believed (hardly a unitary position at any rate), but as highly motivated statements that serve the purposes of the gender ideology of the narratives.

6. Certainly the assumption that transvestism (and hence, by European standards, the violation of gender norms expressed by clothing) is the sign of and therefore the same thing as sodomy, which is the slippage that this narrative supposes, cannot be assumed to apply to native American practices of cross-dressing. The literature on the subject of the *berdache* is extensive; for one recent attempt to think about native cross-dressing and

homosexuality, see Gilbert Herdt, "Representations of Homosexuality: An Essay on Cultural Ontology and Historical Comparison, Part I," *Journal of the History of Sexuality* 1 (1991): 481–504. For a survey of the various accounts of cross-dressing that reviews much of the anthropological literature from the first European contacts to the present day, see David E. Greenberg, *The Construction of Homosexuality* (Chicago: University of Chicago Press, 1988), 40–65. Greenberg usefully stresses the range and diversity of practices, although his conclusion that these reflect differences in notions of gender from one society to another too easily effaces the role that sexuality plays in the definitions of gender. For further bibliography, consult Will Roscoe, "Bibliography of Berdache and Alternative Gender Roles Among Native American Indians," *Journal of Homosexuality* 14 (1987): 61–171.

7. In this light, it is worth adding, as Paula Bennett has urged me to do, that the naked bodies of Indians in the De Bry illustration are feminized. This can be seen in their pose, as well as in reference to the conventions of representation (marked by clothed/naked bodies) that divide the male spectators from the scene that they view. The fact too that the naked bodies are supine and the clothed ones erect, and the insistent eroticization of the relations between the naked bodies and the dogs, furthers this point. Moreover, the usual confusion of sodomy with bestiality is also suggested by the ways in which the slaughter of the so-called sodomites in this image looks like rape. Within the terms of Eden's translation, the "preposterous" effect of substituting sex between men for sex between men and women is played out by making the naked male bodies assume the guise of femininity. But what this also does—much as the ruse in which the righting of sexual wrongs is said to be done for the sake of women—is to punish women by delivering feminized bodies to the dogs. Much as this punishment was meant to reassert "nature" (that is, male/female procreative sexual relations), the image itself is (within these terms) "unnatural." Something congruent to this was suggested by an anonymous reader of these pages, who notes in the image "a . . . subversive reading of the sameness of 'sodomitical' and the *accepted* bonds of men," by which I assume this reader has in mind the ways in which the Spaniards in the scene also seem to be affectively/erotically linked to each other by their poses, perhaps, too, by the presence of their erect standards and swords. For an incisive statement of relationships between normative and excoriated male/male relations, see Alan Bray, "Homosexuality and the Signs of Male Friendship in Elizabethan England," *History Workshop Journal* 29 (1990): 1–19.

8. This analysis has been aided by the insights of a number of postcolonial theorists: Benedict Anderson, whose *Imagined Communities* (London: Verso, 1983) brilliantly explores the constructedness of nationalisms; Homi Bhabha, who, in essays like "The Other Question: Difference, Discrimination and the Discourse of Colonialism," in Francis Barker et al., eds., *Literature, Politics and Theory* (London: Methuen, 1989), 148–72, has writ-

ten on colonial ambivalence and mimetology (in considering mimic mimesis, Bhabha's work opens spaces within the projection of stereotypes and thereby destabilizes hegemonic discourses; he thus moves analysis beyond the model of opposition and victimization); and Gayatri Spivak, who has done similar work in finding the ways in which a deconstructive analytic can produce subalternity (see, for example, "Subaltern Studies: Deconstructing Historiography," in Ranajit Guha and Gayatri Chakravorty Spivak, eds., *Selected Subaltern Studies* [Oxford: Oxford University Press, 1988], 3–32). Important as this work has been for me, and crucial as it is in its approach to questions of nationality, race, and gender, it has not opened the questions of sexuality that concern me here. One study that might appear to do so, Ashis Nandy's *The Intimate Enemy* (Delhi: Oxford University Press, 1983), although full of endorsements of what Nandy calls "androgyny," fails to satisfy: first, because of a masculinist bias, which makes androgyny available only to men; second, because the celebrated cross-gender behavior keeps in place utterly traditional definitions of masculinity and femininity; third, because Nandy explicitly separates homosexuality from androgyny in order to reserve his privileged term for men who are not homosexual. In an unpublished essay, "Where Is Amitabh's Moustache? Violent Androgynes and Subaltern Pretensions," Lawrence Cohen critiques Nandy's work along similar lines.

9. Garcilaso de la Vega, *Royal Commentaries of the Incas,* trans. Harold V. Livermore (Austin: University of Texas Press, 1966). Citations appear parenthetically in the text. Garcilaso mentions versions of the story by Acosta and Zarate; for versions of the story see Guerra, *Pre-Columbian Mind,* 90 (for Cieza), 99 (for Zarate [1555]), 131 (for Juan López de Velasco [1574]), 141–42 (for Pedro Gutiérrez de Santa Clara [c. 1580]), and 155 (for Antonio de Herrera [1601], who dates the story to 1527).

10. For work that asks similar questions (and often delivers rather benign answers to them), see Sabine MacCormack, "From the Sun of the Incas to the Virgin of Copacabana," *Representations* 8 (1984): 30–60; "*Pachacuti*: Miracles, Punishments, and Last Judgment: Visionary Past and Prophetic Future in Early Colonial Peru," *AHR* 93 (1988): 960–1006; and "Demons, Imagination, and the Inca," *Representations* 33 (1991): 121–46.

11. See Ramon A. Gutiérrez, "Must We Deracinate Indians to Find Gay Roots," *Outlook* 1 (1989): 61–67. Gutiérrez distorts his evidence (fetched from Guerra, among other sources); the "fact" of cross-dressing as humiliation is not the only "native" practice. As the Balboa account suggests, it may, in some instances, represent a Europeanization of natives. But even where that cannot be supposed, one cannot argue from the practices of some Indians at some times to all Indians. This is Gutiérrez's argument with Katz and Williams, among others, but it can also be mobilized against his own account.

12. See Harriet Whitehead, "The Bow and the Burden Strap," in Sherry B. Ortner and Harriet Whitehead, eds., *Sexual Meanings* (Cambridge: Cambridge University Press, 1981), 80–115. For all Whitehead's

attempts to get beyond ethnocentricity and to present the diversity of cases of cross-dressing, one must pause over the anthropological knowledge that leads to this conclusion: "In our own culture, homosexual behavior itself tends to redefine a person to the status of an intermediate (and, except in liberal circles, strongly disapproved) sex type" (110). Not only is it hard to know whether Whitehead locates herself as a "liberal," but her "knowledge" of present-day definitions of homosexuality was already old-fashioned a half century ago. In this she follows one of the classic articles in the anthropological literature, George Devereux's "Institutionalized Homosexuality among the Mohave Indians," *Human Biology* 9 (1937): 498–527, which, as Gilbert Herdt points out in his "Representations of Homosexuality," reads the Mohave practices through the late Victorian and Freudian lens of inversion. Similarly, it's thanks to that model of the gay man as having a woman trapped inside of him that Whitehead can elide cross-dressing and homosexuality, can view cross-dressing as a male encroachment upon women, and can reduce cross-dressing and homosexuality to "the dominance of heterosexuality" (110) in all forms of sexual behavior. The notion is attributed to Gayle Rubin in a palpable misreading of "The Traffic in Women: Notes on the 'Political Economy' of Sex," in Rayna R. Reiter, ed., *Toward an Anthropology of Women* (New York: Monthly Review Press, 1975), 157–210. Gutiérrez adopts a position similar to Whitehead's in his brief consideration of berdache in *When Jesus Came, the Corn Mothers Went Away* (Stanford: Stanford University Press, 1991), 33–35.

13. Pierre Clastres, *Society Against the State,* trans. Robert Hurley and Abe Stein (New York: Zone, 1987), 101–28. The book appeared in French in 1974.

14. Clastres refers to "the logic of this closed system, made up of four terms grouped into two opposite pairs" (108) and thinks all the permutations of male and female, bow and basket, are realized when he can produce two male basket carriers.

15. When Clastres celebrates how well Krembegi fits in, it is to relabel him finally as a woman (110); given the misogyny in Clastres's account, this is hardly a liberating move across gender. Like other anthropologists, Clastres does not want to admit the possibility of an indigenous homosexuality. For the ordinary homophobia that circulates as objective anthropological knowledge, see, for example, Raymond E. Hauser, "The *Berdache* and the Illinois Indian Tribe During the Last Half of the Seventeenth Century," *Ethnohistory* 37 (1990): 45–65.

16. Hernán Cortés, *Letters from Mexico,* ed. and trans. Anthony Pagden (New Haven: Yale University Press, 1986), 37. Further citations appear parenthetically in the text.

17. Quoted in Guerra, *Pre-Columbian Mind,* 53, 55.

18. Bartolomé de Las Casas, *The Spanish Colonie,* in the March of America Facsimile Series, Number 8 (Ann Arbor: University Microfilms, 1966), Q3v.

19. Guerra leaps upon the fact that despite himself Las Casas, as he puts it, "proved Fernández de Oviedo's points" (76); Guerra is even willing to suppose that Las Casas was mentally unbalanced. So doing, Guerra endorses the desire to destroy the natives of the New World; whatever the logical consequences of Las Casas's account, he never proved Oviedo's point even if he did, inevitably, share his antisodomitical beliefs.

20. See Jonathan Ned Katz, *Gay American History,* 288–89 for Lafitau. For similar eighteenth-century defenses of native cross-dressing as a spiritual hermaphroditism, see Guerra, *Pre-Columbian Mind,* 208, 211–13.

21. To treat native condemnations as the truth of native belief is, of course, to ignore divisions within native belief systems (divisions that are in no small measure the result of the conversion of the Indians to Christianity), and to ignore the history of Indians.

22. Cecil Jane, trans., *The Journal of Christopher Columbus* (New York: Bonanza, 1989), 3–4. Further citations are to this edition and appear parenthetically in the text.

23. On this subject, see Mary Elizabeth Perry, "The 'Nefarious Sin' in Early Modern Seville," in Kent Gerard and Gert Hekma, eds., *The Pursuit of Sodomy* (New York: Harrington Park, 1989), 67–89; Mary Elizabeth Perry, *Gender and Disorder in Early Modern Seville* (Princeton: Princeton University Press, 1990), 118–36; and William Monter, *Frontiers of Heresy* (Cambridge: Cambridge University Press, 1990), 276–99.

24. Citations from *The Four Voyages of Columbus,* 2 vols., ed. Cecil Jane (New York: Dover, 1988).

25. Peter Hulme, *Colonial Encounters: Europe and the Native Caribbean, 1492–1797* (New York: Methuen, 1986), 84–87. As Hulme remarks, what is projected upon the natives is division within Spain as a means of consolidating the ideological apparatus of projecting European unity as opposed to native depravity. The analysis that I am conducting here (as well as the use of the phrase "ruses of power" earlier) is much indebted to Hulme, and particularly to the ways in which the construction of stabilized self/other projections is always related back to the lack of unity in both colonizer and colonized. It is on the axis of these divisions, along the margins and the slippages that they make possible, that my analysis moves, in the track of Hulme's.

26. Francisco López de Gómara, *Cortés,* ed. and trans. Lesley Byrd Simpson (Berkeley and Los Angeles: University of California Press, 1964), 4, 13.

27. Bernal Díaz, *The Conquest of New Spain,* trans. J. M. Cohen (Baltimore: Penguin, 1963), 19. On phallic worship and widespread sodomy in Panuco, see also the 1519 anonymous relation in Guerra, *Pre-Columbian Mind,* 51; on jewels showing acts of sodomy, compare Oviedo, in Guerra, 56.

28. Octavio Paz, *The Labyrinth of Solitude,* trans. Lysander Kemp (New York: Grove, 1961), chapter 4, "The Sons of La Malinche." A more positive evaluation of La Malinche is provided in Alfredo Mirande and Evangelina

Enríquez, *La Chicana* (Chicago: University of Chicago Press, 1979), 24–31. For the lesbian feminist appropriations of La Malinche, see "La Malinchista," in Cherríe Moraga, *Loving in the War Years* (Boston: South End Press, 1983), 112–17, and Norma Alarcon, "Chicana's Feminist Literature: A Re-vision Through Malintzin / or Malintzin Putting Flesh Back on the Object," in Cherríe Moraga and Gloria Anzaldua, eds., *This Bridge Called My Back* (New York: Kitchen Table, 1983), 182–90. In *Marvelous Possessions: The Wonder of the New World* (Chicago: University of Chicago Press, 1991), Stephen Greenblatt glances at the role of Doña Marina within a discussion of the figure of the go-between, to which I turn shortly. While he notes how Cortés and La Malinche share a name, he treats this as a linguistic space of communication and the sharing of an image (143). Once again, as in his discussion of Hal, Greenblatt posits a site of imaginary identification that manages to elide the question of gender and sexuality—and the violence of imposition—that is entailed in this cross-identification.

29. All citations from Cabeza de Vaca, *Adventures in the Unknown Interior of America,* trans. and ed. Cyclone Covey (Albuquerque: University of New Mexico Press, 1983). A recent essay on this text that offers much pertinent information about the course of Cabeza de Vaca's journey is Rolena Adorno's "The Negotiation of Fear in Cabeza de Vaca's *Naufragios,*" *Representations* 33 (1991): 163–99. In other respects, Adorno's essay is less useful since it uncomplicatedly produces a celebration of Cabeza de Vaca's text that ignores many of the questions of cross-identification raised in the pages that follow.

30. Aguilar, Cortés's translator, had forcibly been captured and returned to the Spaniards; Gonzalo Guerrero, whose history was similar, remained with the Yucatan Indians, leading them against the Spanish; see Díaz, 65. For another instance of a Spaniard who rejoined his countrymen after capture, see the account of the DeSoto expedition in F. W. Hodge and T. H. Lewis, eds., *Spanish Explorers in the Southern United States, 1528–1543* (New York: Scribner's Sons, 1907), 149–53. The man in question, Juan Ortiz, had been in the Narváez expedition to Florida.

31. *The Narrative of Alvar Núñez Cabeça de Vaca,* ed. F. W. Hodge (New York: Scribner's Sons, 1907), 88.

32. *The Journey of Alvar Núñez Cabeza de Vaca,* trans. F. Bandelier; ed. A. F. Bandelier (New York: Allerton, 1922), 126.

33. Samuel Purchas, *Purchas His Pilgrimes,* 20 vols. (Glasgow: James MacLehose & Sons, 1905–7), 17:495.

34. The Spanish text reads: "En el tiempo que así estaba, entre estos vi una diablura, y es, que vi un hombre casado con otro, y estos son unos hombres amarionados impotentes, y andan tapados como mujeres y hacen oficio de mujeres, y tiran arco y llevan muy gran carga, y entre estos vimos muchos de ellos así amarionados como digo, y son mas membrudos que los otros hombres, y mas altos; sufren muy grandes cargas" (*Naufragos y Relacion de la Jornada que hizo a la Florida,* chapter 26, in *Biblioteca de Autores Espanoles,* ed. Enrique de Vedia [Madrid: Rivadeneyra, 1877],

22:538). The earliest translations are more accurate than Covey's; the stumbling block, of course, is the word *amarionado,* the antecedent of modern Spanish *amaricado* and the related *marica* and *maricon,* slurs on homosexuality the equivalent of "queer," "pansy," and "sissy." The term does not mean a man who has "become" a woman through castration or even necessarily through gender-crossing behavior.

35. All citations will be from *Yucatan Before and After the Conquest,* trans. and ed. William Gates (1937; reprint, New York: Dover, 1978).

36. See Inga Clendinnen, *Ambivalent Conquests: Maya and Spaniard in Yucatan 1517–1570* (Cambridge: Cambridge University Press, 1987), 76. Further citations appear parenthetically in the text.

37. Here Landa's opinion is the same as the liberal bishop of the Yucatan, Francisco de Toral, who put an end to Landa's torturing, and in 1564 wrote that the Mayans were "the best people I have seen in the Indies, very simple, even more obedient, charitable, free of vices, so that even in their paganism they did not eat human flesh or practice the abominable sin" (cited in Clendinnen, 107, who is rather snide about the bishop's transformation of the Mayans into innocent victims, in a moment when her attempts to register the ambivalent nature of these contacts leads her to identify with her "hero" Landa; something similar can be seen in her take on the discovery of representations of sodomy in the first venture into the Yucatan—the episode recorded in Díaz and discussed earlier; she writes, "they were not vexed by the grotesque idols, nor even by the possibility, suggested by some strange sculpted figures, that these people lacked a proper abhorrence of sodomy" [8]; as Clendinnen enters into their attitudes, she seems to endorse the enormity and grotesquerie of the "crime" and the propriety of its abhorrence). It's worth mentioning that the few surviving depictions of anal intercourse in native South and Central American art are anything but ambiguous about what act they represent, although the gender of the "passive" partner can be ambiguous; for illustrations, see Guerra, *Pre-Columbian Mind,* following 160 and 256, and the discussion on 255–59.

CHAPTER 7

1. Chicago: University of Chicago Press, 1979. Citations appear parenthetically in the text.

2. A tradition enshrined in Samuel Eliot Morison's edition of William Bradford, *Of Plymouth Plantation 1620–1647* (New York: Alfred A. Knopf, 1952), or its abbreviation in Francis Murphy's Modern Library edition (New York: Random House, 1981). I cite page numbers from Murphy's more widely available text except for some materials from Morison's appendixes omitted in Murphy. One sign of how Morison reads Bradford is the list of "Quotations" provided at the back of his edition, purple passages that are no doubt thought to be inspirational. Murphy concludes his introduction by hailing Bradford as "the first in a long line of American writers . . . who grasped the imaginative possibilities of the essential

American myth: the story of a people who set themselves apart from the rest of the world and pledged themselves together in self-sacrifice and love" (xxiii–xxiv).

3. Bradford's abiding interest in the "First Comers" can be seen in the records he kept of their genealogical histories (see Morison edition, appendix 13, 441–48), and his purpose in writing *Of Plymouth Plantation* was to preserve the past for these future generations.

4. On the practice of putting out children, see Edmund Morgan, *The Puritan Family,* 2d ed. (New York: Harper & Row, 1966), 75–78. Morgan reads the practice as designed to ensure the creation of distance between parents and children, to guard against too much affection; this view is endorsed by John Demos in *A Little Commonwealth* (London: Oxford University Press, 1970), 71–75, who tentatively suggests that the "ancient mother" passage in Bradford may relate to family tensions that were displaced into neighborly disputes about property (189).

5. This contrasts with the virulent misogyny in, for example, John Winthrop's *Journal* or the various accounts centering on Anne Hutchinson and her followers; on this, see especially Carol Karlsen, *The Devil in the Shape of a Woman* (New York: Vintage, 1987).

6. See Francis Jennings, *The Invasion of America: Indians, Colonialism, and the Cant of Conquest* (Chapel Hill: University of North Carolina Press, 1975), and Neal Salisbury, *Manitou and Providence: Indians, Europeans, and the Making of New England, 1500–1643* (New York: Oxford University Press, 1982). One limit to this undeniably valuable work is its blindness to questions of gender and sexuality; the remediation offered, the setting straight of the historical record, still operates within the confines of war and trade and towards a reversal of accounts like Bradford's.

7. Although that is the way in which James Axtell shapes his "moderate" ethnohistory; see, for example, "A Moral History of Indian-White Relations Revisited," in *After Columbus* (New York: Oxford University Press, 1988), 9–33, in which exception is taken to the "extremity" in Jennings and Salisbury; or "Colonial America Without the Indians," in *After Columbus,* 222–43, in which a vision of the cooperative Anglo-Indian venture is offered that mutes the genocide unflinchingly faced by Jennings and Salisbury.

8. See Ann Kibbey, *The Interpretation of Material Shapes in Puritanism: A Study of Rhetoric, Prejudice, and Violence* (Cambridge: Cambridge University Press, 1986), chapter 5 *passim,* especially 105–10.

9. Perhaps even more horrific is the juxtaposition of Bradford's account of the compassion of Plymouth for the Indians killed by a smallpox epidemic in 1634 (302–3), and its representation not merely as God's pleasure, but, as the English settlers wrangle over the spoils, of the land as "the Lord's waste" and rightfully belonging to Plymouth since "it was they that found it so . . . and have since bought it of the right owners" (316).

10. See Alan Bray, *Homosexuality in Renaissance England* (London: Gay Men's Press, 1982), chapter 3 *passim,* especially 67–80.

11. For this broad definition and its significance for the American colonial situation, see Jonathan Ned Katz, *Gay/Lesbian Almanac* (New York: Harper & Row, 1983), 31–65.

12. For an account sympathetic to Morton, see Richard Drinnon, *Facing West: The Metaphysics of Indian-Hating and Empire-Building* (Minneapolis: University of Minnesota Press, 1980), 3–61; Drinnon sets Morton's relations with Indians in contrast to the repressions of Puritan life, and pronounces sexual behavior with Indian women "good clean fun" (57). More puritanically, Neal Salisbury attempts to "save" Indian women from the charge of promiscuity (see *Manitou and Providence*, 160).

13. Richard Slotkin, *Regeneration Through Violence: The Mythology of the American Frontier, 1600–1860* (Middletown, Conn.: Wesleyan University Press, 1973), 61. In "'Things Fearful to Name': Sodomy and Buggery in Seventeenth-Century New England," *Journal of Social History* 12 (1978): 268–81; reprinted in Elizabeth H. Pleck and Joseph H. Pleck, eds., *The American Man* (Englewood Cliffs, N.J.: Prentice-Hall, 1980), from which I cite. Robert Oaks also associates the "worse practices" with homosexuality, opining their likelihood in an all-male community (58). This rather flattens the notion of sodomy, and fails to see its connections with the variety of practices associated with Morton in Bradford. Oaks thinks the "homosexuality" at Merrymount may have been either "situational" or a matter of "preference"—either compelled or freely chosen, alternatives that only appear, I believe, to cover all the possibilities in that dichotomy, and that depend moreover on the quite problematic notion that any man in the period would have self-identified as a homosexual.

14. Cited in John Carnup, *Out of the Wilderness* (Middletown, Conn.: Wesleyan University Press, 1990), 45.

15. The situation in New England was not the same as in Virginia; the first death penalty for sodomy was administered in Virginia in 1624; in New England, in 1646. For particulars, see Jonathan Ned Katz, *Gay American History*, 16–23. Two buggery executions took place in New England in 1641; others occurred in 1646, 1647, 1654, and 1662.

16. See, for example, Oaks, "Things Fearful," 70–71, and Bradley Chapin, *Criminal Justice in Colonial America, 1606–1660* (Athens: University of Georgia Press, 1983), 128. Both authors think that the horror of bestiality was connected to the belief that monstrous offspring could come from such unions.

17. I cite the case as transcribed in Katz, *Gay/Lesbian Almanac*, 84–85, derived from Nathaniel Shurtleff, ed., *Records of the Colony of New Plymouth*, 11 vols. (Boston: William White, 1855–61), 2:35–36.

18. See Bray, *Homosexuality in Renaissance England*, 25–26. In *Facing West*, 28–29, Drinnon finds the metaphor of damming in Freud, and treats Bradford's text as presciently modern in its articulation of repression.

19. As might be expected, Hutchinson's name never appears in Bradford; when Williams's does, Bradford expectedly writes: "I shall not need to name particulars" (286).

20. See Drinnon, *Facing West,* 55, indebted, as he notes, to Larzer Ziff, *Puritanism in America* (New York: Viking Press, 1973). See also Roy Harvey Pearce, *Savagism and Civilization,* 2d ed. (Berkeley and Los Angeles: University of California Press, 1988), 24. It is of course Kibbey's important recognition, in the texts she studies, of the ways in which this equation implicates the bodies of women.

CHAPTER 8

1. *National Review* 42, no. 13 (July 9, 1990): 16–18. Further citations appear parenthetically in the text.

2. For an assaultively insightful set of pieces about these and similar complicities, see David Wojnarowicz, *Close to the Knives* (New York: Vintage, 1991).

INDEX

In this index an "f" after a number indicates a separate reference on the next page, and an "ff" indicates separate references on the next two pages. A continuous discussion over two or more pages is indicated by a span of page numbers, e.g., "57–59." *Passim* is used for a cluster of references in close but not consecutive sequence.

Library of Congress
Cataloging-in-Publication Data

Goldberg, Jonathan.
Sodometries : Renaissance texts, modern sexualities / Jonathan Goldberg.
p. cm.
Includes index.
ISBN 0-8047-2050-9 (cloth) : —
ISBN 0-8047-2051-7 (paper) :
1. English literature—Early modern, 1500–1700—History and criticism. 2. Homosexuality and literature—England—History—16th century. 3. American literature—Men authors—History and criticism. 4. English literature—Men authors—History and criticism. 5. Homosexuality and literature—United States. 6. Sodomy in literature. 7. Sex in literature. I. Title.
PR428.H66G6 1992
306.76′6—dc20
92-3105
CIP

⊗ This book is printed on acid-free paper. It has been typeset by Keystone Typesetting, Inc. in Adobe Caslon, designed by Carol Twombly. This face is an Adobe original release based on the letters cut by William Caslon in the 18th century.